# ADVENT

"Rogers has a knack for storytelling and drawing the reader in. You'll finish this book feeling as though you, too, have spun around the globe."

—*USA Today*

"Engaging and enlightening. Rogers and company show the reader their great good time, giving a sense of the world's true vastness at a time when we perceive it to be getting smaller."

—*Barron's*

"A page-turner. It deserves to be No. 1 on your summer reading list—and unlike most books with economic content, you can read this one at the beach."

—*The Dallas Morning News*

"If Warren Buffett and Bill Bryson were trapped in a car with each other for three years, they might write like Jim Rogers."

—Books on Tape editorial review board

"A fascinating and entertaining account of one man's remarkable journey, and a glimpse into the mind of one of this generation's great business iconoclasts. Oh yes, it's also a love story."

—*The Roanoke Times*

"[Rogers] writes with verve and blessed brevity."
—*The Wall Street Journal*

"Rogers, who has guts of steel, goes where no one else goes and eats what no one eats, and we're all the better for it. . . . Rogers' knowledge of history colors all of his commentary, and his openness to the world is a refreshing change from other investment books."
—*HedgeWorld's Inside Edge*

"Rogers successfully mixes business with pleasure. . . . Great reading for business lovers and armchair travelers."
—*BookPage*

"A must-read book . . . one of the most extraordinary travel adventures since the sixteenth-century expedition of Ferdinand Magellan . . . [*Adventure Capitalist*] rivals the accounts of Marco Polo and Richard Burton for fascination and novelty."
—MSNBC.com

"A wonderfully written book about the world at the turn of the millennium. A must-read for any investor looking for long-term opportunities."
—CNBC.com

"Exhilarating . . . [A] great story and plenty of good insights."
—LewRockwell.com

"This book should be required reading at schools and colleges not just because it beats Phileas Fogg's journey hands down in intellectual stimulation, but because the book is also a compendium of free-market ideas and live comparative social analysis."

—StrategyTalk.org

## ABOUT THE AUTHOR

Born in 1942, JIM ROGERS had his first job at age five, picking up bottles at baseball games. Winning a scholarship to Yale, Rogers was coxswain on the crew. Upon graduation, he attended Balliol College at Oxford. After a stint in the army, he began work on Wall Street. He cofounded the Quantum Fund, a global investment partnership. During the next ten years, the portfolio gained more than 4,000 percent, while the S&P rose less than 50 percent. Rogers then decided to retire—at age thirty-seven—but he did not remain idle.

Continuing to manage his own portfolio, Rogers served as a professor of finance at the Columbia University Graduate School of Business and as moderator of *The Dreyfus Round-table* on WCBS and *The Profit Motive* on FNN. At the same time, he laid the groundwork for his lifelong dream, an around-the-world motorcycle trip: more than 100,000 miles across six continents. That journey became the subject of Rogers's first book, *Investment Biker* (1994). He is also the author of *Hot Commodities*.

While laying plans for his Millennium Adventure 1999–2001, he continued as a media commentator at CNBC, et al., and as a sometime professor.

He now contributes to Fox News and others.

He and Paige now have a daughter, Hilton Augusta Parker Rogers, born in 2003, who is pure ecstasy for them both.

He can be reached at www.jimrogers.com.

ALSO BY JIM ROGERS

*Investment Biker*
*Hot Commodities*

# ADVENTURE CAPITALIST

**L**

*Visas — Départ/Sortie*

*Entries/Entrées*

سفارة سلطنة عمان
بالقاهرة

**EMBASSY OF THE
SULTANATE OF OMAN
CAIRO**

| | | الرقم |
|---|---|---|
| No. : | 40157655 | |
| Type of Visa | Tourist | نوع التأشيرة |
| Date of Issue | 8/11/2000 | تاريخ الإصدار |
| Valid for | one month | صالحة لمدة |
| Purpose of Visit | Tourist | غرض الزيارة |
| Period of Stay | 3 weeks | مدة الإقامة |
| Single / Multiple | | أحادية / متعددة |
| Accompanied By | — | المرافقون |
| Ref. | 269/2000 | المرجع |
| Signature | | التوقيع |

سلطنة عمان

1
RIAL   RIAL   Revenue

SUL   SULTANATE OF OMAN

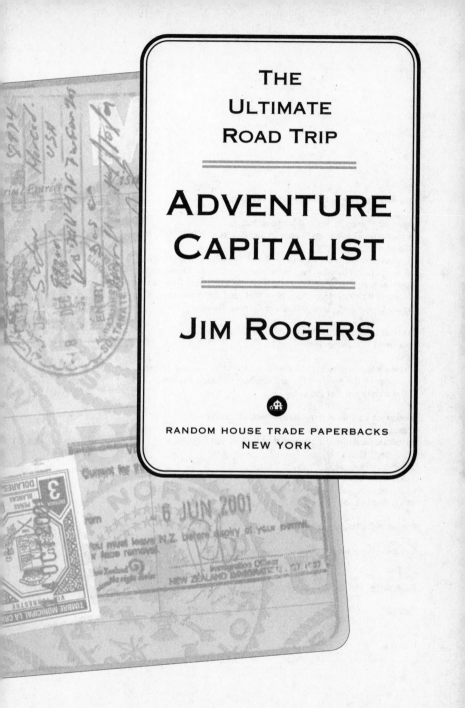

THE
ULTIMATE
ROAD TRIP

# ADVENTURE
# CAPITALIST

## JIM ROGERS

RANDOM HOUSE TRADE PAPERBACKS
NEW YORK

2004 Random House Trade Paperback Edition

Copyright © 2003 by Beeland Interests, Inc.
All photographs and maps © 2003 by Jim Rogers and Paige Parker

All rights reserved under International and Pan-American Copyright
Conventions. Published in the United States by Random House Trade
Paperbacks, an imprint of The Random House Publishing Group, a
division of Random House, Inc., New York, and simultaneously in
Canada by Random House of Canada Limited, Toronto.

RANDOM HOUSE TRADE PAPERBACKS and colophon are
trademarks of Random House, Inc.

This work was originally published in hardcover by Random House,
an imprint of The Random House Publishing Group, a division
of Random House, Inc., in 2003.

LIBRARY OF CONGRESS CATALOGING-IN-PUBLICATION DATA
Rogers, Jim
Adventure capitalist: the ultimate road trip / by Jim Rogers.
p.   cm.
Includes index.
ISBN 0-8129-6726-7
1. Investments.   2. Rogers, Jim—Journeys.   3. Voyages and travels.   I. Title.
HG4521.R684 2003      332.6—dc21      2003041420

Printed in the United States of America

Random House website address: www.atrandom.com

987654

Book design by Carole Lowenstein

*To the greatest adventure:*
*my first child, in the hope that*
*she will always seek, explore,*
*and question, and understand*
*the world as it really is*

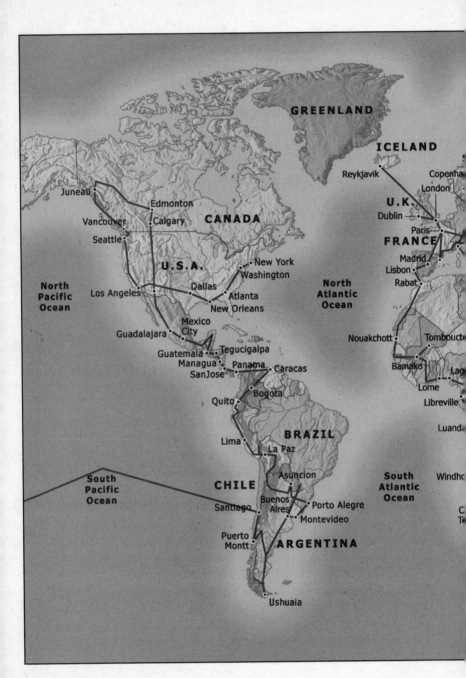

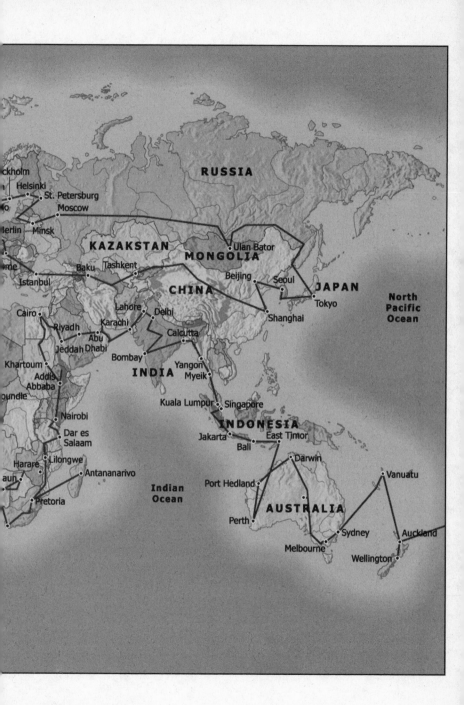

# CONTENTS

# PART THREE: 2001

# PART ONE

## 1999

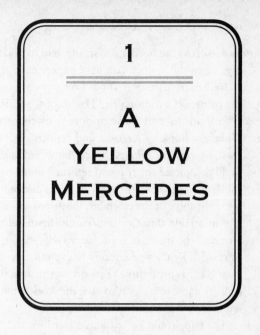

# 1

# A
# YELLOW
# MERCEDES

I ENTERED THE INVESTMENT BUSINESS in 1968 with six hundred dollars in my pocket, and I left it in 1980, at the age of thirty-seven, with enough money to satisfy a lifelong yearning for adventure. As the comanager of an offshore hedge fund, analyzing the worldwide flow of capital, raw materials, goods, and information, I had invested where others did not, exploiting untapped markets around the globe, and it was a significant factor in my success. But what I wanted out of Wall Street, and ultimately out of long-term investing, was not typical of the business. I wanted to buy the freedom to taste as much of life as possible—I wanted to see the world. And I wanted to see the world that other travelers rarely see, the world that can be seen only from the ground up and truly understood only from that vantage point.

I wanted to see what I like to think of as the *real* world.

I have met people who have traveled to more countries than I, but in almost every case, it seems, they have flown from one place to another. You have not really been to a country, I believe, until you have had to cross the border physically, had to find food on your own, fuel, a place to sleep, until you have experienced it close to the ground.

In the late winter of 1990, I set out on a two-year odyssey to circle the planet on a motorcycle. That 100,000-mile journey took me across six continents and through dozens of countries; it landed me in the *Guinness Book of Records* and resulted in a best-selling book of my own, *Investment Biker: Around the World with Jim Rogers.* No sooner had I completed the trip and returned home to New York than I began thinking about something more. I was abetted in my quest to find it by a simple quirk of the calendar: the approaching turn of the millennium. My insatiable thirst to understand firsthand what is going on in the world, to be there, to see it for myself—to dig out the real story—was intensified by the opportunity to capitalize on a historical moment. My plan was to spend three years driving around the globe as the twentieth century came to a close, to take the world's pulse at the end of one millennium and the start of another.

The trip would be both an adventure and a part of the continuing education I had been engaged in all my life, from rural Demopolis, Alabama, where I grew up, through Yale, Oxford, and the U.S. Army, and eventually to Wall Street, where experience taught me that the "experts" were usually wrong. My travels tended to be characterized by the slaughter of sacred cows, the puncturing of various balloons, and the laying to rest of preconceptions of the world held by certain "authorities," many of whom rarely left home. My success in the market has been predicated on viewing the world from a different perspective.

While I have never patronized a prostitute, I know that one can learn more about a country from speaking to the madam of a brothel or a black marketeer than from speaking to a government minister. There is nothing like crossing outlying borders for gaining insights into a country.

Finding promising investment opportunities was not a defined aim of the trip, but just because I am who I am, it is something that happens when I travel. As an investor, I would seek to learn about the markets in China, Africa, and South America, and I would visit promising stock exchanges whenever possible. I had made money in the past by investing in sleepy markets, such as Austria, Botswana, Peru, and others, and would no doubt stumble on some again.

If the trip killed me, I would die happy, pursuing my passion. And that was better than dying on Wall Street someday with a few extra dollars in my pocket.

The trip took me through 116 countries, many of which are rarely visited: Saudi Arabia, Myanmar, Angola, Sudan, Congo, Colombia, East Timor, and the like. The journey took me down the west coast and up the east coast of Africa, through thirty-two countries there. (My previous trip had taken me straight down the center, from Tunis to Cape Town.) It took me from Atlantic to Pacific—out of Europe across Central Asia and China—and from the Pacific back to the Atlantic, by way of Siberia. From the northeast coast of Africa I traveled across Arabia and the Indian subcontinent to Indochina, Malaysia, and Indonesia. After touring Australia and New Zealand, I made for the southern tip of South America, driving from there to Alaska before heading home to New York. No one had ever driven overland following this route. The trip took me through approximately half of the world's thirty civil wars, covered 152,000 miles, 50,000 more than the distance of my previous trip, and resulted in another Guinness World Record.

Studies have shown that traveling around the world is people's single most popular fantasy; many people in many places around the globe approached and said, "You are living everyone's dream."

The trip began on January 1, 1999, in Reykjavík, the capital of Iceland. I did not make the trip alone. I traveled with a beautiful woman, a blue-eyed blonde from Rocky Mount, North Carolina, named Paige Parker. I met Paige in 1996 during a speaking engagement at the Mint Museum in Charlotte. Paige, a fund-raiser at Queens College, had read my book on the recommendation of Billy Wireman, the college president, and come to hear me speak about my motorcycle trip. I tracked her down the next day and invited her to dinner.

"I'm thinking of going around the world again," I said to her on our first date. "I haven't told anybody yet. But I'm thinking of doing it at the turn of the millennium."

She agreed that such a trip could be illuminating.

"Do you want to go with me?" I asked.

She was momentarily dumbstruck.

"Yes," she said. "Sign me on."

Of course, we both thought it was idle banter.

Who knew?

Paige and I had been dating for a little over a year when she quit her job in Charlotte and moved to New York, taking her own apartment there in October 1997. As she began working as a director at a marketing firm and she and I began working that much more on our romance, I began seriously searching for an overland alternative to motorcycles.

There is nothing more exhilarating than driving a motorcycle. I have owned several in my life. I first rode a motorcycle across China in 1988, a trip documented by PBS as part of its *Travels* series, titled "The Long Ride." More than exhilaration, there is a simplicity to a bike. It is a lot easier, for example, to get a motorcycle across oceans, across deserts, or through jungles. And had Paige been enthusiastic to do so, we might have motorcycled around the globe. It was she who encouraged me to think about making the trip in a car. But I was not going to travel in just any car. It had to be a sports car. And it had to be a convertible. I wanted to put the top down and have the wind in my face.

Of course, I knew nothing about cars. Living in New York City, I had not owned one since 1968. And my ignorance was apparent to everyone when I explained that what I was looking for was a convertible two-seater with four-wheel drive and a lot of clearance off the ground, without which, I could guarantee, no car was going to make it around the world.

Everyone in turn guaranteed me that there was no such car on the market.

Every two years there is a big Four-Wheel-Drive Show in Munich, and in the spring of 1998 I attended it. I did not find the car I was looking for, but I met people there who modified cars—I had looked at many vehicles by now and figured I would use a sporty body on a Toyota chassis—and one of them told me about a fellow in California I should look up. It was typical of the quest that I had to go to Germany to find a guy in California. The guy in California told me about *another* guy in California (it was very much like trying to get into Cameroon two years later), and that is how I met Gerhard Steinle. It was Steinle and his team at Prisma Design International who would put together the one-of-a-kind Mercedes-Benz in which Paige and I eventually traveled the world.

By then my requirements had become more specific. More than a convertible, the car had to be equipped with a retractable hardtop. I did not want to run the risk of the top's being slashed, which could prove to be a definite damper on a trip around the world. Furthermore, I decided, it had to have a diesel engine. Trucks, buses, trains, and boats around the world run on diesel fuel, and you can always get it. Gasoline, I had discovered on my previous trip, was often very difficult to find. If you could get it at all, you could not be sure it would be any good.

Steinle, a former president of Mercedes-Benz Advanced Design of North America, came up with the notion of merging the body and interior of Mercedes' SLK roadster with the chassis and diesel engine of the company's sport-utility vehicle, known in Europe as the G-Class, or *der Geländewagen* (G-Wagen). The rugged G-Wagen, designed originally for German military and police use, would be unavailable in the United States until three years later, when it would be introduced as the G500. The SLK, which came with a retractable hardtop as standard equipment, was built on the same wheelbase as the shorter of the two G-Class models. The chassis of the two cars were the same. To marry the two, Steinle figured out, we would not have to cut or lengthen anything.

I told Steinle that I needed an extra fuel tank and a secret compartment in which to hide money. He said that because the hardtop retracted into the trunk, I was going to need a trailer, as well. He would design one to match the car. He talked me out of going with a manual transmission, explaining that Mercedes-Benz was a far better driver than I and that the company's automatic transmission would get me out of predicaments better than I could extricate myself with a stick shift.

"I need everything ready to go by the end of the year," I said.

Steinle, unbeknownst to me, rather than simply order the cars, called Mercedes of North America, told the people there that he had this crazy guy who wanted to do X, Y, and Z, and asked if they wanted to get involved. Apparently, they liked the story. When I next heard from Steinle, he reported, to my amazement, that he had persuaded Mercedes of North America to provide the vehicles free of charge, as long as I paid for the expensive conversion.

"And of course," Gerhard said, "they'll be under warranty."

"Let's do it."

NEW YORK AND ICELAND

Even in the absence of a warranty, I knew, I would find Mercedes service everywhere in the world. Even in the developing world one is never far from a dealership; every dictator and mafioso in the world drives a Mercedes. Even in countries with no roads to speak of, Mercedes service is available—often to the exclusion of things like food—thanks to all the U.S. foreign aid, the International Monetary Fund, and World Bank money being shipped in. It is no secret that this money is aimed at nourishing only those corrupt enough to get their hands on it, while at the same time fattening the bureaucrats on both sides of the transaction who diligently work the trough. And none of them is driving a Chevy.

I knew much of this from my last trip. The upcoming trip, especially as it took us through Africa, would be an eye-opening education into the workings of the latest foreign aid scam: the nongovernmental organization, or NGO. As an American taxpayer, I would be amazed to discover that a lot of the money we send to these countries goes to support Mercedes and BMW dealers and various Swiss bankers.

But more about that later.

The truth is that had we traveled in a different car, we probably never would have made it around the world; this wacky idea of a car was the perfect choice in every way. One of its more important attributes would prove to be its color. Officially Sunburst Yellow, or, as I saw it, Martian Movie Yellow, it would draw crowds everywhere we went, making us many friends in the process, and in so doing save our lives on several occasions. Showing up by surprise in a car so unusual, so weird, and at the same time so downright unthreatening, would spark immediate curiosity. The bizarre, all-terrain hybrid in explosive color was just goofy enough to throw people off balance, to warm them up long enough to get us through a particular situation before anyone had a chance to say, "Hey, we forgot to rob those people" or "Weren't we supposed to kidnap them?"

One of the more frequently asked questions one gets about traveling around the world is "How do you pack?" It is worth mentioning here that when we designed the trailer for this trip, we in effect designed it around the supplies with which we intended to fill it. We got everything we wanted to take with us, put it in a pile, and measured the pile, determining how many cubic feet of space we would need, and gave the measurement to the people who were manufacturing the trailer. Among all the things we carried, the jerry cans for extra water and fuel, the sleeping bags, the tent, and whatever else we packed into the trailer, the most important item, and the first to go into the pile, was the kit containing medical supplies. And it was big—not so big that it could not be carried aboard an airplane, but bigger than the typical household first aid kit.

To determine what went into the kit, we visited a couple of doctors, among them exotic disease specialists, and got their recommendations. We packed syringes because there are many places in the world where syringes are unavailable, or where, if available, they are recycled. We had normal stuff, bandages and disinfectants, and we also had malaria pills and antibiotics. And we had instructions on how and when to use them and what symptoms to look for, in the event that we had to act as our own doctors. It was a pretty extensive first aid kit, and we had a doctor's letter, for what it was worth, to show those border guards who might suspect us of smuggling. I am happy to say that very little of what we carried did we ever actually need. Normally, if we needed something, we would buy it locally, if it were available, rather than invade the first aid kit, which was much more important for emergencies out in the bush.

Before setting out on the trip, I prepared an extra wallet. It contained several expired credit cards, an expired license or two, and what looked like a lot of money—a healthy portion of low-grade currency, Italian lire, Spanish pesetas, and Portuguese escudos—so that I would have something convincing to hand over calmly in the event that I was robbed.

In addition to the G-Wagen and the SLK roadster that he would combine to make the hybrid, Gerhard arranged for Mercedes to donate a second G-Wagen as well. The additional—straight, unmodified—SUV would carry the video cameraman and Webmaster I was seeking to recruit for the trip.

Paige and I knew from the beginning that we wanted to document the trip. And it did not take some youngster's running up to me and saying "You need a Web site" for me to realize that there was no other way to do it. Ten years earlier, there had been many places where the only way I could communicate with New York was by postcard. But the world had since undergone a communications revolution of blinding velocity, and Paige and I were determined to participate in the revolution firsthand. We decided to maintain a multimedia Web site, with audio and video, by way of which we would provide an on-line diary of the trip and interact with those who "traveled" with us. (I was so naïve as to think that this would be a snap. Though ultimately it worked, it was far more difficult and annoying than I had anticipated.)

For the last twenty-seven and thirty-one months of the trip, respectively, we were joined in our adventure by the same videographer and Webmaster, Chris Capozzoli and Fredrik Görander, who traveled in the second vehicle and helped chronicle the trip.

I ran my third consecutive New York City Marathon in the fall of 1998. Just as I finished the race, I asked Paige to be my wife. She accepted. We were not yet in a position to specify plans—who knew where we would be or where we would *want* to be at the time—but we did set a date: January 1, 2000.

Paige had quit her job in anticipation of our spending time in California with a four-wheel-drive instructor, but the company to which Gerhard Steinle subcontracted the metalwork missed several deadlines and we were unable to practice with the car before striking out. We managed to get hold of the car and load it aboard a ship bound for Iceland just in time to meet our January 1, 1999, deadline.

Paige and I had been talking about the trip virtually from the moment we met, but putting your life on hold for three years is not easy for most people. Paige's feeling was that the trip represented a challenge and an opportunity that she would forever regret passing up. Even though she had just received her first big promotion and raise— she had been on the job only a year—she nonetheless felt that after the trip, being that much more knowledgeable and well rounded a person, she would be even more employable.

Several times before we left, I gave Paige a chance to back out of the trip. As the deadline approached, I increased the pressure, encouraging her to think twice.

"You don't really know what you're getting in for," I said. "Everything that can go wrong *will* go wrong. Things that you cannot imagine, no matter how well we plan, will go wrong. Things are always going wrong. Just by the nature of the world. It's going to be very difficult, and our lives will be in danger. There will be deserts and jungles . . ."

"I'm going," she said.

"There will be wars, there will be epidemics . . ."

"I'm tough," she said.

"There will be blizzards . . ."

"I can do it."

And with that we flew off to celebrate New Year's Eve in the Land of the Midnight Sun.

It had to be the worst blizzard that that part of Iceland had seen in thirty years, and it hit unexpectedly on the third day of our trip. Even with our faces pressed to the windshield, we could not see the front of the car. Not even the meter posts could keep me on the road. Driving along with the posts on my right, I suddenly noticed them on my left. When the meter posts finally disappeared beneath the snow, I knew we were in serious trouble.

No visibility. Deep snow. Disaster.

Driving perfectly was not good enough anymore. A slight turn to the right, and we would veer off the mountainside; to the left, and we would drive directly into it. Avoid either, and there was always the possibility of a head-on collision with an oncoming truck.

Setting out in Iceland on our round-the-world adventure, we had not known if we would return alive—but not even at our most pessimistic had we thought we might die on our third day out.

Iceland is the westernmost country in Europe. Also, it was celebrating the one thousandth anniversary of Leif Eriksson's voyages west from there to North America. But what really drew me to choose Iceland as a starting point for the trip was a happenstance of geology. Tectonic plates beneath the Eastern and Western Hemispheres come together in Iceland; it is the only place in the world where you can actually drive from North America to Europe—geologically speaking. What better place to start the trip?

We were in the capital, Reykjavík, on December 31, 1998, in time for one of the world's great spectacles. On New Year's Eve in Iceland, everybody puts on a fireworks display—every town, every block, every household, every family, individually, all at the same time. Imagine a city of 150,000, the sky above it one massive light show, everybody trying to outdo everybody else, and you have Reykjavík on New Year's Eve. The celebration begins with gigantic bonfires all over the city. They start at around ten o'clock. People travel from one bonfire to the next, huge mobs of people, throwing things into the fires. You can look out beyond the city and see bonfires lighting the sky over towns that are fifty kilometers away. Sometime before midnight, the fireworks begin. The sky in every town erupts. Paige and I, watching from Perlan, a revolving restaurant built atop Reykjavík's geothermal hot-water storage tanks, sat there overwhelmed.

We officially started the trip the following day, January 1, 1999, drinking champagne at Thingvellir, on the spot where the tectonic plates meet, some thirty kilometers from Reykjavík. The plates, we learned, are actually pulling apart. As a result of its seismic instability, Iceland is overactive with earthquakes, volcanoes, and hot springs. Sixty thousand years from now this island nation suspended just below the Arctic Circle is going to split in two, but in the meantime electricity here is cheap because of the island's enormous store of geothermal energy.

As far as domestic energy is concerned, Iceland is even better situated than Saudi Arabia. The Saudis will run out of oil some day, but Iceland has vast amounts of perpetual, renewable energy in geysers, natural steam, and hot water—all of it virtually free after the initial investment to capture and harness it. Everywhere you go you find outdoor pools, naturally heated. The night before we set out, we were swimming, doing the backstroke, in one of those outdoor pools, with snowflakes coming down on our faces.

The first day of the trip was wonderful. We set off at daybreak, which at that time of year, that far north, does not hit until after ten A.M. We traveled the ring road that circles the country—fourteen hundred kilometers from Reykjavík to Egilsstadir to Akureyri, then back around to Reykjavík—a rough, jagged, glorious country of glaciers, geysers, fjords, ancient lava flows, waterfalls, and eruptions of steam. Our first night on the road we stayed in a farmhouse about three hundred kilometers east of the capital, heading the next morning to Egilsstadir on the country's east coast. The second day of the trip was more of the same. Absolutely perfect. Glorious winter scenes and no traffic. We ate Arctic char dragged that day from the sea, which even topped the fresh puffin we had eaten the day before.

We could not have been happier.

And then came day three.

Leaving Egilsstadir, we set off across a mountain pass toward the northern town of Akureyri. Conditions became treacherous almost immediately. A light snow quickly turned into a driving, blinding, heavy Icelandic blizzard. Darkness fell in the middle of the afternoon. The meter posts disappeared, I guessed wrong one time too often, drove off the road, and we came to a sudden stop in a snowbank. Jumping out of the car, thigh-deep in snow, we shoveled to clear the tires, but new snow, replacing the old, rapidly outpaced us. It was soon apparent that we were going nowhere.

Soaking wet and shivering, we were rescued a few hours later. A passing truck driver had notified authorities that these hopeless Americans were trapped in the snow. The police showed up, followed by a flatbed truck with a winch. They got the Mercedes up onto the road, we secured it, and we started back to town in the police car— which was when things really turned dangerous. Our driver nearly got us killed along the way. Apparently, he was the town's only policeman. While he was rescuing us, an airplane, caught in the blizzard, crashed at the local airport, and because the policeman was racing to get there, we skidded off the road a few times.

By then Paige had just about lost it.

The rescue squad came as we were about to set off, and the man in charge said, "We'll go with you this time. You're guests in our country. These are conditions you are unfamiliar with. We'll see you over the mountain."

Our arrival in the country had been big news to start with, since a country of only 270,000 people does not have much news in January. Our dawn departure three days earlier had attracted numerous tourists and had been widely covered by the local media. So naturally, our rescue was all over the press. News reports portrayed us as nutty Americans trying to drive around Iceland in January. It was not going to look good if we got killed. So when we set out across the mountain two days later, we were escorted by the rescue squad in its big-time, all-terrain, four-wheel-drive vehicle, custom made to go anywhere in Iceland in the worst conditions conceivable. There was nothing this machine could not do, nobody it could not rescue.

Until the rescue squad drove it off the mountain.

We had to rescue the rescue squad.

You can imagine the Icelandic press. The story played better than the original rescue. Here were these hapless American tourists, up against the Icelandic winter, and they had to rescue the rescue squad. And we had it all on videotape. Which naturally I shared with the media. The tape shows me shoveling snow as fast as I can, trying to save Iceland's experts.

And it shows Paige having second thoughts.

Not five days into the trip, Paige was in shock, literally—ashen-faced, quivering, panicked—showing the clinical symptoms of shock. There she was on videotape, thinking, "Even the rescue squad is a disaster." All the warnings about bandits in Russia and malaria in Africa had not prepared her for this.

I had been around the world before, and I knew that this, our first predicament, was not going to be our last.

"We were trapped in a blizzard, we survived, that's part of the adventure," I told her, exhilarated by our escape.

"We didn't save ourselves," she said. "Thank God the rescue squad came along."

"We're alive," I said. "We made it. That's part of the excitement."

"Excitement, Jim?" she said. "There I was, thinking, 'This is the guy I'm trusting my life to, and he doesn't know how to drive. What on earth am I doing?' There I was, stuck in two feet of snow, wearing tennis shoes in an Arctic blizzard."

"That," I said, "is what's so much fun about going around the world."

Paige did not quite feel that way.

We made it all the way around Iceland, spending two weeks in the country. We met with President Ólafur Ragnar Grímsson, and Paige had more questions of him than I did, specifically on women's issues affecting Iceland. While I toured the stock exchange, she interviewed women business owners. The head of a modeling agency pointed out a fact of local demographics that we found illuminating: that despite the image Iceland has around the world for being home to numerous blonds, it actually has more brunets per capita than any of the other four Scandinavian countries. Icelanders are the descendants of Irish slaves brought by the Vikings to Scandinavia a thousand years ago. There are very few true xanthochroids on the island.

In Iceland we discovered a country in the midst of enormous change. There were young people everywhere we went. The streets, bars, and restaurants all were packed with kids. Well over half the population of Iceland is under thirty years old. People under fifty are heavily represented in positions of influence in the country. Iceland, demographically, is one of the four youngest countries in the world, and that alone will lead to the most dramatic changes in the way it is run after centuries of isolation.

Because agriculture is still heavily protected and there are high tariffs on imported foodstuffs, basic necessities are currently so expensive that many people have to work two or three jobs to maintain their living standard. But the country is becoming more urban. A majority of the population now lives in greater Reykjavík. With fewer and fewer farmers to protect, price supports are much harder for politicians to justify. Subsidizing food production on a volcanic island that is contiguous to the Arctic Circle is perceived by youthful voters as an increasingly ludicrous extravagance. Quotas governing the wild fishery are also being reexamined. Restrictions on foreign investment, especially in the energy sector, have condemned the country to little development in that very lucrative resource as well.

The same outdated thinking behind the protection of those industries is directed at safeguarding the nation's cultural heritage. Iceland was a Danish colony for hundreds of years, and it is still mandatory for all schoolchildren there to study Danish as a second language. Ponder that for a minute. Denmark is a nation of five million people, so there are maybe seven million people on earth who speak Danish. Doing so is hardly a competitive advantage in today's world, and forcing kids to study the language clearly helps hold Iceland back. Their children, you can be sure, will not learn Danish; they will learn English, Spanish, Mandarin, or Cantonese.

We would run into this again and again, everywhere in the world— in Ireland, for example, where all schoolchildren are required to learn Gaelic, or Irish as they call it now. Who in the world speaks Gaelic? Why are they not learning German or some dialect of Chinese? If there are people dying to learn Gaelic, let them do it, but making it compulsory leads to a dead end. When they are thirty-five years old, all Gaelic will get them is a job washing dishes. Irish politicians are now using Gaelic as a form of protectionism—another dead end. The novelist Roddy Doyle was teaching English in Ireland, but was assessed on his Irish if he wanted to keep his job. One must speak

Irish to get a job at Aer Lingus now—not very conducive to attracting talent.

The sad fact of the matter is that sometime within the next hundred
years there may be only about thirty languages left in the world—and
Gaelic and Danish will probably not be among the survivors. It may
be horrible that Gaelic is disappearing, but the world has already lost
hundreds of languages. Take Cornwall on the southwest coast of England. The last person who spoke Cornish died fifty years ago. Are we
going to go back and teach everyone Cornish? There are a lot of native American languages and a lot of African languages that have disappeared. It is nothing to celebrate. But if people were sitting around
still speaking them, they would be even worse off than they are.

People who fight change are fighting inevitability itself. Think of all
the great cities and great civilizations throughout history. The great
city of Carthage, home of Hannibal—gone. It is nothing but a memory, an excavation site. Families, tribes, corporations and nations,
races, languages, entire civilizations—gone. I am not applauding it. It
would be wonderful, and enriching to us all, if the Aztecs were still
here. I am sure the Maya would love to be what they once were. But
cutting yourself off from the world and fighting the forces of history
are not going to protect you from the fate that those civilizations suffered.

In 1962, Burma was the richest country in Asia. The army decided:
We do not need the rest of the world, we are closing the door. Since
then, of course, Burma, present-day Myanmar, has been a disaster in
nearly every way. In 1957, Ghana was the richest country in the British
Empire, richer than England itself. Promptly upon the country's
achieving independence, the great liberator, Kwame Nkrumah, closed
the country, saying, "What do we need the British for?" Seven years
later the country was bankrupt. Two hundred years ago, Ethiopia did
the same thing.

Poor Copernicus was condemned for claiming that the earth was
not the center of the universe. The Catholic Church made him recant.

You can take a similar approach today—tell an Icelandic kid that
he has to learn Danish—but you are not doing your country any
good, and you are not going to stop the wind of change from sweeping over you. History is replete with examples of nations that paid the
price for ignoring reality.

One of the more visible changes the world is undergoing right now is the end of the age of the empire builders. Over the past three hundred years, thanks to technological advances, countries tended to grow bigger and bigger. That tendency is reversing. There are about two hundred countries in the world today. Over the next three to five decades, there will be three hundred or four hundred. Many have already begun to disintegrate. The Soviet Union is now fifteen countries. Yugoslavia is now six, Czechoslovakia is now two, Ethiopia two. Somalia? Who knows? Many of us have heard of the Basque independence movement in Spain, but who realized that three other regions of the country—Catalonia, Castilla, and Navarre—also have separatist movements? And along comes East Timor. In conjunction with globalization, we are seeing tribalization. While we are dancing to Madonna, drinking Pepsi, and driving Toyotas, people are reaching out for something they can understand and control. The emergence of smaller nations from the ashes of collapsing empires may lead to wars but need not necessarily do so. If borders remain open to trade and migration, we will all be better off.

Evidence of the trend is visible in Europe but is even more apparent beyond it, in Africa and especially in Asia. It is in Asia, the crucible of some of the world's oldest civilizations, that many of the more immediate changes of the new millennium are taking place. And Paige and I were eager to get there.

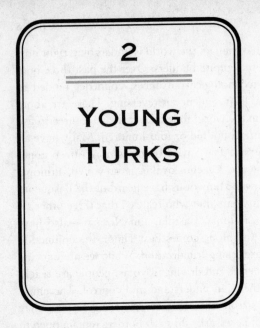

# 2

## YOUNG TURKS

WE SPENT A MONTH crossing Europe, starting in the United Kingdom and driving southeast to the Black Sea. Waiting for the car in Edinburgh, less than two weeks into our trip, Paige, having survived an Icelandic blizzard, came down with a horrible case of food poisoning after eating at a five-star restaurant. On the road for a full three years, touring the more remote, primitive regions of the planet, eating what we could find along the way, Paige would suffer serious food poisoning a total of three times. In each case her falling ill would result from eating at a five-star restaurant.

From Scotland, we drove to Northern Ireland. And I very much liked what I found there. The pubs were mobbed, and talking to the kids was encouraging as well as informative. They do not have all the hang-ups about Protestants and Catholics that are typical of their elders. The Easter Uprising means nothing to them. And when they look ahead, to the future, these kids look to Europe—not London or Dublin—for inspiration.

The changes I saw coming in Northern Ireland were more than

*Ireland is the only country in the European Union
not suffering a fertility crisis.*

merely conjectural. A lot of people are currently investing there. Prosperity, against the efforts of certain entrenched interests, appears to be breaking out. Foreign investors believe in the peace that is promised by the present cease-fire. The throwbacks of Sinn Fein, who are invested in war, are swimming against the current. Companies are moving into the country with jobs, and it is employment, not war, for which everybody is mobilizing.

Convinced that peace was on the horizon, I said to Paige, "Let's buy some land."

Successful investing means getting in early, when things are cheap, when everything is distressed, when everyone is demoralized. On the theory that a rising tide lifts all ships—that even if you are not very smart you are going to do well, if only in spite of yourself—I looked into real estate in Northern Ireland. Unfortunately (for me, not the Irish) I was not the first one to think of doing so. To make a killing, you really need to get in during a time of despair. In Ireland there is little despair.

The Republic of Ireland itself is a European Tiger. It is booming (although it is in debt). Since the onset of the potato famine in the middle of the nineteenth century, Irish have been leaving the country, or have been until now. Now, after 150 years of emigration, Ireland is suddenly playing host to a significant influx of immigrants. The Irish themselves are returning, and foreigners are moving in. Europeans, Americans, multinational companies—they are all building factories in Ireland. Also, thanks to a change in the tax laws, there is a computer boom under way.

One thing I learned from traveling around the world is that when you pull into a large, unfamiliar city, traveling overland, the best and easiest thing to do is to get a taxi to lead you to your hotel. Dublin was the first such city into which we drove. Paige, who was driving, insisted that to find our hotel, no taxi driver was necessary. She could follow the map. We turned down one street . . . it was a dead end. Another . . . it was a one-way street.

"It doesn't say one way on the map," Paige explained.

We drove in circles. And we fought.

"A taxi driver will know exactly where the hotel is," I argued.

"A taxi is a waste of money and time."

"It will *save* us time," I said.

Finally, after two hours, she relented. We got a taxi. And we followed it. From then on—when we got to London, when we got to Berlin—it was Paige who said, "Let's get a taxi."

In England we stocked up on supplies—sleeping bags, camping equipment, guidebooks, maps. It was the last time for a long time we would be able to get some of this stuff, our last shot at a decent selection of printed material written in English. One of my former students, John Durrell, gave us a going-away dinner of fine English lamb washed down with Château Margaux in the very room at the Reform Club where Jules Verne's Phileas Fogg began and ended his fictional journey in *Around the World in Eighty Days*. In Frankfurt, I visited a few financial folks. I toured the stock exchange, talked to a lot of people, and what I heard was far too much optimism and "New Economy" hype to merit any investment. Driving through Austria, we hit a second blizzard—the worst to hit the area in many decades, we were told, which was the only kind we seemed destined to hit—and made it through the mountains just before they closed the roads.

Having not yet driven beyond the geographical confines of the European Union, we had not yet really crossed a border. When we reached Hungary on February 11, crossing behind the old Iron Curtain into what was once known as the Eastern Bloc, Paige got her first taste of a real-world border crossing. The border guards were not as polite as the preacher of her Baptist church in North Carolina. These were guys with submachine guns. They did not say, "Yeah, we remember you, Paige. You were Miss Junior Miss" or anything remotely like that. And Paige was indignant at the treatment we received.

Budapest, once a center of the Austro-Hungarian Empire, is a glorious, beautiful city, a city essentially frozen in time. Nobody has built anything significant in a century, and all the old structures still stand. The entire city could serve as a museum. Little has changed in a hundred years; the country has been nothing but broke. They lost the First World War, they lost the Second, and then the Communists moved in after that. Budapest is the physical expression of a historical moment—the high-water mark of a great, rich culture, gone. The Austro-Hungarian Empire has disappeared; the Habsburgs in powdered wigs and white gloves no longer dance to the strains of Mozart rising over the Danube.

Our plan had been to go from Hungary to Turkey by way of Romania and Bulgaria. But the weather was horrible, the terrain was mountainous, and the second-rate roads would be hazardous. It was the dead of February, and we were no strangers now to the impact of sudden blizzards. Our only alternative was to go through Yugoslavia, the two most prominent features of which were a well-paved motorway, a toll road, running north to south, which we found encouraging, and a recent outbreak of war, running in the same general direction, which we did not. We decided to take our chances.

Yugoslavia presented the first border at which we were charged extra fees. Having traveled extensively, I knew that when one was charged extra money, there would usually be extra forms to fill out. I was paying little attention—the fees were minimal, I was expecting them—though they did take Paige by surprise. Another border, another lesson. But Paige was not the only one who discovered something that day.

In payment of the fees in question, the border guards refused to take dinars.

This caught my attention.

We were crossing the border into Yugoslavia, and the border guards would not accept Yugoslav money—they would not accept their own currency.

Curious to see what would happen next, we headed down the motorway, a government toll road, manned by the military. We did not want to stop. And then it happened again. The toll takers, Yugoslav soldiers, would not take dinars, either—dinars we had purchased with dollars expressly for this purpose. They would accept dollars, deutsche marks, and Austrian schillings, but not their own currency. Now I knew the country was really in trouble. In most places around the world, the currency is like a thermometer. It may not tell you what is going on, but it tells you that *something* is going on, and you know a country is falling apart when even the government will not accept its own currency.

By the time night fell, we were in Niš, headquarters of the Serbian Army's southern command, not much farther from Kosovo than we were from the Bulgarian border. Of course, the hotel would not accept the local currency either. Or credit cards. The proprietors knew, and I knew, that with the U.S. sanctions that were in place, they were not going to get paid. So we had to pay for everything in cash. But not

their cash. We spent some of our dinars on fuel, wasted some on inci-
dentals, and dumped the remainder on the black market as we crossed
into Bulgaria.

That night, we were awakened by what I knew to be small-arms
fire.

"What's that?" asked Paige, almost talking in her sleep.

I lied. Being of the opinion, this early in the trip, that I may have a hys-
teric on my hands, I said, "Oh, they're moving furniture downstairs."

"Oh, okay," said Paige, and went back to sleep.

I suppose I could have said, "Automatic weapons, darling. Sounds
like a very small firefight . . ."

I realized we really had to get out of there.

We left, heading into Bulgaria through scenic countryside. Paige
drove, and I, as was my habit, drifted off to sleep. When I awoke,
Paige painted me a word picture of the dramatic change in scenery
that had revealed itself as we approached the Bulgarian capital, Sofia.
The roadside was lined with prostitutes, she said. The young women,
parading there, raised their skirts as drivers passed, advertising their
wares. Until I saw it for myself, a dozen times in a dozen other places,
I did not believe her.

A few days after we left Yugoslavia, in an expression of far greater
dissatisfaction with things than any we might have offered, the United
States started bombing the country.

As the gateway to Asia, Turkey was the place where I thought I might
get my first good look at the future, observing some of the more dramatic economic and cultural changes overtaking the world. Expecting
positive things to be happening there, I was keen to meet people and
ask questions. In northwest Turkey, overlooking the Sea of Marmara,
is one of the world's truly exotic cities: Istanbul. I had been there a
couple of times before, most recently on my motorcycle trip, and I
was eager to share it with Paige. In whatever era, whether as Byzantium, Constantinople, or present-day Istanbul, the ancient city on the
Bosporus has always been fascinating.

We drove into Istanbul on the day Abdullah Öcalan, the Kurdish
rebel leader sought by the Turkish government, was captured in
Sudan. Tanks and armored personnel carriers patrolled the streets,
and jumpy Turkish soldiers, automatic weapons at the ready, stood

everywhere, prepared to respond to almost certain demonstrations on the part of the nation's Kurds, who represent 20 percent of Turkey's population.

Turkey is where Europe and Asia cleave—in both, mutually opposed, meanings of the word. The Bosporus is where the continents geographically split and culturally embrace, and nowhere is the rich result more evident than in Istanbul. Once the ancient Greek city of Byzantium, it is the site on which the Roman Emperor Constantine, in A.D. 330, built his empire's eastern capital, naming it Constantinople. With the fall of Rome, the city continued as the capital of the Byzantine Empire. It was the major center of eastern Christianity until it fell to the Turks and their Ottoman Empire in 1453. It was officially renamed Istanbul in 1930, two years before Turkey joined the League of Nations.

In our stay in Istanbul, we met numerous people who clearly took their identity from the West and considered themselves Europeans. In this same cosmopolitan city, the largest in Turkey, we watched people sacrifice goats on the side of the road. We dined one night with three successful businessmen, rich, well-educated Turks, and their wives. One of the men was at pains to explain that he and his wife, being Europeans, had nothing in common with those people we had seen on the roadside, people he clearly identified with Asia.

"We're not evil, wily Turks, or whatever your image of us is in the West," his wife added somewhat defensively.

We had first met this couple in the United States through Murat Köprülü, an American friend of Turkish heritage. When we were introduced in New York, I suggested we all go uptown for a unique American experience and took the visiting Turkish couple to a Harlem nightclub, where we danced to big band music. Our dinner in Istanbul was their way of returning the favor. In lieu of an orchestra, the Turkish nightclub featured belly dancers, the first of whom seemed particularly attracted to me. She directed all of her attention my way, dancing right in front of me, for what seemed like a very long time. What I had not noticed, of course, was that every other patron had slipped money into her skirt as she danced by. She finally danced away, no doubt resigned to the fact that I was a cheapskate. An easily understandable faux pas on my part—she was the first belly dancer I had seen up close—and I was forgiven with a smile when, once I realized what was happening, I stood up, crossed the floor, and did as tradition demanded. (This experience would only half prepare me for the belly dancer we would run into in Baku on the Caspian Sea.)

It was Nuri Colakoglu, our host, during the course of the evening, who informed me that there were three Turkish corporations that were the largest of their kind in Europe. I have to admit I was stunned. One was a manufacturer of white goods, or household appliances; another made ceramic goods. The third, Sabancı, a manufacturer of tire cord fabric and industrial nylon, was the largest company of its kind in the world. For Turkey to have one, much less three, European industry leaders was startling. I had to confess that I was guilty of harboring that same outdated image of Turkey that the man's wife was so defensive about.

You do not accomplish something like that in a week or two. It takes brains, the accumulation of capital, and a sound educational system. Something was going on in Turkey, and I decided to look into investing there.

Later Paige and I had dinner with Axel Arendt and his wife, Uta. Axel, the director of Mercedes-Benz Turkey, told me that Mercedes was manufacturing buses there.

"You can get Mercedes quality in Turkey?" I asked.

"Absolutely," he replied. "The same quality we get in Germany."

Quality as high as in Germany. I made him repeat it. Again, I admit, I was stunned.

"And we get the same quality much, much cheaper," he said. "We're adding capacity here."

I was speaking with an executive from Mercedes-Benz, with its worldwide reputation for very expensive, extremely high quality, precision engineering. And he was telling me that the same high quality that comes out of Germany is now coming out of Turkey. Cheaper.

My enthusiasm for investing continued to grow, until, I suppose you could say, etymology intervened. Passing through Germany, we had ordered a car cover to be made for the G-Wagen. It had not been ready by the time we left, so I had it sent to me in Turkey. It arrived at the airport in Istanbul, delivered by DHL.

"Have it sent over here to the hotel," I said.

"We can't just bring it to you," said the caller from the courier service. "You have to come to the airport to get it."

And that is when the derivation of the word "Byzantine" departed the realm of the merely semantic. Redeeming the car cover at Turkish Customs was an intricate mosaic of official procedure. I was forced to spend several hours visiting several offices, purchasing more than a dozen stamps, and buying $75 worth of permits for a tarp that cost no more than $150, as though I were importing it for sale. I went from office to office, filling out countless forms, all for a piece of rubberized cloth, a custom-made car cover that was of no use to anyone but me, that I was taking out of the country. The next day, as luck would have it, my battered laptop arrived from New York. And back to the airport I went. This time I had to see twenty-two separate officials, some of them three and four times . . . more stamps, more forms, back and forth . . . and obtain several dozen documents. After two days in a row of dealing with Turkish bureaucracy, I thought twice about investing in Turkey.

Still I could not ignore the strong indicators of economic progress. With the fall of communism and the opening up of the old Central Asian republics, Turkey is in a unique position to exploit the vast new market emerging on its eastern border, far better situated than any western European country to do so. As part of the Ottoman Empire, Central Asia was once controlled by Turkey. Their languages, religion, history, and cultures are similar. In Turkmenistan, I would discover that the Mercedes dealer was a young Turk—indeed in both meanings of the word, having gone there to exploit the new economic frontier. From the Black Sea to Tashkent, as we traveled east through the land of the old Islamic caliphates, we would find Turks everywhere we went, filling the vacuum created by the fall of the Soviet Union and the withdrawal of the Russians.

For decades Turkey has been trying to become part of the European Union. And as much as Turkey needs that to happen, Europe needs it more. The population of many European countries is aging in dramatic fashion. In Italy, for example, the following November, we would walk into restaurants and look around, and we would see no kids. Everybody was over fifty. The Italians have one of the lowest birthrates in the world. The same is true of much of the European Union.

A demographic time bomb is ticking all over Europe. If you are thinking of building a factory in Europe—in Germany or Spain, for example—think again. In five years you are going to suffer massive pension costs—social security, call it what you will—because the populace is so old. The government is not going to throw the country's old people out onto the street; the government is going to tax its companies, its workers, or both. And with only one or two workers for every retiree, costs are going to skyrocket.

Turkey, by contrast, is young, with seventy million people. It is almost as big as Germany, population-wise. Turks know how to manufacture efficiently, competently, and cheaply, and the European Union desperately needs them. Europe has to have its manufacturing done somewhere. And someone has to pay those pensions. Within the European Union there is free mobility of labor. If Turkey becomes a member, all the young Turks unable to find work at home can go to work for Siemens—pay taxes, donate to the pension fund, and support the aging Germans.

The younger the population of a country, the more open to change it is. A young population embraces change the way an older population reveres the past. One is not necessarily better than the other—and there is nothing particularly revealing in pointing any of this out—unless, of course, you are thinking of the future or thinking of investing.

It is one of the reasons I am so optimistic about Iran, a country where I do have small investments and one I was eager to visit on this trip. Iran is a young country. Right now Iranians are having as many children as possible. Forget about the mullahs. The majority of the population is happy to ignore what some seventy-eight-year-old guy tells them to do. I cannot think of a nation in history where masses of young people have stood up and said, "We like it the way it is. We like it the way it *used* to be even better than the way it is now. Let's go back to the old days."

One reason America became a wealthy country was because it kept constantly adding new markets. We called them states. People went west, filled up a given region, and we added that territory to the Union. That is just adding new markets. The United States became a bigger and bigger market all the time. Companies that were manufacturing horseless carriages or stagecoaches or cars, or whatever they happened to be making, were constantly selling to a bigger market. That is what Europe has done, of course. The European

Union remained strong as it continued adding markets. It started off as six countries. Then it went to fifteen. And admitting a country like Turkey now will only make it stronger.

As far back as 1693, early American statesman William Penn suggested a united Europe that would include Turkey.

For almost forty years Turkey has been applying for admittance. Its application has been denied, continually, for a variety of reasons. The Europeans always have reasons. But the chief reason for their denying the Turks is the reason that is never given. It is quite simple. It is because they are Turks. They are Muslim, they are not Christian. They may be white, but they are not *really* white people. They are a little too Asian.

It is for this reason that Europe will likely take in a country such as Estonia or Latvia, a white, Christian country, first. But taking in Turkey would be the better move by far. The Baltic states are tiny. Lithuania, with two million people, would bring little to the table but welfare problems, without substantially expanding the market. Certainly, the Baltic countries are in better shape than those of central Europe, several of which are applying—the Czech Republic, Slovakia, Romania—but I would leave them all alone. Central Europe is going to be a disaster.

The borders of central Europe were drawn after the two world wars by victorious armies rewarding friends and settling scores; little attention was given to history, ethnicity, religion, or linguistics. Parts of Prussia are in Poland now. The ancient German city of Königsberg—the home of Immanuel Kant—is now all the way east of Poland, a part of Russia yet cut off even from Russia. Most of us do not care much if Moldova is part of Romania or part of the Ukraine or whether it is independent, but many people in central Europe care a lot. Czechoslovakia has already broken into two countries. Yugoslavia is now perhaps six countries. Hungary may well go to war with one of its neighbors in the next decade. Ancient animosities are rising again as aspirations aroused by the fall of the Iron Curtain fail. The central Europeans were promised that democracy meant prosperity. They have all seen the equation play out on the TV programs America sends them. We in the United States know that one does not automatically lead to the other, but many in central Europe are bitter and looking for scapegoats. Why bring into the European Union several small, angry countries with little to offer—most of which are running huge budget deficits in excess of the terms of accession—when Turkey is willing to join?

Admitting Turkey would add seventy million people to the market; it would be one of the largest countries in the Union. Volkswagen could sell a lot of cars if it had another seventy million people to sell to—tax-free, tariff-free, duty-free. The economist understands what the politician does not want to admit. He may look askance at the unknown Turks personally, but as a productive entrepreneur, he knows he needs Turkey. The capitalist knows that whatever the problem a country exhibits, the underlying problem, more often than not, is rooted in its economy. It may pass for a religious or racial problem, but it is basically economic.

Take Germany, for example. As long as the economy was expanding, as it did in the 1960s and 1970s, there were no racial problems to speak of. When Germany was expanding, it was open to immigration and people were content. Give us your tired, your poor, your cheap labor yearning to be free, we want them. When Germany became a high-cost place to do business, one of the more expensive economies in the world, and as a result less competitive, the prevailing response was, "Get rid of them. We don't like those dirty foreigners. It was the Turks who caused our problems." And along came the skinheads. When jobs were no longer opening up and layoffs were under way, everybody looked for someone to blame. And it is always the foreigners who are blamed: the Christians or the Jews or the Muslims or the white people or the black people or the yellow . . . the Americans, whoever.

Everyone blames the foreigners when the economy goes south. Always. It is human nature to blame others, and it is the same all over the world: "We have been here for decades, for centuries, we are patriotic Americans. It is not our fault, it is never our fault. It is the fault of the evil, wily foreigners." Or it is the evil financiers: "It is not the wonderful folks of Iowa, these problems are not caused by us. It is the fault of those horrible people on Wall Street."

At the turn of the first millennium, Córdoba, in southern Spain, with a population of almost half a million, was perhaps the largest and most prosperous city in the world. In the fourteenth century, Samarkand, in modern-day Uzbekistan, was a city in the cultural and economic forefront. In those cities, it serves us well to remember, people from everywhere were welcome and lived peacefully together, Muslim, Christian, Jew, Chinese, Indian, nobody cared. It was their diversity, in large part, that made such places what they were, as artists, scholars, and merchants from all over the world were attracted to them. And this has been true throughout history. All of these places were great melting pots. It is when things start to go wrong and people look for someone to blame that one's religion, culture, and race become noticeable.

In the end I did not invest in Turkey, for a variety of reasons. I felt the Kurds, pushing for their homeland, were likely to keep creating trouble until they obtained some satisfaction. Also, the rising Muslim fundamentalist party was problematic at the time. Businesspeople kept telling me they were the only honest party, but some of their pronouncements were worrisome. The Turkish banking system is a mess, and the government has a long history of debasing the nation's currency; it will be a while before it has long-term value. And then here was my own Byzantine experience, trying to get my property out of Turkish Customs.

The country, then, was inimical to investors. I wanted to wait three or four years and then take another look. A lot of these problems seemed transitional. I had previously invested in Turkey once or twice, but always for the short term. Perhaps a few years down the road, I thought, the country would be a superb choice for the long-term investor.

Interestingly, three or four years have passed now and the religious party has won an absolute majority. Turkey now has a two-party Parliament, which is rare in its history of multiparty chaos. The new government is not pursuing religious fundamentalism and has implemented sound economic policies. It is working toward peace with Greeks over Cyprus as well as modernizing its laws to appeal to Europe. There remain problems left over from decades of mismanagement, but that is why Turkey is cheap. I have invested there again.

From Istanbul, on an early-morning drive, we set out for Nevşehir and the sprawling underground cities of Cappadocia. In nearby Derinkuyu we descended eight stories below the earth into a city whose construction was begun by the Hittites more than four thousand years ago. Between the years A.D. 400 and 1200, Orthodox Christians completed the excavation. The subterranean city was home to three thousand people. Excavated by communities seeking to protect themselves from would-be conquerors, warriors who continually crisscrossed the open valleys of the central Anatolian plateau, this and the other underground cities of the region are an awe-inspiring tribute to mankind's ability to survive.

On our way through northeastern Turkey, along the route from Erzurum to Artvin, we stumbled upon one of the world's most spectacular roads, a glorious stretch through gorgeous scenery, past villages, over mountains, through gullies, over sparkling streams, up and around challenging hills and tight turns. We drove with the top down and the Grateful Dead playing on the CD, Paige, her feet out the window, singing along with the music. None of the guidebooks mention this road, which was in terrific condition, with excellent tarmac, and I suspect it is a military road, probably put in by the U.S. Army during the Cold War. It is on my list of the ten greatest roads to drive in the world.

We were leaving Turkey after not enough time, heading for Batumi, a Black Sea city in the Republic of Georgia that lay just beyond the border. Many look at our map and marvel at all the places we visited, but we see the same map and notice all the places we missed, such as the ruins of Troy in western Turkey. But the short answer to why we missed them is simple: Paige and I had to make Siberia by summer, Vladivostok by July at the latest. If not, we would find ourselves in trouble. Numerous people throughout history—Hitler and Napoleon, to name two—have discovered that Russia at certain times of the year can be tough on visitors. Even I was smart enough to know I did not want to set off in the Russian winter to drive across Siberia.

# 3

## THE COMING CATASTROPHE OF CENTRAL ASIA

O UR CROSSING into Georgia was delayed somewhat by the fact
that all the border guards on both sides were drunk when we arrived. Talk about a changing world. When I had crossed this border a
decade before, in the spring of 1990, Georgia had been part of the Soviet Union, and these same functionaries had been very uptight. Leaving the free world and entering the totalitarian world of the
Communists had brought one face-to-face, all along the Iron Curtain,
with some very sober, very serious, and extremely strict border officials. Now they were falling all over themselves.

There were still a lot of forms to fill out and a lot of hassling back
and forth, and the actual entry itself was a holdover from the old Soviet days: the car was locked in, gates were lowered front and rear of
the vehicle, and the car was inspected. But the search this time was
more casual than in the past. In the old days the undercarriage would
have been inspected, too. (In the old days, when *people* were contraband, antismuggling efforts were directed at traffic both into and *out
of* the country.) Nonetheless, one still had to climb a bureaucratic

mountain to enter. We had to pay a variety of fees, insurance, a road tax—all the paperwork being made that much more complicated because all the guards were drunk.

So it was late, around midnight, when we arrived in Batumi, the first town on the Georgia side of the border.

We followed a taxi driver to the best hotel in town. Formerly run by Intourist, the Soviet state tourism monopoly, it was the same hotel I had stayed in the last time I had come through. The price I negotiated for a room, $25, included parking. I had noticed, behind the hotel, a private fenced-in area overseen by a guard in which several automobiles, most of them luxury cars, chiefly Mercedes, were parked. These were cars obviously owned by members of the local mafia, and the lot was controlled by whichever of them ran the hotel.

We climbed the stairs to our room to find each floor of the hotel monitored by an elderly woman—a practice held over from communism—whose job now, under the new regime, was to oversee the provision of prostitutes to incoming guests. All the members of our party declined the offer of services. Still a "four-star hotel," which under the Communists had been very basic, the establishment had seen significant change under the new government. In a glorious setting, looking right out over the Black Sea, it no longer featured heat, electricity, or running water; in fact, it was completely falling apart. The only thing that functioned was the restaurant bar downstairs, from which loud music was blaring. The hotel was such a dump that Paige returned to the car to retrieve her sleeping-bag sheet, refusing to sleep on those provided by the hotel, and I returned to the lobby, where I obtained a $10 reduction on the room rate.

Later, around three A.M., an old babushka knocked on our door, offering me the services of a bleached-blond, scantily dressed teenager.

"Sorry, he's taken," said Paige.

Later I learned how such state-owned businesses had changed hands with the fall of the Soviet Union. Because nobody owned them—the government had owned them, but now there was no government—whoever had overseen their operation at the time had simply taken possession of them. "It's mine now," the manager would say, and there was nobody to stop him. At some point the mafia would come along and say, "Okay, it's your hotel" or factory or what-

ever the asset was, but "we are going to provide you with a *roof*"—
insurance, as it were, a hedge against disaster—which was the mob's
way of telling him that *he* was going to provide *them* with a payoff.
From that point on he would pay extortion money to the mob, and
often, because he was incompetent and because the business as a result would fall apart, he and his partners would simply milk the assets
until there was nothing left.

Leaving Batumi the following morning and heading for the capital,
Tbilisi, we were stopped every twenty kilometers by the police. This
was yet another holdover from the totalitarian days of Communist
rule. Up to then we had been stopped periodically by the police for a
variety of reasons, but in fact mostly out of curiosity. What they really
wanted to do was see the car. We would pay them a little bit, maybe
give them some cigarettes, and be on our way. But getting stopped in
Georgia was entirely different. There, it felt as though we were being
stopped by the KGB. They did not call themselves Communists anymore, but their behavior was no different. Their mentality had not
changed since the days when their president, that great hero of the
West, Eduard Shevardnadze, had been the Soviet foreign minister.
They, and he, were still the thugs they had always been.

   Tbilisi had changed somewhat since I had been there last, in April
1990, when I had seen statues of Lenin lying toppled in the street.
This time we actually ran across some private restaurants in the city.
But for all its newfound capitalism and privatization, the country was
still in pretty sorry shape—Shevardnadze is as hopeless as all the rest
of the Soviet functionaries who rose to power—although many Georgians to whom we spoke were optimistic about its future.

   I looked up an old friend, Zaza Aleksidze, a university professor
whom I had met and from whom I had learned a lot about Soviet
Georgia on my trip through Tbilisi in 1990. Still a professor, he was
living much less well than he had a decade earlier. Seldom paid on
time, he was earning the same now as then, but the currency had collapsed and the money went nowhere. He lived on the fifteenth floor of
a building that rarely had electricity; residents always knew when a
tenant had died because the elevators would be activated to remove
the body. Nevertheless, he expressed great confidence that Georgia
would one day be a successful country.

"Things have continued to get worse since communism failed," he told me, "but we Georgians know things will get better."

National spirit, he said, was in abundant supply.

I said, "Zaza, you're nuts. You should get out of here."

But he, like a lot of former Soviets, was still convinced that everything would be okay, that Georgia would eventually rise and become a great nation again. After all, I was reminded, it was one of only thirteen or so world cultures with its own alphabet.

"We still love Georgia," he said. "We have pride in our country. The Georgian people still have hope."

As much as I wish Zaza the best, I fear that things will get worse, and worse, and worse, long before they get better.

Azerbaijan, a major oil producer under Russian rule, was the world's first great oil province. At the start of the twentieth century, half the world's oil came from the Caspian region. Since my last trip through Baku, the nation's capital, Azerbaijan had completed a $7.4 billion deal with Western companies to develop oil fields in the Caspian Sea. Other than that, little had changed but the light.

Under communism, in all of these cities—Batumi, Tbilisi, Baku— there had been no light—no streetlights, no market lights, no restaurants, no cars. There had never been more than one café, with one radio or band playing music from the same list of songs. It was very clear by now that things were different. There were markets, restaurants, sidewalk stands, people selling ice cream on the corner. But that was all the change you saw. Much more remained the same. All these places were even more run down than before. Nobody appeared to be putting money into anything.

In Baku, for the first time, I sat down with one of Central Asia's new oligarchs, a man named Namik, one of the opportunistic few who had seized the moment and grown rich while the old Soviet system was collapsing. It was he who explained to me how the hotel in Batumi had come to be controlled. If you were the manager of a hotel or the local vodka factory, taking possession of the asset required a certain amount of sophistication, if only because most Communists did not know what private ownership meant. For others, like Namik, who had not had the advantage of holding down a position as a Communist functionary, a bit more ingenuity was required.

As the country was falling apart, an entrepreneur such as Namik would get an export license for, say, chemicals; such a license would be difficult to acquire, but only in the absence of a bribe. Once he had his export license, he could buy chemicals from the Soviet factory at Soviet prices, which were ludicrous—there was no market pricing at all, because commerce was confined to the Soviet Union. So he would buy chemicals from their manufacturer and, with his export license, sell the chemicals in the West for hard currency at market prices. He was buying chemicals in Azerbaijan for somewhere in the vicinity of a nickel a ton and selling them abroad at $832 a ton. Because he was selling abroad and being paid outside the country, he was being paid in hard currency, not in worthless rubles, and he was keeping his money in Switzerland.

This opportunity lasted only a year or two before everyone eventually caught on. The chemical manufacturer realized *he* could sell the chemicals himself. He did not need the middleman with the export license—export licenses were no longer required. Under the Communists you could not export *anything* without a license, but the license even then had not been worth a whole lot. Why? Because the Soviets did not export much.

The guys who stepped into the vacuum of the collapsing Soviet system were relatively young, in their thirties and forties, and were not so much a part of the establishment that they had much to lose. Knowing a good opportunity when they saw it, they seized the moment and got rich. Namik, now in his fifties, was typical of the breed, an intelligent man who spoke fluent English and wore perfectly tailored suits that looked as if they been handmade in London. And here he was, explaining how the new system worked, how a young businessman had gone from having almost nothing to eating caviar on the Caspian Sea.

At the Grand Hyatt in Baku, they serve caviar in large bowls. They just bring it out and lay it on the table, the way a bartender at some other joint might lay out peanuts. A single serving, more caviar than you have ever seen at one time, would cost about eighteen hundred dollars anywhere else in the world. Anywhere but here, where it is harvested.

On this trip around the world, I would meet quite a few people like Namik. And I found these chance encounters to be invaluable. When in Rome, *talk* to the Romans. That is my variation on the proverb. (Needless to say, I also try to do what they do.) Dining with Namik taught me more about Azerbaijan and the new Central Asia than any guidebook could, and far more than I would ever learn from meeting with a bureaucrat or politician or accepting an audience with a "world leader." I had done my homework—I read the same stuff that everybody else reads, I pay attention to the same information out of Washington—but not until I sat down with this guy did it all start falling together. Not until I listened to Namik, whose story is really the story of Azerbaijan, did I quite understand the context. Paige and I would have dinner with Namik a couple of times.

Azerbaijan is home to an indigenous nomadic people, and long before Baku, under the Russians, established itself as a significant outlet on the Volga River–Caspian Sea route, the city was an important stop on the ancient Silk Road. Into and out of Baku, camels, tethered in groups of about six, sometimes as many as six thousand to a caravan, traveled single file across the desert, carrying spices, perfumes, incense, medicine, fruits, nuts, tea, salt, precious stones, gold, silver, copper, porcelain, ivory, jade, cotton, and silk. Each camel could transport more than five hundred pounds, and the largest of the caravans carried as much cargo as a large merchant ship. The animals were watered at scheduled stops along the way, in walled fortresses that afforded shelter along the trade route. Such oases were called caravansaries.

Some Azerbaijani entrepreneur had recently turned one of these ancient caravansaries into a restaurant. Restored and at the same time renovated, with camel enclosures converted to dining rooms, it had been dolled up in lavish fashion, and it was here that Namik entertained us the second time we got together. As he had when we had first met for dinner, Namik brought along a young woman—a different woman on each occasion, neither of whom was his wife—which this time outraged Paige even more than it had when he had first done so.

Paige was not cheered up by my suggestion that Namik's bringing a young, beautiful mistress, instead of his middle-aged wife, was an indirect way of flattering her. That Namik might have been showing off—escorting a girlfriend as young and beautiful as mine—was a backhanded compliment at best, she explained. If he was showing off, he was complimenting me, not her, and he was doing so by showing off his property. The insult was one Paige took personally, and it was a slap in the face to women in general.

Which brings us, I suppose, to the belly dancer, the most spectacular belly dancer I have ever seen, far wilder and more unrestrained here in the caravansary in Baku than the dancer we had seen in Istanbul. There was no argument on the matter of the young woman's performance. Indeed, the dance sparked a mutuality of opinion that Paige and I, equally appreciative of the art, would have good reason to revisit periodically over the course of our trip. We both marveled at what appeared to be a preternatural ability on the part of various local dancers around the world to do what they did. It was a phenomenon that would make itself felt even more dramatically later, when we arrived in West Africa. I just could not believe—today, it is almost as if I dreamed it—that people could move their bodies that way. As we traveled, we continued to be dazzled by local dancers, in East Africa and in other parts of Asia.

I learned more from dining with Namik and his two mistresses than I could ever have learned from "official" sources. Washington says we are supporting the new oligarchs because they are capitalists who believe in democracy. In truth, what these people believe in is natural selection, a principle best expressed in socioeconomic terms by the mafia. And after talking to Namik, I knew I would be crazy to invest in Azerbaijan.

I am not the type who would be good at brazenly paying big bribes, wheeling and dealing, giving kickbacks, or anything else. But Namik is. He can deal. He can go to a government official and say, "Okay, what do you need? This is what I need. How do I get it?" That is how the system in the former Soviet Union works. It is not a real system at all. It is not driven by an accumulation of knowledge and capital and expertise. If it is capitalism, it is outlaw capitalism. The entrepreneurs there are not building anything. They are stripping assets. As fast as they can.

I had been trying for months to get a visa to enter Iran. I was very keen to visit the country, which I had not yet done in my life. Since 1993–1995 I had been holding small investments there. It had taken me a year of campaigning to get permission to do so, but finally I had been allowed to buy shares that traded on the Iranian stock exchange.

Forget what Washington tells you; there is a lot of positive change coming in Iran. Demographically, it is a very young country. And it is ripe for investment. I am very optimistic about its future. As an investor, I am supportive of the emerging changes there. Furthermore, I am acquainted with the country's foreign minister, Kamal Kharrazi, who visited my class at Columbia University and who had had me to lunch at the Iranian mission to the United Nations. I assumed that if anyone would be granted a visa to drive across the country, it was I. I had been assured that a visa would be waiting for me in Istanbul. No such luck, neither in Istanbul nor in Baku.

Despite the repeated promises of Iranian bureaucrats, the country's equivalent of the KGB, in the person of a hard-line cleric sitting in the back room of secret police headquarters in Teheran—the last stop for all paperwork in Iran—always said "no." Apparently he understood that I was interested in the reforms proposed by the new secular government and, determined not to let me tour the country, talking to people at random, he exercised his clerical veto power, which no moderate could override. No matter how many people say yes, the final decision on everything in Iran lies with a cleric. I learned early, viewing things from the ground up, that reform in Iran was going to be a slower process than expected, no matter how hard the new government and Parliament tried.

Americans were regularly allowed into Iran, of course—just as every other mullah's grandson was allowed to study in the United States—but none of them was driving through the country at will. And my itinerary would take me through Kurdish territory. That we were ultimately refused entry was not the end of the world, but it was probably my biggest disappointment of the trip. Iran was the country I was most excited about visiting and the only one that never allowed us to drive through.

Iran's refusal to let us in with the car, of course, had a consequence that was far more compelling than mere disappointment: we were trapped in Baku.

Cut off by Iran to the south and the Caspian Sea to the east, I was faced with retracing my steps—traveling west and going back through Georgia and Turkey—or going north, across what the current political map of the world refers to as Russia and what the people in that part of "Russia" refer to as the Republics of Chechnya and Dagestan. Retracing my steps was out of the question; reversing course now, with China still to cross, I would court the unwelcome prospect of running up against the Siberian winter. Going north? In the full-blown, flat-out bloodbath of the war in Chechnya and environs, the combatants were not handing out tickets. There was only one way to go, and that was due east: I had to get across the Caspian Sea. By car. Or *with* one, at any rate.

"When does the boat leave for Türkmenbashy?"

I was standing dockside in Baku, inquiring about the old passenger ferry that crossed periodically—I had taken it across in 1990— between Azerbaijan and Turkmenistan.

"I don't know," said the shipping company employee. "When the next boat comes, it will come. And then it will go."

Fascinating.

"Do you have a schedule?" Paige asked.

No schedule.

"Come back tomorrow," we were told.

We went back the next day. And the day after that. Every day, for several days, we visited the dock, until one morning the schedule revealed itself.

"The boat is coming," we were told. "Come here tonight. It will leave tonight."

A man stepped out from the back of the shipping office, took us outside, and told us that if we wanted first-class tickets, he would provide them at half price.

"When you come here tonight, just come and see me," he said.

The ferry had been renamed the *Azerbaijan* after it had been purchased secondhand from Denmark, and its schedule was geared to that of the railroad. It serviced the freight cars that locomotives hauled into Baku. The boat ferried these freight cars across the Caspian. If there was no cargo to transport, there was no crossing. There were very few passengers crossing on this trip, maybe fifty people at the most, and all, with the exception of a couple of truck drivers, were pedestrians, walk-on passengers.

We paid the man for first-class tickets, and he ushered us aboard. We were absolutely horrified by the accommodation. There were holes in the compartment bulkhead, the floor was black with dirt, and the cabin's furniture consisted entirely of a thin, threadbare mattress on the floor, with a single blanket that had probably not been cleaned since the Danes had owned the boat. It was hard to imagine what second class might be like, let alone steerage.

We took the ticket master up on his offer to stay in an empty crew cabin during the overnight crossing.

At night, flares from the offshore oil and gas wells lit up the Caspian Sea.

Docking in Turkmenistan, we were the last people to leave the boat. We were forced to sit there for five hours as one security officer after another pointed, looked, and wondered what to do with us. We were definitely new and different, and all of them were afraid. This was Turkmenistan, one of the worst, most totalitarian of the Communist states, and these simple functionaries had no idea what to make of us.

Finally, after collecting a five-dollar disinfectant fee—and promising not to disinfect us—they allowed us off the boat with the car. We were required to buy a special permit that enabled us to purchase diesel fuel at the local fixed price of something like twenty cents a gallon. We gave them our route to Uzbekistan, they estimated our fuel consumption—they actually had a chart showing how many liters we would consume—and we paid them the difference between the local price and the world price, in advance.

It was midnight when we arrived at our hotel in the town of Türkmenbashy.

Turkmenistan's president, Saparmurat Niyazov, former party chairman under the Soviets—the same party continues to dominate Turkmenistan's politics today—has changed his name to Akbar Türkmenbashy, which means "Great Father of all Turkmen." And his megalomania is not limited to his renaming the town of Krasnovodsk after himself. His portrait appears on the country's currency, on bottles of vodka, on packets of tea. Everywhere we went, driving across Turkmenistan, Niyazov stared down on us from statues and from posters that read: ONE PEOPLE, ONE NATION, ONE TÜRKMENBASHY, as explained to us by our Russian translator, Sergei, who had joined us in Baku. I was shaken when I saw one of these posters for the first time. I have a collection of hundreds of mostly historical political posters I have picked up over the years, including a 1930s Nazi Party propaganda poster featuring a picture of Adolf Hitler and the words EIN VOLK, EIN REICH, EIN FÜHRER (One People, One Nation, One Führer).

Niyazov's cult of personality was in evidence everywhere we looked. On Turkmen television, from the upper-right-hand corner of the screen, his face stared out at the viewer around the clock. It was only by way of significant pressure exerted by the international community that he was prevented from placing his face on his country's flag. (Within a year of my return to the United States he had proposed renaming the months of the year. January would henceforth be known as Türkmenbashy, April would be named for his mother, who died in 1948, and October for a book of his musings, which had been required reading in the nation's schools since its publication in 2001.)

The last time I had been in Turkmenistan, it had been a sterile, hopeless place. There had been one hotel, one restaurant, one road. And not much had changed, not if the town of Türkmenbashy was any example. The only hotel with a vacancy by the time we got off the boat was nothing more or less than a horrible slum that doubled as a home for retired military.

I really do not care where I sleep, but this dump was just too horrific for Paige.

"What would you like to do?" I asked. "It's midnight. This is the only place we can get."

We fought about the accommodations, about food, about the trip in general. It was the same fight we had been having for weeks. But saying "I warned you" was a clear waste of time. The boat had already gone; it was on its way back to Baku. We were about to drive through the desert, and there was no way for anyone to get home from there. We decided to get out of town as fast as we could. We were gone early the next morning, hoping for something better somewhere down the road.

The Kara-Kum (Black Sand) Desert, one of the largest deserts in the world, covers around 90 percent of Turkmenistan, a remote and sparsely populated country. Wild camels, running in herds, traversed our path as we raced down the highway. Following the Silk Road, heading for the capital, Ashkhabad, we crossed the Kara-Kum Canal, now, of course, renamed the Türkmenbashy Canal, which carries water from the Amu Dar'ya to the country's arid regions and which in large part is responsible for the desiccation of the Aral Sea, one of world history's great environmental disasters.

In the Soviet years, the Turkmen, a nomadic people, suffered greatly under forced collectivization and the bloodletting of numerous antireligious campaigns, as well as a purging of their intelligentsia. They were also, and continue to be, victims of economic mismanagement. Entering Ashkhabad, one passes a line of twenty hotels, all of them brand new, all of them financed by money borrowed from the West, all of them empty. The country is bankrupt, the currency is collapsing, and Türkmenbashy is building monuments to the nation's various bureaucracies, the Oil Ministry Hotel, the Agriculture Ministry Hotel . . .

The one good highway in the country—perfectly flat, asphalt, beautiful—is the road Türkmenbashy takes to work from one of the two palaces in which he lives. The country has a spectacular airport but little air traffic in or out, just twenty-five airplanes sitting there empty. Driving into town from the airport, one drives down a well-maintained road lined with fountains on either side. The houses built along this route have no water when dignitaries drive by—which is when the fountains are turned on. And two blocks behind those houses, behind the facade they represent, the neighborhood is a slum, a Soviet-style disaster. A tourist or visiting official traveling to Turkmenistan would see only the facade.

In the middle of town, the visitor to Ashkhabad comes upon a huge monument, a 246-foot arch, on top of which stands a solid gold statue of Türkmenbashy. The statue rotates, so that the great father of all Turkmen can maintain a perpetual vigil, surveying his entire domain, his arms always pointing to the sun.

Every member of the Turkmen legislature and of the Council of Ministers owns a Mercedes that was given to him by Türkmenbashy. None, however, has a Mercedes S600, which in Central Asia represents the top of the line. Only one such model has been allowed into the country: the car given by Mercedes-Benz of Germany to Türkmenbashy himself, as a kind of thank-you for all the foreign aid money the Turkmen president has funneled the company's way. You and I provide Türkmenbashy (and by extension Mercedes) this money by way of our various taxes—all in the name of promoting democracy and in actual support of the politics of petrochemicals. This nation of five million people, under the thumb of an absolute dictator, is rich with deposits of natural gas. And we keep feeding this megalomaniac money in the hope that someday he will let us extract it.

Over the course of the trip, we had been receiving e-mails from an American working in Turkmenistan for one of the U.S. agencies. A young man who had arrived relatively recently in Ashkhabad with his wife, he had been following our trip on the World Wide Web. He was administering one of the funds set up by the United States to funnel money to governments like that of Türkmenbashy. These are funds financed with private money, funds that you or I or anyone can invest in, which were set up when the Soviet Union started falling apart. While they are typically bad investments, these funds are actually indemnified against failure, because all the money—you guessed it—is guaranteed by Uncle Sam.

Characteristic of these was a $300 million Central Asian fund, administered by flunkies who could not make it on Wall Street—and if you could not make it on Wall Street in the nineties, you could not make it anywhere, except maybe in government—who managed to lose all the money the first time around. Either because they were playing fast and loose, maybe making bad loans to friends, or because they were really that much more stupid than everyone else, they were summoned back home. No one's reputation was at stake, because the U.S. government made good on the money. The young fellow who was corresponding with me had arrived in Turkmenistan with his boss, the regional director, to replace the original incompetents.

We had two or three dinners with some of these people in Central Asia. There is nothing about them individually that warrants discussion. When I meet people like these, I think of characters like Lord Jim, who cannot really make it back home. They always find it easier going to work for the government and moving to places like this. They do not have to run quite so hard or think quite so fast. They all have big offices, they all go to restaurants whenever they want, they live much better than they could in the States—they live like kings— and they have a rationale for everything. They will explain to you that they really *have* to have drivers to avoid problems with the police. Here they were, throwing our money and their weight around, living

*Wild camels in the Kara-Kum Desert are the only free spirits in Türkmenbashy's "new" Turkmenistan.*

*We never got sick from dining in the street, no matter how remote from "civilization." Food poisoning struck only three times and only after meals in five-star restaurants. This establishment in Samarkand was not listed in the* Michelin Guide.

very high on the hog, not terribly smart but leading plush lives. They do not have to be right or wrong—when everything goes wrong, the government bails out the shareholders.

Programs like theirs are an absolute disaster, money thrown out the window, all in the name (and out of the utter arrogance) of teaching these countries capitalism. The people who do their kind of work, expatriates all, whether American, British, or German, are the same all over the world. They love the life, would not dream of doing anything else, and smarter people than I—Joseph Conrad, Graham Greene—have written about how they think and act.

I would be remiss in my description of Turkmenistan if I did not mention a discovery we made in Chardzhou, a city of almost two hundred thousand people, the second largest city in the country. Here, on the border with Uzbekistan, we entered Lebab, a delightful restaurant whose proprietor had seen fit to stock the few tables there were with delicate china, lace tablecloths, and fine linen napkins. The place was almost Victorian in the dignity of its appointments, and we were the only guests that night. Few people in Turkmenistan could afford such things or cared about them if they could. But even in the most dismal and hopeless places in the world, one always finds small pockets of optimism where such expressions of spirit flourish. After we had eaten a delicious meal, the owner introduced herself and thanked us for our patronage, and seemed somewhat taken aback at how impressed we were by her establishment. We left Turkmenistan no more bullish on the future of the country but with our faith in human endeavor freshly renewed.

Across Uzbekistan, following the old caravan routes to China, we visited the fabled cities of Bukhara and Tashkent. Just the sound of their names alone was enough to summon visions of the past. Bukhara, with its minarets and ninety schools of religion, was an ancient center of commerce, a wellspring of Islamic power, wealth, learning, architecture, and art, and is still a magnificent city, one the Communists failed to destroy. Tashkent, the Uzbek capital, a vital, modern metropolis, had become the fourth largest city in the former Soviet Union. Samarkand, the oldest city in Central Asia, dating back some four thousand years, became a melting pot of Western and Chinese cultures after its conquest by Alexander the Great. It reached the height of its splendor in the fourteenth century as the capital of Tamerlane's empire.

Tamerlane, the Tatar leader, was one of the early conquerors. He would say he was propagating civilization; others would say he was a horrible, murderous jackass. Whatever he was, he was good at it; he created a vast empire for himself. His conquests led to a huge accumulation of wealth and learning in Samarkand. Once, while Tamerlane was off conquering, his wife, Bibi-Khanym, built a colossal mosque. The stories now are garbled, but there must have been some kind of hanky-panky going on at home, since Tamerlane, upon his return, executed the architect. Women have been wearing the veil since, to avoid tempting men. It is said in Samarkand, where Tamerlane is buried, that he who disturbs Tamerlane's tomb will bring destruction upon his house. A group of Russian archaeologists, it is alleged, opened Tamerlane's tomb on June 22, 1941, a few hours after which Hitler invaded the Soviet Union.

Neither in Samarkand nor in Bukhara, when I passed through in 1990, had there been any tourist industry to speak of. Now Uzbekistan, showing evidence that capitalism had come, was learning to attract tourists. Fairly nice hotels were springing up. Outside the major tourist attractions, T-shirt shops and rug merchants had begun to appear. Neither city was Miami Beach by any stretch of the imagination—this was Uzbekistan, remember—but things had changed a lot since my last time through, when there had been no tourists at all.

In Tashkent we ran up against an obstacle that would cause me sleepless nights for the next week and a half. It was there, in the Uzbeki capital, that we had been instructed by the Chinese to pick up our entry visas, but at China's embassy in Tashkent, the consular official in authority told us he was allowed to grant visas only to those who could show six-month residency in Uzbekistan. It cost us a few days and several calls to Beijing before we finally prevailed, but being handed the documents did not allay my anxiety. As my experience with the Iranians had shown, a traveler in this part of the world could take nothing for granted.

Standing on the doorstep of a given country did not guarantee one an invitation to enter; indeed, it was just as likely to make things more difficult. It remained to be seen if we could get into China with our visas—and that was assuming we could actually get out of Uzbekistan. Someone had tried assassinating the Uzbek president, so the border was closed.

We departed Uzbekistan the third week in March. Across beautiful, mountainous Kyrgyzstan and the vast pastureland of Kazakhstan, passing donkey carts and—as if they were riding out of ancient stories—horsemen, galloping across the steppes, we made our way to China. Between the Kazakh capital, Almaty, and the Chinese border, we traversed four hundred kilometers of near-empty frontier. Having recorded notes on our stay in Almaty (where she had both visited her first Russian Orthodox church and interviewed her first prostitute), Paige was doing the driving, while I organized my thoughts on the future of Central Asia and tried not to think about what the bureaucrats might have in store for us on the Chinese border.

To say I am not optimistic about the future of Central Asia is an understatement of oceanic proportions. The entire region is unstable, with ethnic disputes and conflicts over borders, water, oil, and pipelines disrupting every political discussion. It is debatable whether these countries are in fact countries. Turkmenistan, for example, was shoved together by Stalin out of a vast stretch of desert, incorporating five nomadic tribes. There is no logic at all to Kazakhstan. And Uzbekistan as an identifiable country does not exist. Ethnic and tribal distinctions will drive the region's politics for the foreseeable future. Their current "leaders" are opportunists who seized the moment as communism fell but who have little support. Groups in all the Stans will start to agitate to establish their independence, just as happened in Eastern Europe with the former Yugoslavia and has been occurring regularly over the years in Africa.

The Soviet Union has already broken into fifteen states. People speak eighteen different languages in the five Central Asian republics. There are more than a hundred linguistic, ethnic, religious, and national groups in the region, none of which joined the Soviet Union willingly. (Compare this to the ethnic homogeneity of China, where 94 percent of the population is Han Chinese.) Those in Washington and on Wall Street who think Russia will provide stability in the region are dreaming. The Russian army? After eight years it still cannot handle Chechnya, a country the size of Connecticut or Northern Ireland, with maybe a total of 1.5 million people. This is the mighty

Russian army of which we were all so terrified. The draftees do not show up, and the generals are stripping whatever assets they can, as fast as they can.

Sooner or later, all these "countries" will be bankrupt. The currencies of Kazakhstan and Kyrgyzstan are declining in value rapidly, and both economies are moribund. The Turkmen and Uzbek currencies, when Paige and I were in Central Asia, had collapsed to the point where the dollar, on the black market, went for more than three times the official rate. Big trouble is in the offing: violent strikes, assassination attempts, bombs exploding, and the eventual outbreak of more than one civil war.

What does this mean for the United States? Very little, probably, for these people will be paying little attention to us and blowing *one another* up for a very long time to come. Their nuclear weapons have, in large part, been stripped and cannibalized. Those weapons that are intact have not been maintained. Unless U.S. politicians, in their mindless posturing, make the mistake of replaying the "Great Game" all over again, and dragging us into this mess, as their European counterparts did in the nineteenth century, we in the United States should be largely unaffected. Or so it seemed a few years ago. Now the United States, rattling sabers over Iraq, has established bases in Central Asia, making additional enemies in the region. It constantly grieves me to see our politicians dragging us into terrible situations about which no one has done the homework, in places where no one understands the situation on the ground. Remember Somalia? The revolution in Iran?

At geopolitical stake in this part of the world are immense reserves of oil and gas and vast supplies of other raw materials. Turkmenistan has the world's fifth largest reserves of natural gas, huge oil resources, and large supplies of coal, sulfur, and salt. Uzbekistan is now the world's third largest cotton exporter, a major producer of gold and natural gas, and a regionally significant producer of chemicals. Kazakhstan is a significant source of natural gas, petroleum, coal, gold, uranium, silver, copper, lead, zinc, tungsten, and molybdenum. None of these abundant assets will do any of these countries any good, however, certainly not in the short run; in my opinion, things as they stand are certain to get worse before they get better.

It would be nice to think that the Soviet Union in the twentieth century contributed more to the world than a handful of space hardware, some first-class Olympic athletes, and an innumerable array of chess grand masters, but in the end, it is difficult to come up with much more. History will remember Russian communism and its disastrous seventy-year economic experiment chiefly for having impoverished the lives of hundreds of millions of people around the world. And the future of the former USSR looks a lot like its past. Its destiny can be read—quite fittingly—in the tea leaves of the Aral Sea.

Back in the early sixties, Moscow decided it needed to be self-sufficient in cotton. It implemented a plan to irrigate vast cotton fields in the south by diverting two rivers, the Amu Dar'ya and the Syr Dar'ya. These two rivers fed the Aral Sea, an inland sea or brackish lake of more than 25,000 square miles, the largest lake between the Caspian Sea and the Pacific Ocean and the world's fourth largest lake overall. For thousands of years, the fresh water from the rivers held the Aral Sea's salt levels in balance.

The Soviets built dams across both rivers and dug an 850-mile canal with a far-reaching system of feeder canals. Russian cotton was planted and raised on three million acres, and 60 percent of the country's cotton needs were met by the new southern crop. The party bosses responsible were promoted to plum assignments in Moscow.

Over the next thirty years, the Aral Sea all but disappeared, leaving behind a dry bed of poisonous salts, dead fish, and seaside vegetation. By 1995 it had lost three quarters of its volume. Fishing villages once located on its banks are now thirty miles away, surrounded by desert. Once the source of 13 percent of all the Soviet Union's fish, the Aral Sea today supports no life.

I kept hearing that things had improved in the former USSR since the fall of the Communists. I wondered if I would notice changes in Central Asia. I hoped at least to find the Aral Sea improving but discovered that much had grown worse since my earlier ride. Today more than 100 million tons of toxic silt, composed of salt, sand, fertilizers, DDT, and industrial and household poisons, are swept up and carried away annually by the prevailing winds. The winters are colder than before, the summers hotter and dryer. Rainfall has diminished dramatically. Pasture is gone. Production is down. Local children are ill from the toxins blown off the dry seabed, and adult life expectancy has dropped. The Aral's distinctive poisons, rising to high layers in the atmosphere and carried around the globe, have been found in the blood of penguins in the Antarctic and have fallen on glaciers in Greenland, forests in Norway, and fields in Belorussia, thousands of kilometers away.

Mirrored by the progress of this ecological disaster, one can see the entire economic and political face of the region. Therein lie the outlines of its future. In much the same condition as the Aral Sea, the former Soviet Union is a disaster that is about to spiral into a catastrophe.

# 4

## THE BEST CAPITALISTS ARE IN COMMUNIST CHINA

I T HAD BEEN EXCITING TO LEARN, as I had from the Chinese Embassy and Chinese travel authorities, that I, this crazy redneck from Alabama, would be the first person—not the first non-Chinese, but the first person ever—to drive across China three times. Who could ever know, of course? In fact, I thought it might be too good to be true. Was this really going to work? I asked myself. It was China, after all. Anything could happen, as my experience in Tashkent had proved. While my running around there to secure a visa had ultimately succeeded, it had given me serious pause. Would I get to China and be turned away? There was no way to know, because, as was painfully apparent as we neared the border, no one else was trying to get in. That in itself was probably a pretty good clue. My fear that all our work had been for naught was exacerbated by all the security thrown up at the frontier: a big wall, a heavy fence, soldiers amassed on both sides of the border, and a no-man's-land between the two armies across which I intended to drive. Would the Kazakhs even let us out of Kazakhstan?

Coming upon the border, one could see vivid evidence of the Soviet Union's recent collapse. On either side were the remains of hundreds of stalls where merchants had raced back and forth, getting rich, exploiting the window of free trade and commerce that had opened up briefly after the disintegration of the USSR. Now, in the spring of 1999, when Paige and I arrived at the frontier, the stalls were closed and the border had long since been fortified again. China and newly autonomous Kazakhstan were not particularly friendly. The fall of communism had seen a strong revival of religion and culture among Kazakhstan's Muslims, and tension had arisen between the two countries as members of China's large Muslim population in the west had begun to identify with their Kazakh brothers.

After clearing the Kazakh guards, we pulled up to the border ready to jump through some of the more difficult bureaucratic hoops erected in the path of our pilgrimage. And the Chinese were predictably unpredictable.

Welcome to China. Have a nice day.

What?

Just like that. We were in.

Well, maybe not just like that, but close. They did put everything we had through a scanner, but little else. And I was about to discover that it was typical of the way the Chinese regularly confound the world's expectations.

The Chinese call themselves Communists, but they are among the best capitalists in the world. These are people with a very long entrepreneurial history, and when Deng Xiaoping in 1978 said it was time to try something new, announcing the policy of the Four Modernizations, he called upon that history, unleashing the same spirit of enterprise that had put China in the forefront of world commerce, industry, and technology following the turn of the first millennium.

The rise of the Song Dynasty in A.D. 960 had brought with it the institution in China of an efficient bureaucracy of twenty thousand mandarin officials and a revival of Confucian teachings that reinforced order and morality. The dynasty, which lasted until 1279, spanned a period of unprecedented economic activity during which coal, steel, and armaments industries developed. Market-regulated commerce led to a level of iron production in 1078 that would be twice that of England seven hundred years later. The Chinese engaged in international commerce aboard sailing ships that carried up to a thousand men. In the dynasty's capital, Kaifeng, the second largest city in the world at the time, with a population approaching half a million, businesses of all kinds proliferated and stores remained open all night.

There is evidence that Chinese ships sailed to the east coast of Africa and the west coast of Latin America long before the Spanish or Portuguese. This happened at a time when China and the Islamic countries were far more advanced than Europe. After a period of political upheaval in the early fifteenth century, xenophobic mandarins turned the country inward, destroying all its magnificent sailing ships and the records of their explorations.

China has had a merchant class throughout much of its history, unlike Russia, for example, which never had much of a tradition of capitalism. Under the czars Russia was basically a feudal society; it never had a capitalist class. Whatever capitalists there were, and there were not many, are long since dead and forgotten. Communists took over the country, remember, in 1917. China's strict Communist economy lasted from 1949 to 1979. That is only thirty years. There are still plenty of Chinese who remember what capitalism is. A lot of them had moved to Hong Kong.

One of China's greatest resources is its expatriate class. The country has a vast network of overseas Chinese—in Singapore, Bangkok, Vancouver, Jakarta, New York—who are very successful. They may be fifth-generation Thais, but they are nonetheless Chinese. Many of them speak Chinese. And China opens its doors to these people. They bring in both capital and expertise. The expertise is as important as the capital, because the Chinese absorb it quickly—they are very fast at turning it to their advantage—and their appetite for it keeps growing.

Driving through China, we would see people constantly working the fields, and they would be working from dawn to dusk, literally. Indeed, they worked beyond dusk. We saw road builders laboring under floodlights, and there were almost as many women working as men. We never saw anybody sitting around chitchatting. The Chinese do not take siestas. You will see some old men—really old men—sitting quietly drinking tea, with their caged pet birds keeping them company, but other than that you will not see people lounging around, looking out windows. Upon arriving in Shanghai, later in the trip, I would come to appreciate the international scope of the country's emerging capitalism. But its promise could not be more vividly expressed than in the small desert city of Dunhuang, as embodied individually by my friend Mr. Ji.

I had met Mr. Ji on my first motorcycle trip through western China in 1988. An ex-farmer, then in his early forties, Mr. Ji had started out as a businessman with a small breakfast stand in Dunhuang, from which he served bread to his fellow farmers. When I met him the stand had expanded to a restaurant with a small hotel attached. Dining there on my *Investment Biker* trip two years later, I found both the restaurant and the hotel to be a little bigger, and I remember being impressed at the time by the ingenuity that enabled him to serve fish in the middle of the desert. When on this trip Paige and I arrived in Dunhuang, I asked around for Mr. Ji, wondering how changing times had affected him over the course of a decade.

Oh, yes, I was assured, Mr. Ji was still around. And he was doing better than ever. He owned a factory, he owned big hotels, and indeed he owned more than one restaurant. He was really successful, I was told.

Mr. Ji was the heart and soul of the New China.

Out there in the middle of the desert, Mr. Ji was, among other things, making rugs. Using skilled craftsmen, knocking off classic Persian and Chinese designs, he was manufacturing silk carpets by hand. And he was not cutting corners; he did not have to. Labor and silk were cheap, and Mr. Ji had tapped into a tremendous worldwide market for the merchandise. The rug-making industry for which Central Asia was famous had pretty much collapsed all around him. The manufacturing infrastructure in Iran, probably the world's foremost supplier of fine oriental carpets, had been destroyed by the revolution in 1979, the industry having fallen into disrepute under the Ayatollah Khomeini, who viewed the industry as Western-influenced and branded it imperialist. In the Central Asian republics, famous throughout the ages for Bukharas and other highly prized oriental designs, people stopped making rugs for the government after Communism fell in the 1990s; it was work for which they had never been paid anyway. And more than twenty years of war had put an end to the industry in Afghanistan. Mr. Ji had recognized an opportunity and seized it. It was not as if he were some evil capitalist undercutting others; the others had failed.

I had seen Mr. Ji three times now, in 1988, 1990, and 1999, and he had continued to grow, going on to bigger and better things every time, through the boom years, through the troubled economic times that followed Tiananmen Square, and now, leading up to the turn of the millennium. Working overtime, twelve hours a day, seven days a week, and enjoying it, he was a businessman in the classic mold of those who had flourished in China one thousand years before, an entrepreneur allowed to grow rich some twelve hundred miles from the bureaucrats of Beijing.

Needless to say, I had to buy some of Mr. Ji's rugs. I selected three, of Persian design, and had him ship them to me in the United States. After being introduced to his family and his workers, Paige and I were treated to dinner in one of Mr. Ji's restaurants. There he led us into the kitchen, where we watched him make noodles by hand. He wanted to show us that he could still do it, that he was not above it.

The first time I drove across China, I was lucky to survive the trip. Back then, in 1988, you literally drove across the desert. There were no roads. Now the cross-country route is all motorway. The Chinese have learned from the experience of others—the Germans, the Japanese, the Americans—how to go about building a road, and the Chinese, being the capitalists they are, have built a procession of toll roads, all of which are expensive to drive, even though the Chinese still call themselves Communist. In my opinion, the roads are the best in the world.

Still, there is very little civilization in western China. It is the only part of the country where you will not see somebody every hundred meters. Towns along the way are sparse, grown up from ancient oases on the Silk Road. Hundreds of years ago the Chinese figured out how to irrigate these towns, creating a system of tunnels beneath the desert and drawing water through them from the mountains hundreds of miles to the north. Driving across the bleakest of deserts, we were periodically brought up short by the sight of tomatoes, pumpkins, and melons growing. The people of these oasis towns were so proficient in

*Just in case the car was unable to get us across the Takla Makan—the desert's name means "He who goes in does not come out."*

*Farming has not changed much over the centuries in most of the world, but even using the old methods, the new China can still produce enough to export some crops.*

*The Communists have done their best to eliminate what they call "coolie" hats, which they see as a remnant of imperialism, but the older generation and I find them extremely practical. I still have this one, which I bought in Qufu from a follower of Confucius.*

capturing water, and had so much of it under control, that they were able to hose down the streets to reduce dust.

The desert here is called the Takla Makan. And it is a really badass desert. It translates "He who goes in does not come out." One of the more famous cities out here, along the Silk Route, is a place called Hami. It is a city that for fifteen hundred years has been famous for its melons. So delicious and so famous are Hami melons that they were routinely harvested, wrapped in ice, and delivered to the emperor. Even today, the idea of getting a melon from Hami to Beijing is overwhelming to me, yet the Chinese were doing it hundreds of years ago and it worked.

Our first night in China, arriving in Yining, we stayed at the Yili Post Hotel, one of the many hotels built across China during the inflationary boom of the late eighties, more often than not as status symbols. Usually these hotels were the trophies of various party functionaries, and this one, reflecting the glory of a post office bureaucrat, was no exception. What was most astonishing about the hotel, however, was the huge banner across the reception desk that greeted us when we entered the lobby: THE HOME OF GOD. Merely the management's way of saying "We treat the guests as if they were divine," the sentiment was nonetheless startling in a Communist country. And again China held forth a surprise. For we discovered, as we set across the country, that in this international stronghold of godless communism, the houses of worship—mosques, Buddhist temples, Confucian temples—were packed.

About seventy kilometers outside Xi'an, about two weeks into our crossing of China, as we were making our way out of the desert, we passed a huge Christian church—yes, a church—on the highway. At first, what we saw did not really sink in. We drove on for several miles. Then, almost simultaneously, in the manner of a vaudeville act, we looked at each other and said, "We gotta go back."

We turned and drove back toward the desert, returning the way we came. It was not as if somebody were hiding this church. It was not underground. It stood right at the side of a superhighway, marked by gigantic crosses. In this village outside Xi'an we had run across a Christian community converted by missionaries in the eighteenth century. The entire village was Christian and had been for more than two hundred years. When we walked into the church to look it over, the people seated inside—some children, some elderly members of the congregation—picked up their hymnbooks, gathered around us, and sang "Onward, Christian Soldiers" in Chinese.

Paige is from North Carolina, where Jesse Helms froths at the mouth over China's persecution of those who practice religion.

"I bet Jesse Helms has never even visited the country," she said. "I'm gonna go home and invite him to drive across China with us."

The people of this village, the people singing to us, all of whom were Christian, apparently did not know they were persecuted; they told us the government paid their preacher. The Communist government in Beijing.

As we saw, entering the country from Kazakhstan, China fears the influence of fundamentalist Islam on its western border. Equally apparent to us was the fact that there are a large number of Muslims in China who are religious. But nobody we could see was persecuting them for being religious.

In Pingliang we climbed a holy mountain to a Taoist monastery. As we walked the thousand stairs to the top, we were periodically overtaken by Chinese men, their backs loaded down with supplies for the monks. Up and down they went every day, because everything on the mountain had to be carried there by hand. While unable to keep up with them, we did outpace our thirty-four-year-old Chinese interpreter, Mr. Yuan, who had joined us at the border and would be with us until we departed the country.

Arriving at the top of the mountain, expecting to see an interesting temple, we stepped out into a small courtyard, startled to find six Taoist priests. Down on their knees, clad in clerical robes, they were conducting a ceremony to bring rain, as it was explained to us by Mr. Yuan after he finally caught up to us. Kneeling there, chanting, burning incense and yellow rice paper, they glanced up and were surprised to see us. This was not a place with foreigners. The priests were just as stunned as we. They were praying for rain, and they got white people. ("Wrong prayer," I imagined them whispering.)

It was just one more religious service—unfettered, unhampered, its practitioners unpersecuted—of the many we would run across as we traveled through China. We found extensive religious freedom and religious practice everywhere we went, and we went just about everywhere. In Qufu we visited the huge complex that has grown up over the centuries around the home of Confucius, whose ethical system has been observed in China since the fifth century B.C. Operated freely and openly, the site, covering several acres and housing numerous shrines within it, is the focus of an ongoing pilgrimage on the part of followers.

The Taoist priests, once they got over their shock at seeing us, were quite happy to have us sit and watch as they continued with the ceremony. It actually started sprinkling while we were up there, so the ceremony, one has to assume, was sanctioned not only by the Chinese government but by a higher authority as well.

In Pingliang, walking the streets in the evening, we came upon hundreds of people dancing in the park. Following the lead of a young woman instructor, they waltzed to Western ballroom music playing over a loudspeaker. No sooner had the music stopped than Paige and I were surrounded by townspeople who engaged in excited chatter about our eyes being round and blue. Our interpreter, Mr. Yuan, explained to them that we were Americans traveling the world.

"They love China," he told the people of Pingliang.

Mr. Yuan was right about that.

Mr. Yuan was from Beijing, and it became pretty clear pretty quickly that we were showing him more of China than he had ever seen in his life. A not particularly intrepid man, he was always telling us what we could *not* do—not because of any official restrictions, but simply out of his own timidity. Of course, we did all those things and more, in the process opening his eyes to things he would never otherwise have seen. Mr. Yuan was simply the translator; we, in fact, were the tour guides.

One of the things he insisted we could not do was patronize a teahouse.

Though they have been around for centuries, teahouses, if not strictly illegal, are still officially frowned upon in China. They are seen as a holdover from colonial days, as decadent establishments that promote indolence, and for fifty years the Communists have been trying to shut them down. That had not prevented me from visiting one on my previous trip through the country, and it would not discourage me on this trip. In the city of Lanzhou in 1990 I had visited the Culture

*Little did I know what we would find after another five hundred steps up the holy mountain in Pingliang.*

*I loved my pre-Revolution sunglasses, but the fellow who greeted us at the teahouse in Lanzhou felt they were a bit old-fashioned.*

*"She" was my favorite performer in the teahouse.*

Palace Teahouse, a small thatched-roof affair where elderly men lounged around smoking and drinking, playing cards, dominoes, and mah-jongg, and ignored the music of a four-man band. Much like the pool halls and barbershops I remembered from my youth in the South, the Culture Palace, though with a uniquely Asian flavor, had its parallels in men's clubs of all kinds all over the world, and I wanted to show it to Paige.

"Let's find it," I told Mr. Yuan.

"Oh, no, we can't go to a teahouse."

"Follow me."

We took to the streets of Lanzhou. A thriving city of three million people, alive with young people wearing five-pocket jeans and running shoes, Lanzhou had since my last visit given birth to numerous modern high-rises, but they rose neither numerous nor high enough to completely overshadow the squat, colorless concrete structures from the bunker school of Communist architecture that flourished in such ubiquity there.

Teahouses, of course, are not easy to find. Like floating card games in the United States, such places tend to fly under radar. But we did not let that deter us. When we discovered that the Culture Palace was no longer in business, that the Communists had shut it down, we were that much more determined to locate another. When we succeeded in finding a teahouse—not far from where the Culture Palace had operated—Mr. Yuan was afraid to go in.

"This is a first for me," said Mr. Yuan.

"Stick with us, and we'll show you China," I told him.

When the three of us stepped through the door, we were greeted by an ancient fellow in large, round-rimmed eyeglasses, who escorted us to a table. Seated in plastic lawn chairs, we ordered, you guessed it, tea. The tea was served to us in porcelain bowls, with litchi nuts and rock sugar, by beautiful young women, who were the only members of the fair sex I could see. All the patrons appeared to be men.

A teahouse would not be a teahouse without entertainment, and under way onstage when we arrived, to my utter astonishment, was an opera. A Chinese opera. It was all very dramatic, very elaborate, heartrending and fraught with tragedy, and just as ludicrous in its own way as Western opera, I was pleased to see. The performers were all men, heavily made up, extravagantly costumed, many of them im-

personating women, all wailing and posturing and singing theatri-
cally of doomed love. The management sold, for the equivalent of a
quarter each, large, brightly colored scarves or towels, and to show
appreciation of the performance patrons were invited to throw these
swatches of fabric onto the stage. Presented passionately by dedicated
amateurs, the production was the darnedest thing I ever saw, so I kept
buying all kinds of towels and throwing them up there. As a result, I
was very popular, as you can imagine—all for $5.25.

That night, after walking a few blocks past several establishments,
we selected a restaurant, passing up one that served only mushrooms
and choosing instead to eat in one that served snake. The first restaurant served about forty varieties of mushrooms, which was about
thirty-nine varieties more than I could identify on a good day. All
were on display, and diners were encouraged to mix and match. Presumably you could select from a variety of recipes, as well. From
what I could see, however, with the exception of tea and possibly beer,
there was nothing other than mushrooms on the menu. Next door
stood a restaurant where items on the bill of fare were similarly displayed, the chief difference being that the food was not yet dead.
There were several tanks stocked with fish, a cage of snakes, a small
pond filled with turtles and frogs, a cage of ducks, another of chick-
ens. This was the restaurant we chose.

I selected a snake. The young man tending the provender lifted it
out of the cage, squirming, and with a large pair of scissors clipped off
its head. Running the blade down the length of the snake, he opened
the animal up and pulled out its internal organs. He drained the
blood, then skinned the snake, before sending it off to the kitchen to
be cooked. (Paige asked him to save the skin, thinking it might make
a nice belt.)

Paige ordered duck and immediately took a seat, saying thanks-
but-no-thanks to the opportunity to watch as her dinner was slaughtered in front of her. The duck was served with broccoli and rice. The
snake was dipped in a light batter and fried to a succulent pink.

"Tastes like chicken," I said.

That is what everybody says, of course, but unlike everybody else I
know, I can now bite into an overpriced slice of chicken at one of
New York's finer restaurants and pay my compliments to the chef
with the following remark:

"Mmm, tastes much like snake."

After the meal, the snake's gallbladder was delivered to me, like an oyster on the half shell, soaked in a shot of Chinese schnapps.

"Custom says to drink this for your eyes," I was told.

As much as I was in the mood for an after-dinner drink, I was not particularly keen on ingesting gallbladder, neither that of a snake nor that of any other animal that came readily to mind. (That a snake actually possesses a gallbladder, until then, was not something I had known.) But I am curious by nature, and I was going around the world to do the kinds of things that people around the world do. I was determined to try everything I could. And I did not want to be rude. I ate the gallbladder, washing it straight down with the liquor, swallowing it whole, not chewing it. And I survived. Which I thought might be worth celebrating. Alas, a second waiter approached the table and served me another traditional drink.

"To improve your skin."

The blood of the snake. Drained earlier for my delectation.

"You know," I said, contemplating the exotic elixir, "my skin's just fine."

Later, in Beijing, I would make amends for this affront to reptiles when, after dining on turtle one evening, I joined my Chinese dinner companions—she, Yiwen Zhao, was a doctor, he, Qun Wang, was a diplomat—in tasting at least a small portion of the animal's blood.

We never had a bad meal in China despite eating in all sorts of places. And we ate lavishly. In crossing the country, we were invited to several Chinese banquets. The only downside to our culinary experience was mao-tai. The typical Chinese banquet, which consists of several courses, is traditionally followed by consumption of the most repulsive after-dinner drink on the planet: mao-tai. A lot of it. It is worse than gasoline with rotted milk of magnesia. It is absolutely horrible, but the Chinese love it. Finally, I had to tell my hosts, I will come to your banquet, but I am not going to drink mao-tai afterward. Thankfully, these days in China you can get good local beer everywhere.

From Lanzhou we headed east to Xi'an, where Paige was awed by the sight of the thousands of life-size terra-cotta statues—of warriors, chariots, horses, entire armies—unearthed by archaeologists in 1974 that constitute the country's major tourist attraction. So, of course, yet again, was I. I saw far more tourists on this trip than on my last. I had seen the boom's stirrings on my last trip to Xi'an, but the site's visibility had clearly, and consciously, been raised. Vendors were everywhere. That tourism was flourishing, and was being encouraged, was one more indication of emerging capitalism in China. Xi'an, still not completely excavated, has been written about countless times by countless numbers of people, including me. Words do not do it justice, and neither do pictures: there are certain places in the world that should never be photographed. For their grandeur and for their glory, these places have to be seen in person to be appreciated, or even, in some cases, to be believed, places like the Grand Canyon, the Taj Mahal, the Registan in Samarkand. The underground museum that is Xi'an is one of those places. Go there and see.

I have pointed out how the Chinese work from dawn to dusk. But not only do they work hard, they also save and invest more than 30 percent of their income. We in America at the moment save about 1 percent of our income. It is because the Chinese work so hard and save so much of what they earn that their economy is growing faster than ours.

(In China, savings are not taxed, whereas here in the United States the government, by taxing them two or three times, discourages savings. Surprisingly, as I write this, President Bush has proposed shifting the U.S. tax system to one that taxes consumption rather than income. The change would be as historically significant as America's shift from a tariff-based tax system in the nineteenth century to an income-based tax system in the twentieth. Such an approach is critical; it is essential for the future health of the nation. So I hope it actually happens.)

In the city of Zhengzhou I observed the Chinese work ethic in action in its most simple and primitive form: the attentiveness of a waitress, Mae Wang. Employed by one of the restaurants in town, her behavior was simply an exaggeration of that which was typical of all the workers in China. Mae Wang, when a restaurant patron caught her attention, literally ran to the table to be of help. Like a sprinter. Across the room. She ran to see what she could do to serve you. For me she was something of a metaphor, a motif, if you will, stated as part of an overture to the symphony of Shanghai.

Shanghai lay before us like Oz. We were approaching what I predicted would be the Emerald City of twenty-first-century capitalism—

within our lifetimes. Zhengzhou was the first stop on the beeline we were now making for the city. Nanjing was the final stop. In Nanjing, I looked out our hotel room window and saw building cranes everywhere I looked; it was here, in Nanjing, that someone informed me that fully half the building cranes in the world were currently in China. My itinerary, it appeared, was trying to prepare me, to educate me, for what lay ahead.

We finally arrived in Shanghai, and I instantly fell in love. Again. Yet again, Shanghai had changed. This was the fourth time I had been there, and every time it was a different city, a different country. Had it changed for the better? The city is modern, full of high-rises. It is trendy, fashionable, sophisticated. And rich. I happen to like big cities. I do not dream of returning to Demopolis, Alabama, where my phone number, as late as my college years, consisted of a single digit. For me, Shanghai is one of the great, exciting places in the world. And I would be very happy to live there. It would be like moving to New York in 1903, as New York was really blossoming.

Before 1949, before the revolution and the establishment of the People's Republic, the Shanghai stock market was the largest in Asia, the largest between London and New York. Shanghai was the center of commerce—and sin, the axis of everything in the Far East. In 1988 I visited the Shanghai exchange. To reach it, you walked down an unpaved road into a somewhat ramshackle storefront featuring little more than a thousand square feet of office space, and to buy stock you simply walked up to a counter, overseen by a single attendant, and paid for your shares. An over-the-counter stock was exactly that. The attendant totaled the transaction on an abacus. And in 1988 there were only a handful of stocks publicly traded. I bought a bank stock, more for its historical than intrinsic value. (The certificate hangs today, framed, on the wall of my home in New York.) At that time, in remarks recorded by a television crew, and later broadcast on PBS, I predicted great things for China:

"This is history being made," I said, in voice-over as I purchased my shares. "This is the way American stock markets evolved over two hundred years ago. Someday I'm going to invest a whole lot of money in China, so it's important to know how things work now. Before the revolution, China had the largest stock market in the Orient, and if I'm right, someday it will again."

The stock exchange in Shanghai today, a little more than a decade later, is located in a brand-new office building, a gigantic, broad, square structure containing a vast, ultramodern trading floor, where maybe three hundred people work at computer terminals. Completely electronic and growing, it technologically dwarfs the New York Stock Exchange, where, thanks to powerful anachronistic interests, brokers are still running around exchanging pieces of paper.

Naturally, I opened an account.

Earlier, to accommodate the growing number of foreigners who wanted to invest there, the Chinese had begun creating a class of shares known as B shares. The market's A shares were limited to purchase by the Chinese. By the time Paige and I arrived in 1999, all the foreigners, having failed to get rich quick as they had expected to do, had started bailing out, victims of just one more of the many bubbles that had burst, and the market in B shares had bottomed out.

You know a market has bottomed out when everybody gives up in despair and does not even want to talk about it. That is the way B shares stood when I was in China. It was purely fortuitous—it happened to be that way when we were there, and I happened to notice because I have been around markets for decades. There was nothing but despair and disgust, outright animosity toward the B shares. They were selling for twenty cents a share, and I stocked up. I bought a lot of shares in a lot of different companies, first because they were so cheap, and second because I believed China to be the wave of the future; not knowing how any stock in particular would perform, I expected all of them to do well.

Had A shares been available, I would not have bought them; there was not the necessary hostility toward them. It was the foreigners who had all dumped their stock, screaming, "Get me out of these B shares!" It so happened that within a year or so the Chinese made some changes in the law. The A shares and B shares became the same. And the B shares went through the roof, along with the entire Chinese stock market. For a lot of reasons my investment turned out to be a good one, but that is irrelevant (although the lesson of buying totally depressed shares usually works out—if not always so quickly). I have no intention of selling. I do not know what my shares are worth today. I do not want to know what they are worth. They are not for sale. I still own these stocks and hope to own them forever. I hope that they are in my estate. Certainly China will suffer setbacks along the way, just as the United Kingdom and the United States did in their rises to greatness. But I would have to be a sucker to sell my shares. It would be like buying shares in New York in 1903 and selling them in 1907.

While I was on this trip, Zhu Rongji, the Chinese premier, was at Harvard Business School making a speech. And somebody, some aspiring something-or-other, raised his hand and asked, "Are you going to devalue the Chinese currency?" There had been a lot of speculation that the Chinese government was going to devalue before making the yuan convertible. We are not going to devalue the currency, Zhu answered. If you really think we are going to devalue the currency, he said, I suggest you buy puts on the currency.

Now, buying puts is an extremely sophisticated way to profit when something collapses. But here was the premier of a Communist country telling this whippersnapper to buy puts, essentially telling him, "Call my bluff, if you don't believe me."

The Chinese understand money, finance, capitalism. This was the premier of the country. This was not his treasury secretary or the head of the central bank or the president of the stock exchange. This was the guy running the country. He knows money, and that sophistication permeates the whole society—finance, getting rich, saving, investing for the future, educating your children.

Compare that economic sophistication to the demonstrable ignorance of a fellow like George W. Bush, who recently, in remarks of his own, showed that he did not know the difference between devaluation and depreciation, an absolute embarrassment, especially for someone who attended business school. Forget that he is the president of the United States and not the voice of Communist China.

Do not get me wrong; it is not just Bush. No recent U.S. president has understood basic economics. Bill Clinton did not even know that the biggest stock market bubble in decades was occurring while he was president. He did not even know it popped when he was in office. I would cast a pox on both their houses—the Democrats *and* the Republicans.

Arriving in the spring of 1999, we were in Beijing during the buildup to the fiftieth anniversary of the revolution. It had been on October 1,

*Nothing is wasted in China.*

In Jinan, the kids were as keen on America as we were on China.

These schoolchildren in Jinan had never practiced English with an American. They enjoyed the lesson, but it was Paige's round blue eyes that stole the show.

1949, that Mao Zedong had proclaimed the establishment of the People's Republic. Thus, Tiananmen Square was completely closed down—for renovation, in anticipation of celebrating the event, according to the official line. Western press reports had it that the government had closed the square out of fear of political demonstrations. Other famous sites, such as the Great Wall and the Forbidden City, were open. Thanks to Paige, and much to my chagrin, we also found it necessary to pay a visit to Beijing's Hard Rock Cafe—where she bought a T-shirt and I demurred.

While we were in Beijing, the United States, conducting the bombing campaign over Serbia that we had just barely managed to escape, blew up the Chinese Embassy in Belgrade. Anti-American demonstrations immediately broke out in the Chinese capital. Seeing the press reports, you would have thought all of China was up in flames. The truth is that, while vast and quite vociferous, the demonstrating was confined chiefly to the area around the U.S. Embassy. We had been scheduled to give a press conference, and about seventy Chinese journalists had gathered to interview us about our trip. But the event was cut short out of fear that the appearance of Americans might inspire riots.

Paige pointed out that if the Chinese were worried for our safety— going so far as to whisk us away—there was probably good reason to be concerned.

"This is serious, Jim," she said. "Many Chinese are furious with the U.S., and rightly so."

While nothing came of our being American, it was nonetheless anxiety-provoking to be in Beijing while all of this was going on.

The notion that the bombing had been an accident, of course, was laughable on its face, and I said so in an article at the time. What I found frightening was that the U.S. media never questioned the government line. Not until six months later did the Western press, first in Britain, begin corroborating the facts: that we had blown up the Chinese Embassy intentionally, because it was riddled with electronic intelligence-gathering equipment and the Chinese were sharing the information being collected with their friends in the Yugoslav military. Of course, neither the Chinese nor the U.S. government felt it could admit the truth without looking bad.

One night while in Beijing we went to dinner with Mr. Yuan, his wife, and their five-year-old son, Wan Shan. The child ate almost none of his dinner, which came as no surprise to his parents. Nor was it a surprise to Mr. Yuan when his son asked for three desserts. Paige and I thought this was a joke of some kind, until Mr. Yuan and his wife indulged the boy's request.

"My goodness, Mr. Yuan," Paige said, "my parents certainly would make me finish one dessert before ordering another."

I mention this episode, not because I find spoiled children particularly interesting, but to make a point about Chinese children in general, most of whom, I noticed, are spoiled rotten.

This is the legacy of China's one-child policy, instituted in 1980 (and just officially ended in 2002). Studies have shown that only children and firstborns are usually smarter, more driven, and more accomplished than other children. And, of course, they are more often spoiled. In China one finds an entire country of only children. Everybody's child is special, smarter, more driven, and more accomplished— or so every parent believes. (That there is a premium placed upon boys versus girls is a dark phenomenon the implications of which would become much worthier of study when we arrived in Korea.) Springing up all over China to accommodate these "special" children and to indulge their parents' need to secure them the best education available is an endless crop of private schools. Their emergence is something of a movement. Young entrepreneurial schoolteachers are doing things never before seen in China. You want to get rich? Go to China and open a chain of private schools.

Looking at China, a country that over history has not been terribly aggressive, I see a country that will become even less aggressive in the future. Not because all its young men of fighting age are spoiled—and each, as an only child, is spoiled rotten—but because people who have only one child are going to be very reluctant to send that child to war or to send an only grandchild to war.

Whereas the nineteenth century belonged to Great Britain and the twentieth to the United States, the twenty-first will be the century of China. But before this happens, there is one very significant, giant step it must take, and that is to allow its currency to be freely convertible and freely tradable on the world market. A country can never achieve greatness or secure its ultimate power in the absence of a currency that people can use without hesitation or transparency, an open system of transactions.

Today the yuan, or renmimbi, is fixed, one of the few currencies left whose value does not fluctuate. It is presently pegged to the U.S. dollar. The dollar may go up and down, but the yuan is worth the same amount of dollars every day. There is no valid intellectual argument in support of fixing a currency. It has never worked and never will. No fixed currency has ever been able to maintain its peg. And some have failed repeatedly; there are plenty of people who still do not get it.

That the Chinese currency is not completely tradable, not convertible, is a holdover from communism, from the mind-set of socialists in the fifties, sixties, and seventies. The convertibility day is getting closer. If there is any currency that can conceivably replace the dollar, the euro, and the yen, which at the moment are the only three possibilities when it comes to a world currency, it is the yuan. Why? The Chinese have a huge population and a big economy that is getting bigger all the time. China is now among the largest importers of goods in the world, having surpassed several nations by 2003; everyone wants the Chinese as customers. They sell more to the world than they buy, and they have gigantic international reserves—they are second only to Japan in international currency reserves. The United States, by contrast, is a debtor nation. We have no net reserves. We have stupendous obligations. China is the world's second largest international creditor nation, while Japan, the largest, has a horrible problem; it has vast internal debts and an aging population. The Japanese now spend 25 percent of their GDP on their government, up from only 20 percent in 1991. The world may owe the Japanese, but the Japanese owe one another. The government is in massive debt to its citizens. China does not have that problem. It has neither huge internal debt nor foreign debt (it is a net creditor), and it has the second largest international currency reserves in the world.

There are those at the central bank in China who understand they must let their currency float to let the international market determine the yuan's value. Historically, they have been afraid to do this, fearful that the currency would collapse in the rush by the nation's citizens to get their money out of the country, with a lot of foreign investors following suit. And they were right to feel that way twenty years ago.

China is different now. This is not 1984 nor even 1994. Let the currency go down. Let all the people who want to dump it dump it. I for one would be buying. And I am not the only investor who would. Nor would all the overseas Chinese who continue to send money home stop doing so. In fact, more funds would flow into China. Capital is always more likely to go places where it will not be trapped by currency controls.

China, when I was there, had yet to be accepted as a member of the World Trade Organization. Now that its application has been accepted, it will be required to have convertible funds. The WTO's predecessor, the General Agreement on Tariffs and Trade (GATT), was created in 1948 in realization of the fact that the war just ended was in large part a consequence of the worldwide economic collapse of the 1930s. Serving as midwives of the Great Depression were the tariffs, quotas, and trade restrictions that had gone into effect as countries around the world, beggaring their neighbors, started closing off their economies, until every nation, reciprocally beggared, went broke. The survivors of the war and the depression are now gone, and those railing against globalization and the WTO have forgotten the lessons of history that those people learned the hard way.

The exchange controls and trade restrictions that China still embraces—and that antiglobalization protesters endorse—were very much a part of the international behavior that led to depression and war.

China, of course, is not the only country that is trying to have it both ways.

The United States, for example, recently put tariffs on tomatoes grown in Canada. Now if you look at a map, Canada, if not an entirely ice-bound nation, is still a place you are unlikely to point to first when you are looking for somewhere to start a farm. But for whatever reason, American tomato farmers cannot produce tomatoes as cheaply as they are produced in Canada. So the U.S. government, in effect, says, "We know there is free trade between the two countries, free movement of capital, and we want to buy the cheapest produce we can. But we have to protect the Florida tomato growers from Canadian growers, who can produce more cheaply than our guys can, even though they are in the Arctic and our guys are in the tropics. We will come up with something. But don't worry—it's only temporary."

Such restrictions are always initiated as "temporary measures."

But now, with Canadian tomatoes burdened by tariffs having gone up in price, I, the American grower, do not have to work as hard—I can go to the beach, leave work at three o'clock every day—and I know I can sell all the tomatoes I grow because I have no competition. And if I get a little sloppy and my income falls, I can simply raise my prices. Which is what has always happened throughout history, throughout the world.

The steel industry in the United States has been going on this way for fifty years. Every few years the industry persuades the government to protect us from the foreigners. "We just need to reorganize." But instead of reorganizing, getting more efficient, and figuring out what the foreigners are doing right, politicians just keep upping the protection. George W. Bush, who claims to be one of the great free traders, just put us through another round of this. There are more than 275 million citizens in the United States. Let us say, for the sake of argument, steelworkers and their beneficiaries amount to half a million people. To give a few of them a few extra bucks, more than 275 million of us have to pay more for our steel. Now, most of us are not out in the street screaming, because we do not really notice what has happened, and if we do notice, it is going to be after a year or two, as the price of a car goes up. But it is always temporary, we are told, and there is always a good reason for the protectionism. We protect rice in this country, we protect mohair, for reasons of "national defense."

All U.S. citizens pay higher prices for rice to help a few rice farmers. We would all be better off if we gave each of our rice producers a guaranteed income, a Corvette, and a place at the beach. In return they would stop growing rice.

Protectionist distortions always go farther too. Since rice producers are guaranteed fat incomes, they buy more land, which drives up the price of farmland. They then use high-priced land as another reason for needing protection. The land might be better used for corn or cotton, but it becomes too expensive for those crops as the more heavily subsidized farmers drive up the bidding.

The distortions keep rippling through society. College kids study farming rather than nursing or languages, since that is where the money is.

Will this sort of madness change? To my delight and astonishment

President Bush proposed in 2002 that all manufacturing tariffs be reduced to zero by 2015. It is one of the most exciting proposals ever to come from a U.S. president. The United States needs free trade and free movement of assets, or we will never be able to finance our debts. At the moment the U.S. tariff system has 10,200 categories with tariffs as high as 48 percent. Unfortunately, poor countries such as Bangladesh bear the brunt of many of these tariffs. Tariffs worldwide total about $300 billion a year and have begun rising in recent years. We would all be so much better off if the president's proposal takes hold, but I cannot imagine it will ever happen—we even protect lentils and chickpeas in the United States, and I expect to be eating expensive soup for years to come.

This recurs throughout history. In the 1930s, in a drying up of liquidity and trade, the world economy collapsed. The inability to move money, to buy and sell, led to the eventual establishment of what is now the WTO and to the expansion of trade that defines it. International trade has expanded dramatically in the last fifty years—and average national tariffs have fallen from 55 percent in 1945 to less than 5 percent today—thanks to an organization of which China, once a pariah nation, is finally a member. And a requirement of that membership, a sine qua non of free trade, of an open society, is the ability of people to come and go with their money.

Because the yuan is pegged to the dollar, because it is not convertible, there is naturally a black market in the currency. There is a black market in virtually everything that is officially controlled, anywhere. Whether it is wheat, gold, currency, alcohol, or marijuana, somebody is going to figure out a way to get around the restrictions and to capitalize on them. To find out if anything is wrong with a country and how bad it happens to be—to "take the temperature," as I like to think of it—it is always instructive when visiting a country to visit the local black market. It is one of the things I like to do whenever I travel, and was one of the first things I did when I arrived in China.

In Urumqi, in western China, our second stop after crossing from Kazakhstan, I went looking to see if there *were* a black market; it would tell me where China stood in the process of what I saw as its positive transition. One of the ways to find the black market is to go to the bank, because that is one place black marketeers tend to gather. They go where the money is. In Turkmenistan I exchanged money on the black market outside the five-star hotel in Ashkhabad. The bell-boys and maids always know about the market and often change money themselves, though their rate is never very good. I have some-times had police lead me to the black market, but only in countries where things have not yet collapsed. In some countries I have had em-ployees at the bank direct me there. Sure enough, outside the Bank of China in Urumqi, there were about fifteen guys, all of them relatively young, hanging out, changing money.

And they were not paying much of a premium. It was hardly worth my while to do business with them. After negotiating with several to no avail, I announced that I was going into the bank to change my money. One of the bosses—there is always a boss—happened to be on hand that day, and one of the youngsters pointed him out. So I went to see him. When he refused to give me a better rate, I headed for the bank, which I would have done anyway at some point. I always get *some* money from the bank. Sometimes on the black market you get counterfeit money. The money you get from the bank is legitimate, and I needed it for purposes of comparison.

Walking into the bank, I was followed in by the money changer, and there he stood, in front of the teller's window, pleading quite openly with me not to sell my money to the bank but instead to sell it to him. Whatever transition China was undergoing, I thought, things could not be terribly bad. I had just learned, out on the street, that the black market was not paying a significant premium for foreign ex-change, and the fact that it was charging a premium at all did not seem to trouble the government—if this scene were any example. The premium was low because the yuan was sound and one could get it out of the country with relative ease. If one had been unable to do so, the premium would have been exorbitant, and the black marketeer would have been far more circumspect.

Has China changed for the better? Sometimes I bemoan the loss of the old Shanghai. I remember going down to the park in the morning, mingling with the throngs of people, and watching the boats come in from across the water. Men would step off the boats onto the dock, coming from the farms out in the countryside with hundreds of eggs on their backs. No longer does that happen. I have gone back every time, to that park, to that dock. The produce boats do not come in

The new entrepreneurs in western
China waste not an inch, nor a minute.

A clear message in Shanghai:
women in Asia will soon be
asking for more—and getting it.

Long-standing protectionism
in Korea means no access to efficient,
foreign equipment, and a lack
of quality control at home.

anymore. It is over. That is not Shanghai anymore. That is not China. I snapped a picture of a young woman on a motor scooter talking on her cell phone in Shanghai, and she was dressed as stylishly as any woman in New York, Paris, or Milan. I flashed back to Wren Shan, a seventeen-year-old in the western-desert city of Urumqi, whose only aspiration in life was to play in the NBA. The walls of his bedroom were covered with nothing but pictures of U.S. basketball stars about whom I knew nothing. Is that better or worse than twenty years ago? Who knows? Better or worse, it is.

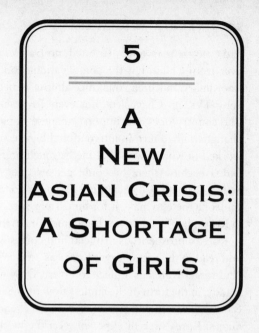

# 5

## A NEW ASIAN CRISIS: A SHORTAGE OF GIRLS

M Y FIRST REACTION to South Korea was how extraordinarily modern and rich it is, one of the twenty richest countries in the world, by most measures—its GDP per capita is eight times India's and fifteen times North Korea's—and in its way a phenomenal success story. As recently as 1965, after all, even North Korea was richer than the South.

South Korea owes much of its success, and the speed of it, to the U.S. Department of Defense, which, in addition to a magnificent highway system, has built thirty-seven military bases in the country—a country only slightly larger than Indiana or Hungary. While injecting billions of dollars into Korea, the U.S. military, for most of the last half century, has propped up the system of draconian dictatorship there responsible for closing the country's economy and society. And Korea's particularly heavy-handed form of protectionism has been richly rewarded, if only in the medium run.

Korean protectionism all but slaps you in the face. It took us two days of dealing with bureaucracy to get into the country, although we had everything in order. Granted, no traveler had ever brought a car over from China, but the complications and expenses were still extraordinary. In Korea you notice almost immediately that there are no Sony TVs, no Chevrolets, not even Toyotas. Everything is Korean. The country does not import Japanese films or Japanese music. In Shanghai, I had met an international businessman who had lived and worked in Korea, who told me he much preferred doing business in China because there he could get anything he wanted. Not so in Korea. If he needed something for his factory, he would have to find someone there to make it for him. To be sure, he could live like a king in Korea, but he could not have much of anything a king would want.

Korea's prosperity is artificial and comes at a price. Despite what you read in the press, forget Korea as a place to live and do business. And forget Korea as a place to invest. Only with a Big Mama or Big Daddy, in the form of the endless flow of U.S. military money into the economy, can such a system work. And even then there are no guarantees. Korea's recent experience on the world market is a textbook illustration of what can go wrong when a country adopts the trade restrictions I mentioned earlier, restrictions similar to the ones currently being enjoyed by the American tomato farmer.

Korean companies, because they were protected, naturally got bigger and bigger. Arrogance crept in. They thought they were smarter than everybody else in the world. "We can compete with the Japanese," they told themselves. Well, the only reason they could compete with the Japanese was because the Japanese could not sell in Korea. Korean companies continued to sell televisions in the United States and automobiles in Europe, but internally they were getting complacent, borrowing gigantic amounts of money because they thought they could not fail. And why not? After twenty years, you start believing you are as terrific as Western banks and *The New York Times* say you are. These companies actually forgot that they had an economic fortress around them.

So they got bigger and bigger, borrowed larger amounts of money, and got sloppier, less competitive, deeper in debt. And it all started falling apart in 1997, when the Asian crisis hit. Thailand, Malaysia, Korea . . . all of them had been borrowing short. All were violating one of the most easily understandable and long-standing adages of the financial world: Do not borrow short and commit long. When the crisis hit, they could not repay their loans, no matter how good they were at manufacturing shoes. It does not matter how smart you are—if you get overextended, you are overextended.

With corporate rot having set in, many Asian companies, while successful at home, were not very competitive on the world market. Also, in several cases, their countries had pegged their currencies to the U.S. dollar. They pegged them to the dollar at a time when the dollar was very low in the market. For a variety of reasons, the dollar got stronger and stronger, which meant the Thai and other currencies got stronger and stronger. So at the same time that the Asian companies were rotting from within—growing inefficient and noncompetitive—their countries' currencies were going up. For both reasons, their goods were getting more expensive overseas.

I will say it again: No pegged currency has ever worked long term, no matter to what it is pegged.

So all these countries got nailed. The whole thing started falling apart, and a lot of companies started going bankrupt. When Thailand gets in trouble, Malaysia gets in trouble. Why? Because we in the West think Thais and Malaysians are the same thing—they're all out there somewhere, we Westerners figure; they all have yellow faces. Koreans can say, "Hey, we're five thousand kilometers from Thailand, different race, different language, different religion, different customs, and different economic models." In Geneva, people don't know that. Or care. When *Time* magazine says it is the decade of Asia, mom and pop cannot wait to invest in Southeast Asia mutual funds. But as soon as something goes wrong, they find themselves asking, "Where the dickens is Asia?"

One thing we need to learn is that all bubbles are the same.

If my mother loses money in IBM or in her Fidelity mutual fund, do you think, even if there is any "expert advice," that she is going to say, "Well, I'm going to take my money out of IBM and put it in Malaysia." She is so furious that she lost money in IBM, which is on every street corner, and in Fidelity, which is in the newspaper every day—do you think she will take her money out of IBM, look around the world, and say, "Well, I've heard the Ivory Coast is a good place to put money"? That may sound crazy, but it always happens when something is booming and the "experts" open their mouths.

That is what was happening in 1997.

Korea was actually a bit sounder than some of its neighbors—thanks to those trade barriers, the country was not so deeply in debt. It did not suffer the balance-of-payments disaster that some of the others did. In Bangkok, by contrast, it seemed as if every twenty-three-year-old guy and girl in town was buying a Rolex and a Porsche. If you think the dot-com cowboys got carried away, you should have seen Thailand. With tons of money coming into the country, the citizens of that big Asian Tiger were spending it as fast as they could.

There's nothing wrong with borrowing huge amounts of money—as a country, as a family, as an individual—as long as you're putting it into productive assets, building for the future. In the nineteenth century, the United States borrowed stupendous amounts from all over the world, mainly from Europe. We were a gigantic debtor nation. We put the money into productive infrastructure such as railroads and factories. And by 1914 we got our payoff. We became a creditor nation for the first time in our history. We then became the world's largest creditor nation and the most powerful country in the world. We borrowed all that money, but we invested it wisely. But if you borrow a lot of money and buy Rolexes and Porsches and big houses, or give it to charity or welfare or spend excessively on armaments, you are not going to thrive long term. (The impact of war, even a victory, on a nation is the same as burning a large part of its wealth.) In 1997, before the crisis, parking spots in Hong Kong sold for HK$1.5 million—more than entire houses in greater London. That kind of borrowing is going to bite you in the behind someday.

As Korea grew richer and richer, people could afford to travel abroad. What they had seen on satellite TV—Japanese poppies in season, the changes taking place in China, all the excitement of life in America—they could afford to investigate for themselves. Young people visited their cousins in Queens, New York, and saw them driving Toyotas and Chevy Blazers and listening to music unavailable in Seoul. (Korea is the fourth youngest country in the world, with 22 percent of its population under the age of fifteen. By that measure, the top three are Mexico, Iceland, and New Zealand, in that order.) More and more people traveled to the West, and more and more of them returned home unhappy. They pushed for an opening of borders in Korea, for an end to crony capitalism, to an economy run by a dictator, banks, and a few big capitalists, all of whom belong to the same club.

So things have begun to change. Some of the country's leaders are currently trying to make good on promises to open Korea to the outside world. But it is still a protected economy. And that is why I did not want to invest in Korea. If these companies ever really have to face serious competition, it is going to be a difficult test. And I do not think they will pass that test.

Certainly I am as capable as anyone of making money in such a climate, of investing in the very short term, getting in and getting out fast. But that has never been my style. I differentiate between trading and investing. Traders are the short-term guys, and some of them are spectacular at it. I am hopeless at it—perhaps the world's worst trader. I see myself as an investor. I like to buy things and own them forever. And what success I have had in investing has usually come from buying stock that is very cheap or that I think is very cheap. Even if you are wrong, when buying something cheap you are probably not going to lose a lot of money. But buying something *simply* because it is cheap is not good enough—it could stay cheap forever. You have to see a positive change coming, something that within the next two or three years *everybody else* will recognize as a positive change.

The difference between investing and trading is the difference between Sam Walton, who rarely sold his Wal-Mart shares, and Roy Neuberger, who sells shares in things he owns every few minutes. Roy Neuberger is one of the legendary traders, and I worked for him once, when I was young. He would get to work five minutes before the market opened, start reading *The New York Times,* then suddenly say to me or one of the others in the office, "There's a hundred thousand IBM for sale on the floor. Buy it at eighty nine and five-eighths."

We would sit up and stare at each other. How does he know? we would wonder. He's sitting there, reading the *Times.* But he had such a sixth sense. The ticker was running by on the other side of the room, and somehow or another, just from the action on the tape, he seemed to know what was going on.

So we would go down to the floor and check. Sure enough, there were a hundred and twenty-five thousand shares for sale. He would always come within a few thousand shares of the amount that was for sale and come in at roughly the best price, no matter what he was sitting around doing. We never saw him look at the tape. He had an instinct, a paranormal power of some kind. After fifty years, he could almost do it blindfolded.

I am hopeless at that. If I do have a strength, it is the ability to look at Industry X or Country Y, on which everybody is really down, and exercise the courage, the sense, the stupidity, whatever it is, to buy it, even though everybody is telling me I am nuts to do so. If people become hostile when you say you are buying, it's probably the right thing to do. Hostility is a great indicator. Everybody has lost so much money that they have sold the disgusting thing, and as a consequence it is really cheap. Conventional wisdom is something I honor in the breach. When I am in the same room with a hundred investors and most of them come out of the room, saying, "Gosh, that's the greatest thing going," I often contemplate selling it short. There is some distance between information and judgment, and I think I have heard something the others have ignored. Besides, I know most investors already own it. Who is left to buy?

Everybody likes to follow the crowd. If you walk out of that room and you say the emperor has no clothes, everybody looks at you with loathing and pity:

"Did you hear that guy? He says the emperor has no clothes? He's crazy. We all know the emperor has clothes."

"Yeah, don't worry, I own that stock, too."

They all reinforce one another's opinions. They call up the emperor, who tells them, "Of course, I'm wearing clothes."

They call up Enron: "Everything's great over here."

They call one another up: "Everything's okay. I called up a guy who works at Enron, and he told me everything's okay."

Three more then go on TV and declare how great everything is with the emperor.

I did not invest in Korea, as cheap as it was, because everything was not okay. The foreign editor of *The New York Times,* even in late 2002, raved about Korea's high foreign currency reserves, totally oblivious to the fact that much of it was borrowed. And unlike the typical trader, who likes betting on the action, up or down, I do not want to be on the Street every day watching the ticker. Roy Neuberger is still down there trading every day at the age of ninety-nine. It is his

*In Korea, it did not take long to notice the shortage of girls—*
*outnumbered ten to five in this class on a school outing.*
*In a few years, young Korean women will be able*
*to pick and choose among men.*

passion, it is in his soul. I took a different road. I literally took *to* the
road.

South Korea features mountainous terrain in the north and east and
broad plains in the south, where a majority of its population is
densely concentrated. About a quarter of all forty-six million South
Koreans live in Seoul, thirty miles south of the demilitarized zone. But
the more significant demographic issue currently facing the nation is
not *whether* it is overpopulated but *how*. We arrived in Korea in May,
just in time for school holidays, a time of picnics and family outings.
We saw plenty of children in our travels. They were gathered everywhere we went.

And not enough of them were girls.

Throughout history, Mother Nature has skewed birth figures in
favor of boys, roughly 51 to 49 percent. Population figures, of course,
skew the other way—there are more women in the world than men—
and that is probably why the dice are loaded to favor the birth of
males. The advantage is meant to account for the fact that men die
younger, are more likely to go to war, to kill each other, and to get
drunk and drive their motorcycles into walls. But in the overall number of births the advantage is only 2 percent. In Korea, noticing relatively fewer girls around, I started asking questions, and learned that
in Korea at the time, there were 120 twelve-year-old boys for every
100 twelve-year-old girls, a 20 percent premium, if you will, which
was way out of line. Indeed, it was several times the norm.

Until recently, the reproductive paradigm for humans has been to
have as many children as possible. In the past, doing so provided a
family with workers in what was a predominantly agrarian society; it
provided parents with someone to care for them as they grew old; and
it provided a necessary counterweight to the high mortality rates of
the period. Today, throughout the world, for the first time in history,
people, for cultural and economic reasons, are purposely having
fewer children. It costs a lot of money to have children, and the time
and energy children require put a serious strain on the modern married couple's freedom. Many nations, for different reasons—e.g., so-
cially engineering themselves out of a population crisis—are actively
working toward lowering their birthrates. In China until recently, it
was official policy.

(China's one-child policy was actually a one-boy policy. If your first child was a daughter, you were allowed to have a second child if you were over thirty and it had been at least eight years since your first child was born. You were not allowed to have a third child under any conditions. If you failed to obey the rules, you lost your job, and your second child was denied an education.)

In Korea, couples are having fewer children for personal rather than social reasons—they are doing so voluntarily rather than under pressure from the government—but the results are no different from those in China, where the ratio for current births is 117 boys to every 100 girls. In fact, the demographic shortfall holds true in much of Asia: Japan, Taiwan, and other countries. In Asia females are second-class citizens, merely servants or handmaidens to their husbands, their parents, or their in-laws. And you do not have to execute your girls or give them away (as happened in China and in other countries in other periods of history) to tilt your population figures in favor of boys.

You have a child, it's a boy, you stop. Even if those with a boy try again, half the second children are boys. That alone skews the population. You have a girl, you try again; if the second child is a boy, you stop. If the second child is a girl? Numerous girls are given up for adoption. But many couples, using sonogram technology, especially when it comes to a second child, simply abort the females. The situation became so bad in Korea that the government outlawed the use of sonograms to determine the sex of a child. So parents fly abroad to have them done.

Where is all this leading? One thousand years ago, at the turn of the last millennium, for a variety of reasons—principally because girls were seen as a drag on the economy—the same situation arose in Europe. There were more men than women in the population. And girls suddenly became very valuable. A nineteen-year-old boy whose libido was bubbling over was out of luck in the absence of being able to offer an appropriate inducement—so back then it was the boy's family that paid the dowry. I believe that today's twelve-year-old Korean girl, in a decade or so, is going to realize she can have almost anything she wants. Just as in China, there will be a surplus of spoiled, testosterone-laden bucks running around, and in the face of an inadequate show of respect from a suitor or even a husband, she will have dozens of others from which to choose. And that 20 percent premium will be even higher given the increased mortality rate of males. Korean women, who currently constitute almost 40 percent of the workforce, a third of whom labor on family farms, are looking at far more independence in the future. Professions will be open to them, higher education in general will be more accessible, and divorce rates will no doubt escalate. Huge sociological changes of every kind will ensue.

So I changed my mind about investing in Korea. I tried to figure out how to profit from the major changes on the horizon. I brainstormed with Paige about how women's lives were changing. I could not find any health clubs or educational institutions, but I did find companies that manufactured birth control pills. For cultural reasons, few people in Asia use the pill, just as was the case in the West once upon a time. (In fact, the pill was illegal in Japan until 2000. Japanese women were furious that it had taken only six months to legalize Viagra but decades to legalize the pill.) With so limited a market for the product, the companies had gone bankrupt during the Asian crisis, but I thought I could see a dramatic positive change on the horizon. And obviously, the bankrupt companies were very cheap. I remembered how the fortunes of such companies in the United States had skyrocketed when women finally began using the pill, so I opened an account and bought shares in all three of the bankrupt Korean companies.

The demographic phenomenon I observed will be a significant factor in Korean reunification. Boys in Korea are going to need girls, and where are they going to get them? They are no different from anyone else; they want to marry their own kind. They will find a few young women among the Korean-American residents of Queens and Los Angeles, but the only real place they will be able to find Korean girls is North Korea.

I also contemplated, if only briefly, buying real estate in Seoul. Land on the south side of the river dividing the city is much more expensive than land on the north because of the constant fear of war. All assume the North Korean Army could cover the thirty miles to Seoul easily enough but would be halted on the north side of the river. Recent South Korean governments have been working with the support of their people toward opening normal relations with their neighbor to the north. I am convinced that peace and reunification will come eventually, but I am not a real estate investor, so I regretfully passed. The North Koreans should buy as much as possible of the cheap land on the north side of the river. They could then declare "Peace!" and become stinking rich.

Our two-week drive across Korea culminated in the city of Pusan, and there, before boarding a boat for Japan, I had one last piece of business to address. Adventure, as I pursue it, takes numerous forms, and my adventure would have been incomplete without my partaking of a legendary culinary delight.

The Korean people, indeed many Asians, have been eating dog for thousands of years. And of course I had to give it a try. Some Korean restaurants actually specialize in the preparation of dog meat, and in Pusan I was directed to the best dog restaurant in the city. There, I was served a very tasty, very lean portion of what I took to be the canine of the day and discovered to my surprise, when I asked the animal's breed, that I was not eating some stray taken off the street but indeed a dog raised to be eaten, presumably of hybrid stock. The proprietor excitedly showed me recent studies illustrating how healthy it was to eat dog. Even so, I ate just enough of my meal to know it was very good, and I do not intend to eat it again, perhaps out of the same vague sense of unease that caused Paige to decline the opportunity in the first place. As I was savoring the specialty of the house—very easy to chew, more like lamb than chicken, I would say—Paige was entertaining memories of her beloved Snoopy and Caesar. Paige also said no to dining on silkworms, which I think was a big mistake. They are available grilled, from various vendors on the street, and I found them to be delicious. Each about the size of a fingernail, the succulent larvae are sold by the cupful, and I personally could not get enough of them. Thus far in the trip (in Kazakhstan we had dined on horse) I had drawn the line only at eating monkey—much too close to home.

From Pusan we took a car ferry across the Korea Strait headed for Japan, arriving in Hagi on the southwest coast of Honshu on the first of June. We would spend almost five weeks driving the country, with stops in Hiroshima, Himeji, Nara, Shizuoka, Yokosuka, Tokyo, and Kyoto (where we were joined for a week by Paige's parents), Hakone, Kanazawa, and Fushiki. We even climbed Mount Fuji.

An absolutely glorious tourist destination, befitting its rich cultural history, Japan also boasts a modern infrastructure the wealth of which is truly remarkable. The highways feature electronic signs that display the estimated time required to drive to various cities down the road. Computers calculate the figure based on weather, traffic density, the occurrence of any traffic accidents, and the current speed limit. Speed limits, posted electronically, are adjustable based on conditions. The software in use must be designed to assume that everyone will drive a certain percentage over the limit, for many do—including us—and inevitably the time estimates hold up. Inset in the paved surfaces of all the major roads are flashing lights that enable drivers, well in advance, to see curves coming up ahead.

Many of the sidewalks in certain Japanese cities are overhung by awnings built into the sides of buildings, allowing pedestrians, especially in large shopping districts, to go about their business comfortably in inclement weather. The color of traffic lights—and an upcoming change in the color—are signaled by the sound of bells, a boon to the blind as well as to those pedestrians who are simply too lazy to look up. The blind benefit further from parallel ridges inscribed in the pavement—approaching an intersection on foot, one encounters a kind of sidewalk Braille that indicates the approach of an intersection and directs one to a route across it.

The wealth of the country is more than impressive—it is dazzling, and it is visible in almost everything you see. Indeed, by traditional measure—international monetary reserves—Japan is the richest country in the world. But it does not take more than a second look to see that this economic Goliath is in longer-term trouble. A pitiful, helpless giant, Japan has serious problems. And its desperation is something it has brought upon itself.

Its problems begin with demographics. Japan has one of the lowest birthrates in the world, and the median age of the population is one of the highest. If the trend continues, its population will be reduced by half well before the end of the century. The country's massive internal debt, one of the highest in the world, continues to grow while the number of people necessary to pay it off continues to shrink. The same demographic prevails in Europe, of course, but the Europeans have nothing on the Japanese when it comes to discouraging immigration. So rarefied is the racism in Japan that not even

third-generation Korean Japanese, for example, qualify for citizenship. If you are Japanese-born but not Japanese by blood, notwithstanding the fact that your parents and grandparents were born in
Japan, you will not be granted a vote. Today's voters are opting
against outsiders despite the certainty of forcing the country into decline. The current group of kids will be unhappy when they reap the
legacy over which they had no say.

Exacerbating the problem, politicians of the Liberal Democratic
Party (LDP), which has controlled Japan since 1955, have enlarged
the debt, building hundreds of "bridges to nowhere," pork-barrel
public works projects that serve no useful economic purpose beyond
currying favor with local voters and ward politicians. Huge amounts
of money and votes lie with the rich Japanese rice farmer, which ex-
plains why rice prices in Japan are several times what they are even
in the United States, though you would not get anyone in Japan to
admit it. They will tell you that their rice is protected because Japanese rice is different from other rice, that the Japanese digestive system
is therefore different, and that therefore the country's *plumbing* system is different. If everybody started eating foreign rice, they will go
on to explain, not only would the nation's health collapse, but its
plumbing would collapse as well. I have heard this argument from
academics in Japan, Ph.D.s, not just the LDP's double-talking politicians. One would not believe some of the arguments the Japanese
come up with—mysticism about rice as part of the nation's culture,
history, and society—all to justify the farm subsidy and protectionism, the real reason for which is the delivery of votes, jobs, and
money to the LDP.

Heading west, as we did to board the boat to Siberia, traversing
vast rice fields, one can see the enormous wealth associated with the
rice-growing industry and easily understand the power controlled by
the region's political representatives. Magnificent highways lead to
these villages, roads of little practical use to anyone, just more political pork returned to the district. Our fat cats in Washington are political amateurs compared with those of the LDP. Japan spends 40
percent of its national budget on public works, versus about 9 percent
in the United States. And the system subverts the health of the entire
society. The cost of a house in Japan is astronomical in part because
the price of land is so high, and that in turn is due in large part to the

value of rice. No farmer is going to build an apartment house on a field that will support a crop so valuable.

In Kobe we ate Kobe beef, which is famous around the world, an extremely expensive delicacy. In Japan they will tell you that Kobe beef is so astronomically expensive because the cows are specially fed and treated—they are massaged, rubbed down by hand so that their muscles develop in the right way, and prevented from exerting themselves. All of which is true, by the way, and Kobe beef is as tender as any beef I have ever eaten, the only meat I have ever tasted that you barely have to chew. But the main reason a Kobe steak costs $100 is quite simply because beef is protected in Japan. If Japan enjoyed free trade, the famous delicacy would still be expensive, but it would cost about half of what it costs now. Always look for the real reason when you hear about something as patently ridiculous as a $100 steak or a $50 melon.

Japan's absurd protectionism will continue to erode the country's economic position in the world. In an effort to keep two coal mines from failing, the government, shortly before our visit, forced Japanese power companies to buy domestic coal at three times the world price and pass the cost on to consumers. To protect a very few workers in a politically influential industry, 125 million citizens and an entire economy were subjected to higher energy costs.

One of the things leading to Japan's success over the years is its insularity. The island nation benefits from a homogeneous population, racially distinct and of a single mind-set. When the Japanese collectively decide to do something, they usually get it done; in so centralized a society there is very little dissent. The downside of this national trait is an enormous rigidity, an inflexibility that is all but insurmountable.

I entered a restaurant near Mount Fuji and ordered a bowl of rice with my meal. My first surprise, in a Japanese restaurant, was to be informed that there was no rice on the menu. Of course you have rice, I told my waitress, pointing out that the menu featured ample varieties of sushi. No rice, she insisted; it was not listed on the menu. I ordered tuna sushi. I asked for a dozen. When the sushi arrived, I asked the waitress for a bowl, which she willingly delivered. I removed the tuna from the sushi and poured the rice into the bowl, explaining to the waitress, "See, you do serve rice." I did not do this to insult the woman, nor do I tell this story to demean her personally. But my demonstration made no impression. It did not compute. No rice, I was told; it was not on the menu.

I wish I were making this up. This country with an overseas reputation as an efficient entrepreneurial power is strangled by inflexibility and overregulation, to the point where the creativity and innovation that made the country great is rapidly evaporating. Japan has reached that very stage of development reached by a complacent United States when the latter dominated television and automobile manufacture, the point at which the Japanese pretty much took over our business, making better cars and better TVs. The Japanese are not about to go bankrupt, but in what is now a protected Japanese society, the drive and spirit of the immediate postwar generation are in short supply.

This is the richest country in the world, a country supposedly technologically ahead of every other, a country with commerce in its blood. This is the country we are supposed to fear and emulate. Yet traveling its motorways, driving its toll roads, which are extremely expensive, you will discover that, both there and at the nation's gas stations, while the use of credit cards is encouraged—they take MasterCard, Visa, American Express, Diners Club—only those drawn on Japanese banks are accepted.

How rigid is the country? I tried to open a brokerage account. And so many brokerage houses told me that I could not do so that I finally had to call up the stock exchange itself. I was informed that it was perfectly legal for a foreigner to open an account to buy and sell stocks, but only one brokerage, Toyo Securities, eventually consented to do so. In the end, as it happened, my VP account executive claimed he did not know how to convert dollars to yen and was unwilling to figure out how, which was one of the more creative ways of achieving something at which the Japanese, in my experience, have become absolutely world class: saying no.

Why, after all I have said, would I want to open a brokerage account in a place like this? you might well ask.

After my last trip through the country, traveling by motorcycle ten years before, I sold the market short in Japan and made some money. The chief reason I am long Japan now is the almost universal belief worldwide that the country is a basket case. As a result, it is very cheap—more than 75 percent below where it was fourteen years ago. That, of course, does not mean it cannot go down another 75 percent. But the market does show the classic signs of bottoming out, at least for the medium haul, the one measured in years, not decades. Right now there is tremendous despondency in Japan. The suicide rate is the highest in recorded history, the birthrate the lowest. People are refraining from having children because they are economically fearful. Polls of college students show the most popular career choice to be working for the government. Everybody is frantic and insecure.

I am convinced that the Japanese economy has hit a temporary bottom and that a prosperous time—call it a rebound—is coming. I am looking for stocks to buy for the medium term. Furthermore, the Bank of Japan—in time-honored, economically blundering fashion— has made it pretty clear that it is going to start printing money. And when governments print money, one of the first places the money winds up is the stock market. I believe that in the short term the yen will rise against the even more fundamentally weak dollar, so not only will certain stocks do well, but the currency will also advance along with stocks, doubling the impact of my purchases. Again, I am speaking of the short or medium term. The Nikkei is not a place I expect to have money for the next ten or twenty years. Japan is sailing into the wind rather than with the wind at its back.

There is hope, however slight, that things will change. After a decade of stagnation, with the entire system becoming more and more rotten, the Japanese electorate can see everything about to collapse under the weight of all the bloat and corruption. Voters— especially urban voters, who do not benefit from most of the graft in the system—recently sent politicians a message. The new premier knows the problems and says the right words. It will be interesting to see if he can produce.

Outsiders have been urging Japan to clear out its system by requiring failed companies to liquidate and requiring banks to write off all the worthless loans they carry. Ironically, the United States is the most vociferous in preaching this as the course for Japan, when the U.S. Federal Reserve is practicing exactly the opposite. It has driven down interest rates at home dramatically and printed money, allowing our banks to carry numerous losers. Joseph Schumpeter taught us that the marvel of capitalism is its creative destruction. Eliminating dead wood enables fresh growth. But both Japan and the Federal Reserve have been impeding the pruning process.

We spent five weeks in Japan, a long time given the size of the country in relation to the world, not so long given Japan's importance in the world. We were enchanted by the ancient temples, the art, music, dance, and other expressions of culture; we were fascinated by our visits to the country's medieval forts, and we wanted more. A professional baseball game and the Osaka Aquarium each held us for hours. Hiroshima hardened my antiwar sentiments and made Paige weep. But it is a long way from the Pacific to Scandinavia, which is where we were headed—a long way across Siberia—and it was time to get going. We did not want to wind up in Scandinavia in the heart of winter, not that we could not handle the weather, necessarily, but we had other plans for January. On the first of the month—the first day of the new millennium, or the first of the last year of the old millennium, however you like to calculate it—on January 1, 2000, Paige and I were to be married. Though we had not yet figured out where, or how.

On my previous crossing between Japan and Russia, I had traveled on a passenger-and-auto ferry that made the trip monthly from Yokohama. That boat no longer existed. The boat on which Paige and I finally managed to book passage, which left from Fushiki, and only in the summer, did carry a few passengers but was designed principally to ferry used cars.

The Japanese have a law, many laws, in fact—very rigid inspections and upgrade standards—that make it cheaper for a Japanese citizen to buy a new car every two or three years than to try to keep his present vehicle on the road. These completely draconian and artificial standards are designed to ensure that the nation's automobile industry prospers (in typical fashion, at the expense of the nation's citizens). Consequently, three-year-old cars are very cheap in Japan; indeed, they are practically worthless. Because they are so cheap to buy and so expensive to own, there is an entire industry, and a very lucrative one, devoted to selling them all over the world.

It is astonishing in how many African countries, for example, these automobiles show up, easily recognizable by, among other things, the placement of the steering wheel on the right-hand side of the car. (In

Japan, as in the United Kingdom, one drives on the left-hand side of the road.) All through our travels, all over the globe, we saw minivans with steering wheels placed on the right and ads printed in Japanese on their side panels extolling the merits of some Tokyo furniture store or a meat market in Osaka.

There is a brisk trade in the aforementioned cars to brokers in Siberia, and the boat on which we sailed was loaded with close to a hundred of them, as many as could be carried. We squeezed aboard with our vehicles, and off we went, on a forty-hour crossing of the Sea of Japan, to Vladivostok.

# 6

# DIGITAL
# MONGOLIA

BEFORE LEAVING JAPAN we had taken care of some housekeeping, or the overland-traveler equivalent of it. Among other things, I picked up the last of my hepatitis B shots. The hepatitis B vaccine is administered in a series of three injections, the second following the first by thirty days, the third by six months. Paige, who had started a little earlier than I, had received her third shot in Pusan. A trip like ours requires more inoculations than most people receive in a lifetime. Paige's vaccination card, when we returned to the States, would show a total of twenty-four shots in a series that began nine months before we left.

Shots were not all we accumulated on the trip. Both Paige and I haunted the markets everywhere we went as a way of understanding the various societies. I am an inveterate collector, and between the two of us we rapidly filled up the sack in the trunk of the car into which we stuffed the things we bought that we did not have shipped home directly by various merchants. In just about every country through which we passed, we allotted time to visit the local post office, con-

stantly shipping home the contents of the "send-back sack." Sometimes, if something were particularly urgent, we would use DHL, but
more often than not we would just walk into a post office, each of
which had a lot to teach us about the country in which it was located.
(In Mongolia, prominently displayed, there are nude calendars for
sale. Kazakhstan's postal workers take hours to hand-sew and seal
everything with wax. Russia forbids film to be mailed and goes so far
as to forbid the mailing of matryoshka dolls, which are considered cultural artifacts, although one can drive or fly out with both.) In Japan,
as you can imagine, the postal service is very efficient.

We picked up our Russian visas in Tokyo. Had we applied for
them in the United States, they would have expired by the time we
needed them. As it was, it took us a week to get them, and they cost
$65 each. But visas are just one of the many things you have to deal
with when you travel—part of the necessary housekeeping—and
traveling the way we did, you have to be mindful of them on a regular basis, trying where possible to pick them up maybe two countries
in advance. For the international overland traveler, staying on top of
visa procurement is like servicing a car. And that is another thing we
were always attending to, auto maintenance, especially in places like
Japan—especially when driving the car from a place as up to date as
Japan to a place as out of date as the former Soviet Union. In Japan
we put on a new set of tires, even though our old ones were more
than adequate. Who knew what Siberia would bring?

In Vladivostok, home of the Russian navy and the country's principal port on the Pacific, we spent twenty-nine hours wrestling with
all the paperwork necessary to get our vehicles into the country. There
we were rejoined by an old friend fluent in English and Russian who
had traveled with us between Georgia and the border of China. He
would travel with us for the remainder of the summer and the better
part of 7,500 miles.

The four hundred miles between Vladivostok and Khabarovsk was
the last substantial stretch of paved road we would see until we
crossed the Urals later that summer. In Khabarovsk, checking into the
former Intourist hotel in which I had stayed on my last trip through
Siberia, we noticed a lot of young Russians, dozens of them, all
smartly dressed, milling about the lobby, and assumed that there was
a birthday party or some similar function under way. Making our

way through the crowd, we joined a large number of Japanese tourists who had already checked in. Not until a few minutes later—about the time that we were informed that there were no rooms available—did we notice that all the young Russians were women and all the Japanese tourists men.

The hotel had been booked entirely by six local madams catering to Japanese men on sex tours. And it was only one of several hotels that had been similarly booked. Siberia and the Pacific Far East are a lot cheaper to get to from Japan than are places such as Bangkok or the Philippines, where such Japanese tourists have been going for years. The hotels in Siberia are a lot cheaper as well, and, being new at the game, so are the women themselves, undercutting their competition in the time-honored fashion typical of any new market opening up. A hundred dollars, we were told, would buy a woman's services overnight.

Free trade had finally come to the former Soviet Union. In the new Russia, after centuries of enslavement, people now had freedom, but they still had no jobs, and these young prostitutes would earn as much in a night as they would earn in a month doing regular work. That is, if they could find regular work in a country where the unemployment rate hovers somewhere between the official 12 percent and what appears to me to be closer to the 20 percent of the Great Depression in the United States.

Without Japanese men, the hotels in Khabarovsk would be empty. As it was, all of the hotels were full. It was only due to the cancellation of some flight from Tokyo that we were finally able to get a room in town. We left the city after being forced to evacuate that room; another planeload of tourists, we were told, was scheduled to land.

Khabarovsk, in the absence of prostitution as an industry, was basically unchanged since my last trip through. There were a few clothing shops in town selling Western labels, but Paige quickly ascertained that they were counterfeit. A large city not far from the coast, Khabarovsk offered amenities, if you could really identify them as such, that would be absent as we made our way across Siberia. I knew that as we headed west it was going to be more and more difficult in every way. Siberian cities, Khabarovsk among them, had been seedy and run down under the Communists. Since the fall of the Soviet Union they had become seedier and more run down.

A hundred and twenty miles west of Khabarovsk, one enters the Jewish Autonomous Region. Proposed by Stalin in the 1920s as a Jewish homeland (his way of removing the Jewish population of the Soviet Union to Siberia), the region was established amid a lot of excitement. At the time, the prospect was met with enthusiasm by Jews around the world—until those Jews who made the move arrived in Siberia, and discovered that it was . . . Siberia, and that the whole thing was a scam. Today, although the region's name is unchanged, its population is, at best, 1 percent Jewish. There is still a single synagogue, a small wooden building. When we arrived, some oligarch or politician who had made a killing on the USSR's collapse was building a church, a Russian Orthodox cathedral, which when finished would be six times the size of the synagogue.

In Birobidzhan, the regional capital, we checked into a hotel where the prostitutes—it did not take them long to approach us—charged only fifteen dollars a night.

Blagoveshchensk, an industrial city and regional capital on the Amur River, which separates Siberia from China, had changed in the nine years since I had been there. There were signs everywhere of the rush put on by the Chinese as the Soviet Union began to collapse. Much like the opportunistic capitalists in the Central Asian republics, the Chinese had come in and bought everything they could at ludicrous local prices to sell on the world market. The boom had fizzled out as the Russians wised up, but there were signs of continued investment from over the border, including a Chinese amusement park.

There is an economic vacuum in Siberia that is currently being filled by Chinese labor and Japanese capital. The vast wastes of Siberia contain untold quantities of raw materials. The northern reaches of the territory are peppered with gold, diamond, and palladium mines. China is desperate for raw materials. It needs everything it can get. Siberia, on the other hand, is desperate for labor and capital. The region is virtually uninhabited, and China has 1.2 billion people who wake up every day ready to work. Japan is supplying its enormous capital to develop Siberia's vast resources with China's excess labor. This will be one of the great frontiers of this century, especially now that technology aimed at overcoming the cold has advanced sufficiently. After all, the United States can now produce oil up near the Arctic Circle.

As far north of the border as Krasnoyarsk, Russians complain that the Chinese have stolen everything from them. What they mean is that the Chinese have crossed the border, espied opportunities, and opened businesses to which they bring their usual long hours and business acumen. The Chinese, by contrast, will remind anyone within earshot that Lake Baikal was settled by the Chinese before there ever was a Russia; the name originated with two Chinese characters, *bai* and *kal,* which mean "holy lake" in Chinese.

All of Siberia, including the Pacific Far East, at one time used to be China, and the Chinese are returning steadily. Until the nineteenth century, throughout most of the region's history, the area north of the Amur River was populated by Chinese almost exclusively. Russia, sending prisoners to Siberia, expanding the scope of its military, started pushing things farther east. China grew weak during the nineteenth century, and Europeans rushed into the vacuum, with Russians taking the north. Then came the Trans-Siberian Railroad. At a time when China was weak, at war with itself in the nineteenth and early twentieth centuries, Europeans exploited the country in general, effectively dividing it up. The time will soon come when the Chinese reclaim the territory—de jure or de facto, more likely by default. One way or another, it is going to happen. Eventually Siberia will be Chinese again.

In Blagoveshchensk, when we pulled up to our hotel and saw fifteen young, nicely dressed women standing outside—not in the lobby, as was the case in Khabarovsk—this time we knew what was up. Only here, the men on holiday were Chinese, a boatload of sex tourists who had been ferried across the Amur from Manchuria.

Between Skovorodino and Chernyshevsk lies a gigantic swamp across which there has never been a road. To traverse the swamp, one must take the Trans-Siberian Railroad. I had learned this on my last trip through the region and had spent two and a half days aboard a flatcar going from one city to the other. Arriving in Skovorodino this time, Paige and I drove directly to the train station.

"Remember me?"

The old stationmaster, Anatoli Pirog, was surprised to see me.

With the look of a classic Communist bureaucrat when I had met him nine years before, he was unchanged but for the fact that he was now a non-Communist bureaucrat. He had laughed in 1990 when our interpreter had knocked on his door, walked into his office, and said:

"I have a couple of Americans who need a flatcar."

"Sure," he said, "bring them in," thinking it was some kind of joke.

In we had walked, and he had jumped out of his chair. Nobody had ever crossed the country by motorcycle. And now here I was again. And this time, no less surprised by our presence, he shook his head in disbelief.

"This time I'm not on a motorcycle," I told him. "I have two cars, a trailer, and a total of five people."

Prices had gone up dramatically, of course, and he offered to accommodate us with an inexpensive alternative to a flatcar.

"I can give you a missile car."

"A what?"

"A missile car."

"What's that?"

He directed me down the line to where I could take a look at one. And of course, as I should have guessed, the train car in question was of a kind used to transport guided missiles—the very intercontinental ballistic missiles the Soviet Union had aimed at us.

An enclosed car, with no windows, the missile car was not advertised as such. It was painted on the outside to resemble something employed to carry mail. Not surprisingly, there were lots of missile cars on hand in Russia these days. The stationmaster recommended it not only for its price but also for what he saw as its amenities. At one end of the car there were four bunks for the soldiers who would have guarded the cargo; and, in addition, there were toilets on board. But the accommodations overall were just about as horrible as those aboard the boat on which we had sailed across the Caspian Sea. We opted for a flatcar and would have done so in any case, because we wanted to see Siberia as we crossed it. In the absence of a car with windows, we were prepared to travel al fresco.

Our next step was to visit Victor, the queue master. There is always a queue, a line for everything, in Russia. And it is no different when it comes to flatcars. The higher the price you pay, the sooner you get your flatcar. It is capitalism at its worst, or best. We drank a lot of vodka with Victor, an ex-convict, gave him some presents, and moved

*This, in Siberia, would qualify as one of the better toilets
we found in much of the world.*

to the front of the line. Paige went searching for a well and filled four of our water bags using a hand pump. It was the first time she had ever used a well. Hooking up to the next available freight, we took aboard all kinds of food and a bucket to be used as toilet. We were the last of sixty-six freight cars—the caboose, if you will—some of which were loaded down with those same secondhand automobiles that had traveled with us across the Sea of Japan. Traveling overnight, we slept in the car atop the flatbed, surprised and delighted to discover that we had been put aboard the fast train. I had fully expected the trip to last two or three days, just as it had nine years before. Making very few stops, the train made the run of some four hundred miles in twenty-four hours, and, arriving in Chernyshevsk surprisingly refreshed, we took to the road again.

Across the wasteland of Siberia, villages are few and far between, and what little population exists is found mainly along a single road, which parallels the railroad line. For the most part, the road is not paved, and driving it is treacherous. You might be driving along a paved section at a hundred kilometers an hour, and then, all of a sudden, without any warning, there will be a crater or the pavement will end. It is almost as if the road were designed to tear up your car. Just outside the city of Chita, a former Communist military outpost, we came up with a flat tire, the trailer brake failed, and for what would be only the first time in a continuing series of their falling apart, we broke the trailer's leaf springs.

While I admit to feeling somewhat panicked—there was no Mercedes service anywhere around—the truth is, had we not suffered these automotive disasters so distant from mechanical service, we never would have met the illustrious Eugen. But before introducing you to the towering, nationally celebrated figure of Eugen, one of the more highly acclaimed citizens of contemporary Russia, let me digress to a brief background on the sorry state of the leaf springs on the trailer of the Millennium Mercedes.

Gerhard Steinle, designing the hybrid that would go around the world, worked with a company called Metalcrafters in California, a top-of-the-line builder of one-off and prototype cars, which among other things did a lot of work for the movie industry. If a production company needed a car to blow up, or if, in another example, Mercedes needed a prototype for the Detroit Auto Show, Metalcrafters would often get the call.

There is a difference between show horses and workhorses. Entering a beautiful mount in a horse show is one thing; you need a different horse to plow your field. The people at Metalcrafters are phenomenal at show horses. They were a disaster at our workhorse. I needed a high-quality workhorse, and they were not up to giving me the quality I needed.

"Listen, this car will go anywhere," I was told. "We've tested it on dirt roads."

Dirt roads in California are pretty hard to find. And a horrible road in California is a great road in most parts of the world.

"We've tested it in the California desert."

Well, the California desert is a joke.

"It'll go anywhere."

Sure. Anywhere in California.

Nearly everything Metalcrafters did on the car broke at least once, and frequently two or three times. We came to call them Metalmashers before it was over. Everything Mercedes—and they do not pay me to say this—was fine, just about perfect. Nearly everything California went wrong. We broke eleven sets of leaf springs in the trailer, plus its axle. The extra fuel tank in the car? The seams came apart at three different places three different times. To give it more of the feel of a sports car, the suspension in the car itself was changed. Special springs were made—which proved too soft for the roads in Azerbaijan. We hit something, the car bounced, and the axle hit the oil pan. It was a Mercedes oil pan, but anybody's oil pan, if you smash it with an axle at over a hundred kilometers per hour, is going to break. In China we replaced the springs with the original-equipment, I-dare-you-to-break-me G-Wagen springs, and they lasted for the rest of the trip. They are still on the car. But not until we reached Darwin, Australia, were we able to find someone to correct the problem with the leaf springs on the trailer permanently.

Not even the mythic Eugen was up to the task.

Eugen, a short, wiry fifty-year-old, lived and worked in Moscow and was Mercedes' number one mechanic in Russia. Unable to find a Mercedes mechanic anywhere near Chita, we called Mercedes headquarters in Moscow for information, and because Mercedes has a deal in Russia that it will provide roadside service wherever you are, the company flew Eugen from Moscow to Chita—which is like sending someone from Los Angeles to Hawaii—to fix our car.

Eugen, who spent a few days with us in Siberia—we liked having him around, and he liked the adventure of being away from Moscow—carried a card identifying him as a Chernobyl Volunteer. He was one of a number of people who had rushed into Chernobyl to help out when the nuclear plant there blew up. Many later died of radiation poisoning, and those who did not, including Eugen, were living on borrowed time. He was the first Russian we met who did not drink—he could not drink because alcohol interfered with all the different medicines he was taking to keep him alive. Honored as a hero, he was given the identification card, which enabled him to walk to the front of every queue—as I have pointed out elsewhere, there were queues everywhere in Russia, and they were endless—and entitled him to other privileges, not the least significant of which was a government stipend.

Eugen did not bother trying to repair the brakes on the trailer; he simply disconnected them.

"You don't need these," he explained, adding, "They'll just break again."

He replaced the broken leaf spring with the leaf spring removed from a Russian army jeep. We bought the used part from the nearby military base—it was simply stripped off one of the vehicles parked there and sold to us.

Everything owned by the Russian army these days is for sale, stripped by some general or some sergeant. With looted equipment flying out its quartermasters' doors, with its soldiers going unpaid, the Russian army is like Eugen: its days are numbered. It is certainly nothing for anyone to fear.

As one might expect of the Russian jeep, neither was it new nor well maintained, and its leaf spring would be one of the several we destroyed as we continued our drive around the world.

Before departing for Moscow, Eugen gave us his business card.

"If you have any problems in Russia, show this card," he advised us.

Eugen, being the crack Mercedes mechanic he was, was known to anyone of any importance in Russia. When President Yeltsin's car broke down, the Kremlin called Eugen. When the KGB's G-Wagens broke down, they called Eugen. And likewise the mob.

His business card was the best passport you could hope to have throughout the former Soviet Union. Paige held it close for the next two months.

(Eugen told us how both sides in Chechnya once called a truce so he could fly in and repair vehicles for the respective combatants. The shooting started again as soon as he left. We did not believe it until people in Moscow confirmed the story. We realized, of course, that the leaders of neither side would be caught dead in a Lada.)

Because Russian air transportation is no different from anything else Russian, it took Eugen three days to get to Chita from Moscow, and we made the best of our wait in the city. As luck would have it, there was a circus passing through town, which we attended. We had our picture taken with the dancing bears, and as with everything we did in Chita, we really had a delightful time. We did not want to leave. We attended a kickboxing tournament—between bouts there were very amateurish performances by women who danced and took off their clothes—and on the advice of the local mafia chief we took in some interesting nightclubs.

The chief's name was Alexei, his nickname was "Panama," and he and I became fast friends. He earned his nickname from the name of the hotel he controlled, the Panama City Hotel, which is where we happened to be staying. I never figured out for sure how the hotel got its name, but I now assume it had something to do with all the money laundering the Russian mob does in Panama. When we got to Panama two years later, it clicked. We ran into scores of Russians there who were involved in a fair amount of illicit trade: drugs, prostitution, and other endeavors.

Russian mobsters all look the same. They all wear the signature European-cut black suit. In Siberia they all shave their heads. They call it their summer haircut. And at the hotel restaurant in Chita they were all sitting at the same table, which was not far from ours. After an hour or so, one of them came over to the table at which Paige and I were sitting—he later introduced himself as Alexei—and asked how we had gotten so far in Russia without paying anybody off.

"How do you know I didn't?" I said, thinking I might bluff my way through the encounter.

Never missing a beat, he said, "I know you haven't paid anybody off, because I checked."

Immediately, I was scared. The most efficient thing in Russia is the mafia. And this was the guy in charge of this particular stretch of the country. My first move was to buy him a drink. I drank a lot of vodka with him and his friends, and over the next two or three days we got to be pretty good friends. Paige danced with several of them. Eugen's arrival in town made things that much better; it made us that much more legitimate in the eyes of the mob. When we left Chita, Eugen traveled with us. He was having a fine time riding around Siberia with his crazy American friends. He had carte blanche from Mercedes to do what he wanted—he was their ace, after all, and besides that he had his Chernobyl card.

As we were about to leave Chita, Alexei took me aside. By now, I had gone to a barber and had my own head shaved—a summer haircut to match those of my new friends.

"I have called ahead," he said. "You won't have any problems."

He had called his people two or three cities down the line to smooth our passage.

"If you do have problems, let me know," he said, "and whoever it is, we will have them killed."

He was serious. This was not bravado. (For the price of a decent night out in the United States, you can have somebody killed in Siberia, and in Siberia these days the latter seems to be the more common practice.) So we had the mafia's protection, and we had Eugen, and, very pleased with both, we continued heading west.

Our next stop, Ulan-Ude, the capital of the Buryat Autonomous Republic, is home to the Buryat Mongols, the descendants of Genghis Khan and one of the 126 official linguistic, ethnic, and religious groups that make up the former Soviet Union. It was Paige, checking the map, who pointed out what lay just to the south and within easy reach of us.

"Why don't we go to Mongolia?" she suggested.

This was something I had never considered, not even having passed this way nine years before. For some reason, I had been traveling with blinders on.

"What a terrific idea," I said.

This was not some American Express around-the-world package tour, after all. This was a get-down-and-go-there, do-whatever-the-heck-you-want-to-do adventure. We found the Mongolian Consulate, purchased the necessary visas—got them immediately by paying a little extra—and off we drove to Mongolia.

Outer Mongolia, as it was known then, achieved independence from China in 1921, and in 1924, with Soviet sponsorship, the Mongolian People's Republic was established. When Stalin opened the international border in 1937, the only way for foreigners to cross the border was by train. There were no roads to speak of, no cars—locals crossed regularly by foot—and even with the construction of the road that now exists, Soviet communism was unable to surmount its own bureaucratic thinking. Today, though a paved road crosses the border, foreigners are not allowed to drive it. They are still required by the anachronistic law—another of those temporary regulations that take on a life of their own—to cross the border by train as they did in 1937.

Around this insanity, a cottage industry has grown up, wherein various locals have found self-employment driving vehicles of foreigners across the border for a fee. You, the foreigner, hop aboard the train, which takes eight hours to go twenty-five miles, an entire business day—it is the Russian Communist mentality, it is a border, everything has to be checked and double-checked—and when you finally arrive, you go looking for the local guy who has your car.

Needless to say, I was not having any of this. I was not giving my car to anyone.

"Find a flatcar and load it yourself, and we will let you take it across."

"Where's the loading platform?" I asked.

"There is no loading platform."

I was not going to give up and go home.

I tracked down a fellow I had met on my motorcycle trip through Ulan-Ude, a young reporter and Communist Party functionary named Victor from whom I had bought some contraband in 1990. He had sold me a Soviet army uniform of the kind used in the Afghanistan desert—I collect this kind of stuff—and a tank commander's cap, and he and I had spent some time drinking vodka together. He was now the editor of a newspaper that was making the transition from communism to capitalism, but, being a former Soviet functionary, he still had influence with the army general who oversaw the border. I explained the situation to him, and Victor called the general.

"Let them drive across the border," he said.

That is all it took.

It occurred to me, in a kind of Orwellian epiphany, that I was not beating the system, I was working within it, for the very corruptibility of the Russian system is what enables it to function in the face of its own stifling bureaucracy. The system is designed to work best when it fails.

Crossing the border, we got the Polaroid out, gave the soldiers pictures of the car, pictures of themselves—we were snapping photos, literally, right and left—we gave them cigarettes, making sure everybody would remember us when we returned in a few days. Polaroid film goes a long way in situations like these.

Mongolia is about the size of Iran or Alaska, which makes it about a fifth the size of the lower forty-eight states, and its total population of 2.6 million is about the same as Kansas City's. More than a quarter of its citizens live in the capital city, Ulan Bator, leaving a very small number of people spread over a very large geographic area. It is hard to believe that as recently as the mid–fourteenth century the Mongols controlled most of Eurasia from Korea to Hungary, having conquered it more than a hundred years earlier. It was against invasion by the Mongol hordes that the Great Wall of China was begun. They were invading Japan when a sudden typhoon sank their ships and drove them away. The Japanese have used the word *kamikaze,* "divine wind," ever since. Marco Polo claimed to have traveled from Venice to visit the Mongol Empire. The Mongols swept the world as the great horsemen of their day, and a simple invention gave them much of their power. Their use of the stirrup gave them control of their fast ponies at a time when others were using horses mainly as beasts of burden. Eventually everyone had the new technology and the Mongols faded into history, outpaced by even newer technologies.

Outer Mongolia is now a name almost synonymous with the word "backwater," evocative of the remote, the retrograde, the unimproved. Yet Ulan Bator, the capital of Mongolia, is perhaps the most technologically up-to-date city in the world, totally digital. With the fall of the Soviet Union, a free and independent Mongolia benefited from numerous sources of foreign aid, and with no infrastructure to upgrade, it leapfrogged about three generations of technology. The

*Women control the currency black market at one end of the bazaar in Chita, Siberia; men control the other.*

*The woman who served us salted tea in her brightly decorated yurt in Mongolia.*

*Yurts in Mongolia still house large, nomadic families, as they have for centuries. Cell phones are a recent nod to modernization. Absent from this picture: Mom and the child whose shirt needed changing and hair needed combing to make him presentable for the photograph.*

whole city is wired with fiber-optic cable, enabling you to jack into the Web from almost any phone in town.

You can't do that in Russia. There, it is hard enough to make a phone call out. To send e-mail in Russia, you have to pay a physical, not a virtual, visit to an Internet service provider—which we did all along our route. As it happens, every decent-sized town in Russia has an ISP, often a battered office jammed with half a dozen aging computers and half a dozen roughly dressed youths staring at their screens. Descending on them, we would find them shocked and delighted to greet visitors from the exotic West.

"How much to plug into your lines?" we would ask, brandishing our laptops.

At a dollar an hour, they were wildly overcharging us, but we were overjoyed to be able to update our Web site. In the absence of these entrepreneurial outposts, we would have been out of touch with friends and family for weeks at a time. It was just one more example of how dramatically the world had changed in the space of a decade.

Another change spawned by the digital age, and one of the more significant changes for the world traveler, was access to money. Paige and I had been through twenty-two countries, and to my surprise I had suffered very few of the problems I had experienced on my last trip regarding currency. Last time, crossing borders, both entering and exiting countries, I had had to hide my cash, confronting border guards who wanted me to declare it on special forms. (Of course, many border guards had simply been looking for a bribe.) Back then I would hide currency in the frame of my bike, my shoes, my helmet, anywhere I figured border guards would not look. To avoid carrying large amounts of cash, I would have funds wired to me at banks in capital cities, so I would have money for food, hotels, and gas. On this trip none of that had been necessary. I did not need to carry a lot of money. Now, on the verge of the new millennium, Visa, Master-Card, Diners Club, and American Express were accepted everywhere. And even in Russia, not to mention up-to-the-minute Ulan Bator, we could just march off to the nearest ATM and take out whatever cash we needed, when we needed it, sometimes even in dollars. One had to be attentive, however. In Siberia I once obtained some cash, but while I was putting my credit card away, the machine took back the money! It took two days to get the cash back.

Running phone lines across Mongolia, a country so large with a population so small, would be both a technological nightmare and economic insanity. So the country, in another instance of leapfrogging technology, went straight to digital communication. Everybody in Mongolia has a digital cell phone. The nation's nomads, crossing the country on horseback, carry them. There is a cell phone in most yurts.

This leapfrogging of technology has impacted history for centuries. In early-nineteenth-century America towns were desperate for canals to put them on the trade routes. Those unfortunate cities without canals went straight to the newfangled railroad. Soon the old canal routes disappeared. (Remember the Erie Canal?) Then along came the Interstate Highway System, and the old railroad towns that ignored the impact of the highway disappeared. San Diego is a major U.S. city now, but not Tucumcari, New Mexico, a major railroad interchange. So figure out what will replace the highway system and jump on board while everyone else is angling for the new interstate.

On the road to Ulan Bator we saw nomads moving their camps, uprooting themselves and all their horses, camels, and goats, and traveling to new grazing grounds. These were the descendants of Genghis Khan, who had swept across the steppes on horseback. The women, we noticed, were expert riders just like the men. We started snapping pictures. Photographing a yurt, we were invited inside by the woman who owned it. She showed us around the humble dwelling and served us salted tea. In this part of the world, I was surprised to discover, they do not put sugar, honey, or milk in their tea; they drink it with salt. (Of course, there has never been much sugar grown in Mongolia.) Just one more culinary adventure.

We wanted to take Polaroids of her and all the kids, about eight of them, of all ages, several photos, so we could give some to the family. She grabbed her youngest and asked us to wait. And then like any mother, anywhere in the world—do not let anyone tell you that people are fundamentally different—she combed the child's hair and changed his shirt before letting him pose for the pictures. The second shirt was slightly less dirty than the first. She wanted him to look his best. That mother could have been in Greenwich, Connecticut, as easily as on the steppes of Mongolia.

When we arrived in Ulan Bator, the Mercedes dealership had just opened. One of its owners, Laurenz Melchers, a German—his partner was a lawyer, David Reiner, from Los Angeles—had been traveling in

Mongolia on business with his father a few years before when he had noticed what we were beginning to notice: an ever-increasing number of Mercedes as we crossed Siberia east to west. It was obvious to anyone paying attention that most of the cars—virtually all of them—were stolen. Massive numbers of luxury cars, some BMWs but mostly Mercedes, were being stolen worldwide and sold in Russia and Mongolia in a flourishing illegal enterprise that had gotten under way as soon as the Soviet Union started falling apart.

The young German went to Mercedes and told the company he wanted the Mongolian franchise. Obviously, he was not planning to sell a lot of new cars right away. How could he compete with the mob? But based on the number of cars in the city already, thousands of aging models with no source of spare parts or service, and based on the number of diplomats he projected would be in the market for new cars, he convinced Mercedes to give him the franchise. His equipment was scheduled to arrive the week after we met him.

In Russia when we were there, the number of Mercedes in the country was estimated to be one hundred thousand, most of which had been stolen outside the country. When we got to southern Brazil two years later, the Mercedes dealer there told us of a car stolen in Rio de Janeiro that had turned up in Siberia. It had been taken in to the Mercedes dealer in Krasnoyarsk, who had punched the car's serial number into his computer in the routine search for a spare part. Stolen in Rio four weeks earlier, according to the report that came up in the computer, the car had made it from southern Brazil to *Siberia* well within that space of time, almost as efficiently as the computer data itself.

Not until the fall of communism did Mercedes have much of a presence in Russia. Under communism nobody could afford such a car. In Novosibirsk, Siberia's largest city, I met the local Mercedes dealer, Oleg Edinov, who was rather new to the whole thing. In the back of his shop he had a top-of-the-line S600 owned by one of the "new Russians," which is what the new mafia types call themselves, they and the other opportunists who are feasting on the carcass of the old economy. The gangster in question had paid so little attention to the maintenance of the car that he had never bothered to check the oil. He had driven it until the engine exploded. He had towed it to the dealer and said, "This car doesn't work; get me another one." He bought a new S600 from the dealer and paid the dealer to order a new engine for the disabled car, but he never bothered to come back for it.

That is how deep the money flows in the new world of the "outlaw capitalists."

How did these "new Russians" become so rich? Much like my recent acquaintance Namik, who had taken us to dinner in Azerbaijan, they grabbed the factories, inventories, and stockpiles of raw materials they controlled and, during the first years of communism's collapse, sold them to the West in what amounted to a gigantic fire sale. And much of the proceeds from the sale of these commodities, billions of dollars' worth, stayed in the West in Swiss bank accounts. These "new Russians" are the third-millennium version of the warlords of old; their fiefdoms are refineries, aluminum plants, vast farms, oil fields, gold mines, and factories, as well as private armies.

I was told that there were more top-of-the-line Mercedes in Moscow than in any city in the world. If there are 100,000 Mercedes in Russia, even if you take a very low figure, and say each is worth $10,000, that is one billion dollars in hard currency needed to import them. Where does this money come from? It pours in from the IMF and the World Bank, which are funded by the world's taxpayers. In 1998 I testified before Congress, which, following the collapse of the ruble, was planning yet another Russian bailout. I said then that both the IMF and the World Bank should be abolished.

Self-perpetuating and ever-growing bureaucracies founded after the Second World War, these institutions have long since diverged from their original mandates. Their analyses are hopeless, and their prescriptions are worse. There are no external, independent audits to determine the long-term efficacy of their projects. The greatest beneficiaries of their programs are the twelve thousand bureaucrats who work for them and their well-funded and well-protected pensions. I have made a career of analyzing financial statements, and I have yet to see a financial statement of either the World Bank or the IMF that I can understand, nor have I ever met anyone who could explain them. Whenever I have found this to be true of corporations, it has always been a sign of serious problems.

I urged Congress not to do what it eventually did, which was to pony up billions of dollars more, funneling it through these institutions for them to sink into the rat hole of Russia.

*My father, despite terminal cancer, traveled with my mother
to Siberia from Demopolis, Alabama,
to see my Russian mafia summer haircut.*

Russia claims to have a balance-of-trade surplus, and Western bankers and academics buy the story. I have crossed the border at ten different places, I have gone into Siberia, I have gone to Mongolia and back, and I am certain that these claims are wrong. Smugglers are everywhere. You can bring anything across the border that you want. That $1 billion in hard currency just for the Mercedes is money you and I are paying, money we give to the IMF to give to the Russian bankers who send it out of the country again in exchange for those stolen luxury cars. The gullible may accept the "official" numbers, which are worse now than when the Communists were feeding us propaganda. Fortunately the currency market knows better—just as money markets throughout history have always ignored the phony proclamations of rulers—and the man in the street knows the truth, which is why the ruble always declines.

And it is not just the Russians, the IMF, and the World Bank that need external audits. Everybody needs them, even that paragon of exactitude, Germany. The German state employment agency for years reported a 51 percent rate in placing workers; a recent independent audit showed that the true success rate was 18 percent.

Crossing back over the border, heading to Ulan-Ude, we had no trouble. The soldiers all remembered us. Those who had worked there on the day we had first crossed came rushing out because they wanted more photographs. Nobody said anything about taking a train back across the international border.

From Ulan-Ude, passing deep Lake Baikal, the largest freshwater lake in the world, measured by the volume of water it contains, we drove west to Irkutsk, where Paige and I were scheduled to rendezvous with my parents.

# 7

# THE
# WEDDING

M Y FATHER HAD BEEN DIAGNOSED with terminal cancer in
October 1996, and, defiant in the face of his prognosis, refusing treatment, he continued to thrive. A tough, adamant man, who
had never struck me as much of a traveler, he told me, when I announced that I was undertaking the trip, that it was the one thing in
life he would envy.

"No matter what you do," he told me, "don't come home because
of me. Do not interrupt the trip or change your plans."

I was surprised when he told me this. I had never thought of him as
having much of a travel bug. He had always told me that he did not
need to travel, having done so during the Second World War. He had
seen Europe, he said. In the past he had declined to travel with my
mother, who had once visited Russia with a group of friends and had
driven to Canada and the West Coast without him, taking one of my
brothers instead.

Not knowing when he might die, I had been calling Demopolis a
lot since leaving New York, more often than ever before in my life,

and I kept asking him to join us. We had hoped to talk him into meeting us in China. We were unsuccessful there, but we continued to invite him, and finally we persuaded him to meet us in Russia. And so at the age of eighty-two, he and my mother, who was eighty-one, got themselves from Demopolis, Alabama, to Irkutsk in Siberia.

Not long after their arrival in Irkutsk, we all found ourselves in the local marketplace, where, as is typical throughout Russia, we could see various old soldiers, wearing their medals, taking the air. There my father passed the time with an eighty-two-year-old veteran of the Russian tank corps who had served on the Russian front in the Second World War. My father, who had served on the western front, shared memories with him of the Russian soldiers he had met at the time, how they and the Americans had come together at the end of the war, swapping vodka and chocolate. On a fine summer day in Irkutsk, the two former allies, members of a generation that was dying out, closed a gap that stretched across more than fifty years and more than seven thousand miles, reliving their victory over Hitler, recalling the days of their youth.

My parents traveled with us for ten days across Siberia, covering about one thousand miles between Irkutsk and Krasnoyarsk. When one imagines Siberia, certain things come to mind more readily than others, things like prisons, Russian sables, and maybe vodka. Vodka, of course, comes to mind when one imagines any part of Russia. In Irkutsk, we went to a vodka factory. Not many visitors came around, so the manager, Vladimir Komorov, was delighted. (Our leaving the factory when the visit was over was somewhat less organized, thanks to the lavish tasting in which we were invited to participate. I did not know there were so many types of vodka.) Built under the czars in 1905 and taken over by the Communists, the factory had been grabbed by its manager when communism fell. Despite its monopoly and the extraordinary demand for its product—all over Russia, we saw drunks at night, drunks in the afternoon, and drunks in the morning—the factory ran only one shift.

We then tried a fur factory, where I bought my mother a sable hat for virtually nothing. As poorly laid out and inefficient as the vodka factory and so many other factories in Russia, it was reminiscent of the old loft buildings in New York that turned out piece goods fifty years ago. Today, no modern owner could afford to move his raw materials or goods through such a factory by means of such inefficient elevators and narrow stairs. The place was a health hazard, with primitive machinery to the extent that it had machinery at all. The conditions under which the women worked would have landed the owner in jail in New York. The factory processed wild sables and lynx; the prices paid to hunters and trappers were posted on the wall. As with all goods in Russia, the quality of the coats was poor and the price was low. Under the Soviet system, quality did not matter; it was enough simply to manufacture the product. If boots were poorly stitched or a bucket unsound, a Russian or a Pole would make do. The same mentality prevails today and will continue to cripple Russia's attempts to capture a share of the world's markets for decades to come.

How he managed to do it, I still do not know, but our friend Sergei, who was from Irkutsk, persuaded Valeri Vasiliyev, the warden of a prison there, to give Paige, my mother, my father, and me a tour of his facility. A Siberian prison, I thought—it doesn't get much more interesting than that. For a 2,500-ruble ($100) contribution to the prisoners' welfare fund, we jumped at the chance.

I do not know what I expected of a Siberian prison, but what I did see came as no surprise: hopeless faces, apathetic and lifeless, hollow eyes looking out from above sunken cheekbones. Never having been to an American prison, I presume the picture would be pretty much the same.

It was not the prisoners but the prison itself that surprised me. Everywhere we traveled in Siberia, we found Russia falling apart. In every town, city, and village, there were weeds, dust, mud, rust, peeling paint, and crumbling cement. With their balconies about to fall off, many buildings that would be condemned in most other countries are still in use. In most public buildings in Russia, nothing works, and no one takes an ounce of pride in keeping things up. The prison in Irkutsk, however, was the best-kept public building we had seen.

"This looks like a kindergarten," said Paige. "There are primary colors everywhere."

Freshly painted, the institution was more than clean, it was spotless, better than the restaurants and hotels we had patronized. I expressed my surprise to the warden.

"I have a lot of cheap labor," he said, "and they do what I tell them."

Father Valentine, on my previous trip, was a dissident, outcast priest, reaching out for support from Suzdal to the Russian Orthodox Church in New York. Now he is a power in the new Russia, with houses, antiques, and underlings.

In the yard the prisoners had built a little white church, a Russian Orthodox chapel, of which they were proud. Under the Communists, obviously, there could have been no church. Where in 1990 I had seen only the palest of green shoots of religious revival in Russia, I now saw lots of churches being restored there. Services were being held every Sunday in churches aflame with devotional candles. These were Russian Orthodox churches, but we also saw a Roman Catholic church and a synagogue on top of which the Star of David was boldly displayed. Buddhist temples in Russia are being revived.

In Krasnoyarsk, with Sergei and Natasha Ivanovich, some local people we met, we hired, for very little, a Russian military helicopter, a great big troop carrier, and flew three hundred miles or so into the mountains for the weekend, very high up into the wilds of Siberia, to a place called Bear Lake. And there we indulged in a Siberian *banya*. You cannot be Russian in Siberia and not go to a *banya*, which is essentially a sauna. It was not the first one we had visited, but it was certainly the best, especially after three hundred miles in a questionable helicopter. We put our vodka and beer in the crystal-clear lake to chill it—the cabin had no electricity—and we ourselves chilled out for the weekend, after which we returned to Krasnoyarsk and put my parents on a plane headed home.

By the time we reached Siberia, Paige and I had narrowed down our search for a wedding location. Based on where we expected to be by January 1, 2000, we had reduced the list to Morocco, Portugal, Spain, and the United Kingdom. From the road, Paige began to investigate our options, and one by one, our options began to evaporate. Morocco, for example, had a six-month residency requirement. It is hard enough to plan a wedding in your hometown. Planning it in a foreign country is that much more complicated. Planning it *from* a foreign country other than that in which it is to be held borders on the impossible. Planning it from Siberia . . .

Paige was undaunted.

By the time we reached Irkutsk, we had settled on the United Kingdom for a variety of reasons, only one of them being that it was logistically simpler. Henley-on-Thames, northwest of London, site of the Henley Royal Regatta, was where Paige and I had fallen in love. I had coxed a record-setting, gold-medal-winning crew at Henley as an

Oxford student in 1965, and after retiring from Wall Street in 1980, I started going to Henley a lot. It is held the first week of July every year, and it is one of the most glorious places in the world to spend a week. Boaters and blazers, champagne and Pimm's, strawberries and cream, the women all done up in long dresses and extravagant hats—it is one of the last vestiges of Victorian England, and I would always see a lot of old friends there.

On our first date, as mentioned earlier, I asked Paige if she wanted to travel around the world with me. The next day I called her up and invited her to the Henley Regatta, which was a week away. She said yes, after discussing it with her parents. We went to Henley. And if you don't fall in love at the Henley Royal Regatta, you are never going to fall in love, because it is the most absurdly, ridiculously, extraordinarily romantic thing you can imagine. It is like the horse races they have at Ascot, only longer. If you cannot knock the socks off an American girl from North Carolina who has not been away from home much, it ain't ever going to work. Fortunately, it worked. We fell in love with each other that week.

We decided to marry at Henley, and from that point on, for the next six months, by cell phone and e-mail—all the way across Siberia and from parts of Mongolia, from Moscow, Scandinavia, and all over Europe—Paige worked on the wedding plans.

At Ufa, crossing the Ural Mountains, we left Asia and re-entered Europe. As we got closer to Moscow, the roads got better, the cities larger and closer together. We seemed to be constantly stumbling upon weddings, partly, I suppose, because weddings and wedding receptions are held in hotels, and we were often staying in one or another. Frequently, the mother of the bride would grab us and parade us into the wedding, or the bridesmaids or the grooms would be ogling our car and taking pictures, and the next thing you knew, we were swept into the wedding.

Foreigners can be deceived into thinking Russia is a real country if they visit only Moscow and perhaps Saint Petersburg. Unlike twelve years ago, when it was hard to find a place to eat even the simplest of meals, Moscow today is abundant with restaurants, video and music shops, chic stores and sidewalk cafés. The well-heeled traveler can even stay in a five-star hotel in Moscow, though it is likely to be German-owned and -operated. The collapse of communism released a tidal wave of consumer demand.

But there are no signs of new productive assets. All the tractors we passed were aging models held together with baling wire. Factories were so neglected we could not tell whether they were still producing goods. There were new shops but no new farm implements; new restaurants but no new plant machinery; a new face-lift for the Kremlin but no soundly run commercial banks. Not only has very little been added to the infrastructure, but little of the old has been maintained.

Russia was the first vindication of my decision to use a diesel engine. One night in Siberia there was no fuel of any kind to be had. Early the next morning, miraculously, a local woke us with ninety gallons for sale. We paid his price without questions.

"We don't want to know where this came from," said Paige.

Later we learned he had siphoned it from the local locomotive.

Russia is really a third-world country, one with a vast wealth of natural resources, a well-educated population, and a diverse but declining industrial base. It continues to experience formidable difficulties moving from its old centrally planned economy to a modern market economy. Why? Partly because it never had much of an entrepreneurial class, partly because it hoped it would never have to change too radically, and partly because the Russian soul still does not trust or understand the marketplace. Until Russia begins to obey the simplest economic laws, it will remain a third-world country. Capital has its own laws as inexorable as those of gravity. Until Russia comes to respect capital, to provide for its safety and nourishment, capital will not come to its aid. Intelligent capital does not aid thieves. Russia's transition to a market economy is likely to take decades and is more than likely to produce much misery.

This, of course, assumes that there will be a Russia. One night, in the luxurious Manezh shopping center in Moscow, we were having dinner and a bomb went off nearby. There had been about a dozen bombings over the previous three years, which had not been publicized much in the West. Before we left Russia, five more bombs went off in and around Moscow. By then I had begun to theorize that Vladimir Putin had taken over from Boris Yeltsin in a silent coup, supported by his mates from the KGB (now known officially as the

*We tried to exercise every day on the trip and tried to experience as much as possible wherever we were. Entering the Moscow Peace Marathon, we satisfied both goals. (We were surprised to witness so much cheating.)*

*The new Russians have quickly adjusted to outlaw capitalism. Here a Lenin impersonator in Moscow matches strategy with a personification of the free market.*

FSB, but still called the KGB by most Russians). A cover-up of the coup would have been necessary to avoid terrifying the IMF and Western capital.

My analysis, after talking with many people, was that the KGB had planted the Moscow bombs to stir up anti-Chechnya hysteria; Putin had needed to gather support for his new government, and what better mechanism than the threat of the evil Muslim Chechnyans? Raising the specter of war is a technique that leaders have used for centuries all over the world. (Soon Putin sent the Russian army back into battle in Chechnya.) The Chechnyans' denial of involvement is what first raised my suspicions—they had never been loath to boast about hitting Russia in the past. Why not do so this time? The reports of several Russian journalists have subsequently supported my analysis.

Russia is defined by political unrest and treachery. Moscow has little control over the rest of the country, which will continue to dissolve. All those who believe the Russian army will hold things together should drive across the country a time or two.

Moscow is the center of what was until recently the largest contiguous empire in human history. And yet, unlike the capitals of other empires, unlike Rome, Istanbul, Seville, or London, it has left behind virtually nothing of value, culturally, artistically, or financially. The other great cities of history attracted people of every nation. The best and the brightest from all over the known world traveled to them to amass wealth and power and took great contributions with them. Nobody ever went to Moscow to become successful. Russians themselves, more often than not, tried to flee the country.

As I have pointed out, one reason China has a great future is that overseas Chinese are pouring back into the country, bringing capital and expertise. Few expatriate Russians are returning home to rebuild. They are heading to the Riviera—anywhere but Russia.

As we were leaving Russia, we met a man whom we would later bump into in Liechtenstein, a country of nothing but banks. He came running over to us, saying, "Remember me?" When we asked him why he was there, he nervously changed the subject to a discussion of cars.

We covered seven thousand miles over the course of eight weeks of driving between Vladivostok and Moscow. We spent another three weeks getting out of the former USSR—traveling from Moscow to Minsk, up through the Baltics, and then to Saint Petersburg—and arrived in Helsinki in the middle of September. Paige almost kissed the border guard when he stamped us into Finland.

From Finland we traveled south through Sweden, Norway, and Denmark.

With its low birthrates and high debts, Scandinavia is no longer an exemplar of social progress. In Denmark, when we arrived, Kurds were demonstrating against the anti-immigration backlash sweeping the country. Formerly tolerant, receptive, and open, Danes and Swedes were now claiming, "We have too many immigrants." Danes will not grant an outsider citizenship even if he or she marries a Dane—nor will they grant it to the child of such a union. In Sweden, with the lowest birthrate of the five Scandinavian countries, notions of social justice and welfare have little influence with young people. Twenty-two-year-olds are asking why taxes are so high and why they have to pay off so great a national debt.

Norway, with five million people and gigantic oil reserves, should be rich but keeps adding debt, spending the oil money on public works projects that offer no return on investment. A journalist complained to me about a tunnel recently built to an island with only one thousand residents. (A new sixteen-kilometer bridge and tunnel combination connecting Denmark and Sweden, by contrast, will have a positive impact. It, together with a new eighteen-kilometer bridge in Denmark, now makes it possible to drive from Finland across Scandinavia directly into western Europe.) Finland recently outlawed prostitution for the first time in its history in an effort to close the country off to Russian women pouring in to work as prostitutes.

Across Scandinavia there is a noticeable brain drain as many of the best and brightest, usually because taxes are so high, are abandoning their birthplace for more favorable environments. They had no say in this legacy so they are now voting with their feet.

We arrived in Germany in the middle of October. Between the end of October and late December, we toured Europe, hitting the spots that most other tourists visit, spending more time on the continent than we had originally intended. But for the wedding, we would have left Europe much earlier. In retrospect, I have to say I am glad we did spend the extra time there. While I had already seen much of Europe,

Paige had not, and in showing it to her—she chose the itinerary—I was able to fine-tune my position on the European Union's adoption of a single currency, the euro, three years down the line.

Put simply: the world needs the euro badly. Unfortunately, I do not expect it to survive in the longer term, although I do own some as we speak.

The world needs the euro because the dollar is a fundamentally flawed currency. The United States is the world's largest debtor nation, and we Americans are not putting the borrowed money into anything productive. We still have a $400-billion-a-year trade deficit, and it is getting bigger. We are not competitive. We do not have enough productive capacity, despite what the figures released by the government show. Every month the U.S. government releases massaged figures professing that our productivity is improving steadily against the rest of the world's. Yet every day the real numbers show that we are not competitive and are buying more and more from abroad. And with Japan's serious internal problems, the yen is in trouble too. As a medium of exchange, as a store of value, the euro would be the perfect solution.

With the euro as the world's chief reserve currency and medium of exchange, the world's central banks, which hold nearly 60 percent of their foreign currency reserves in dollars, would sell off many of those dollars and buy euros. The European Union has an economy and population that are larger than those of the United States. It has the size and depth needed to support a world currency, plus it has a balance of trade surplus compared to our massive deficit and debts. It is estimated that 30 percent of the world's trade would be denominated in euros. The euro's success would make Europeans more efficient, more competitive—with the Japanese, with Americans—and that would bring prices down for all of us. Just as the European Union itself is a great concept—to prevent war, to increase trade and mobility—so is the concept of a new, single currency, which the Union has tried and failed to establish two or three times since the 1970s.

In 1992, the Union succeeded, and twelve of its fifteen member countries adopted the Treaty of Maastricht, which among other things established the euro. Unfortunately, when they had conceived of it, all fifteen countries had had many different financial and economic underpinnings. Some were debtors, some were creditors, some had weak currencies, some had strong currencies. Putting a collapsing currency together with one going up would have been impossible, so the treaty stipulated that each country put its economic house in order. The term was "convergence"—all countries had to achieve and maintain internal budget deficits below certain targets and pay huge fines if they failed to do so.

Now, if a country is in economic trouble and you come along and fine it, that is going to make its economic problems even worse. And the more draconian you make the fines, the worse trouble the country will be in. But those who signed the treaty were essentially sound-money types; they understood the value of money that does not suffer periodic devaluation. When the late nineties rolled around, most of the sound-money governments were replaced by easy-money governments. The treaty stipulated deficits of less than 3 percent, and as the various governments' deadlines started getting close, they all started cooking the books. The French, for example, came up with an outrageous proposal whereby they would take huge amounts of money out of the national pension fund, use it to balance the budget, and return it to the fund the following year, after the deadline passed. They actually announced the plan out loud. Even the Italians were stunned—the Italians, who had been outrageously cooking the books for decades. Then the Italians found their own new way to manipulate the figures, as did the Germans. In the end, everyone cooked the books.

(Just as we do in the United States. Every year in the late 1990s, as the government reported a "budget surplus," strangely enough, the government debt kept going up. Politicians said they were paying down the debt—and they were. But they were borrowing more money to do it. In real money, the deficit continued to rise. In addition, U.S. Treasury Under Secretary Peter Fisher recently reported that the government has off-the-books, hidden liabilities "that have a current value $20 trillion or so in excess of the revenues that it expects to receive." So much for the government's railing at the rest of us about the need for "transparency" in our dealings.)

So along came the euro. Britain, of course, along with Sweden and Denmark, opted out of the plan altogether.

Under the old system, when bad times came, there were certain things countries could do. One, they could print money. It would debase the currency, but that did not matter to the politicians who won the election. The stock market would go up (temporarily), the economy would get better (temporarily), people would have more money in their pockets (temporarily), and everything would be okay (temporarily). They would pay the price later. Another thing governments could do when times got tough was *borrow* huge amounts of money.

With the euro as a common currency, governments can no longer print money. They will be forced to run sound economies and make sure everybody becomes competitive. Take the United States as an example. Right now, if things get bad in the car industry, the State of Michigan cannot turn around and print a lot of money. The Michigan governor can *borrow* a lot of money, just as New York State did in the 1960s. What Nelson Rockefeller built in Albany to buy votes makes some of the great cathedrals of the world pale by comparison. But it helped damage New York's credit.

Look for the same thing to happen in Europe. First, politicians will paper over their problems with fiscal Band-Aids, and then, when this ceases to work, they will point their fingers at others, outsiders— those evil, wily foreigners—particularly those in Brussels, the headquarters of the European Union. Europe's leaders today have no answer to what will happen when Portugal's needs diverge from Finland's or Austria's, or to how they will resolve the regional pressures that must arise as the union grows out of its infancy.

One of the reasons I was so keen on the euro initially was because Germany was the paragon of sound currency for fifty years, and the euro as originally proposed was seen as a deutsche mark in disguise. Cut to 2003. The concept is in crisis. The Portuguese have not been minding their manners, and worse still, neither have the Germans, who elected a left-wing government in the mid-1990s. Two of the countries in most serious violation of the treaty are Germany and Portugal. In the lead-up to the 2002 election, they started spending money as fast as they could. They could not print money anymore, under Maastricht, so they went on a deficit spending spree the likes of which had been unseen in Germany in decades.

A chain is only as strong as its weakest link. The only way for the euro to work the way it is designed to work is for all the member countries to run their economies properly. You are not going to get twelve countries to do that, and when things really get bad, I do not expect the euro to survive.

Several governments are now running big deficits. The French have even said they will ignore the contract. Eventually some populist politician is going to blame the euro and Brussels for his problems and threaten to pull out. Will Brussels send tanks or give concessions or print money? Either way, it will damage the euro. In the meantime, I own euros, but only because the currency is less sick than its competitors.

It could have worked. What the members of the Union could have done is start with a small experiment: Germany and Austria, already tied pretty tightly, having the same currency, for example. After ironing out the kinks, they could have added, say, the Dutch, who also have an economy and a currency tightly tied to Germany's. Then added another, slowly. It might have taken a decade or two. That is the way America did it—we slowly but surely worked our way west, adding new "members," to our country, our market, and our currency. Had the Europeans done it that way, they would have been hard pressed to blame their failure on the evil bureaucrats in Brussels.

The euro looms extremely large in world events today. Trillions of dollars have been invested on the assumption that it is going to work. Bank systems have changed, parking meters have changed, accounting systems, tax codes, everything. If it does not work, the experience of unwinding it is going to be disastrous.

If it were to work, it would be even more important to us all. A sound alternative to the U.S. dollar would have the world abandoning the greenback. The resulting change in U.S. power would have far-reaching and disastrous ramifications, as history shows.

As recently as the 1920s, the United Kingdom was believed to be the richest and most powerful country in the world—as we are today—but its currency, the world's medium of exchange and reserve currency, was already fundamentally flawed. By the end of the 1930s, there were exchange controls on sterling that lasted forty years, and in that forty-year period the United Kingdom lost its empire, its power, and its prestige. Things got so bad that in the 1970s the nation, no longer able to create money and credit at will, could not meet its obligations in the world market and had to be bailed out by the IMF.

Removing the barriers to the free movement of people, labor, capital, and intellectual capital is what the European Union is all about and what the euro is designed to promote. If you are a member of the European Union, you no longer need a visa or passport for internal travel—no more than does a U.S. citizen to go from Tennessee to Texas. The whole world should operate that way.

Sound radical? The world managed without passports for thousands of years. Christopher Columbus did not have a passport or a visa. Those great waves of immigrants into the United States in the nineteenth century—those people did not show up at Ellis Island with passports and visas. They just came. Had visas been required, most of our grandparents would have been denied them, and denied entry. Great cities, countries, and cultures grew as people unrestricted by passports and visas headed to the new frontier. This has always been, and *is,* good for society.

Passports were conceived by the British as a way to control their people and their empire. They did not want a lot of foreigners leaving the outposts of the British Empire and coming to England, or even going to other parts of the empire, unless they could control such movements. The last thing they wanted was people of color showing up in the mother country. The "White Man's Burden" was not something to be shouldered at home.

The passport, in its earliest incarnation, under the Chinese or perhaps before, was a medallion of safe passage given to a courier or emissary of the emperor, for example, attesting to the bearer's bona fides and saying, "Please look after him," or "Let him pass." In time, the notion was inevitably corrupted and was expanded to the point where every citizen was required to carry a passport in order to travel. And soon even that was not enough, and along came the additional requirement of a visa, creating even more control and restrictions.

Think of the tens of thousands of people who do nothing but sit around at borders checking passports, checking visas, issuing passports, issuing visas, stifling mobility, creativity, and efficiency. Think of the massive amount of resources that could be opened to the world in the absence of their being there.

I remember the case of a Cuban who strapped himself onto a barrel and washed up onto the shore in Florida—whereupon he was immediately arrested. I would love to have that guy working for me or living in my town. Those are the kinds of people we need in America—risk takers, driven, brave, bright, ambitious people.

I hold up the famous Leaning Tower of Pisa. Closed at the time, undergoing stabilization, the tourist attraction is now open to visitors again, to the delight of the prostitutes lining the roads into the city.

We went from Atlantic to Pacific and Pacific to Atlantic— the first ever to do so in a car—beginning and ending here in Dunquin, Ireland.

The world, and this country especially, got along quite well without passports and visas in the past and could get along without them in the future. What keeps them in force today is basically inertia. The concept of a world without them is foreign to most people, for no other reason than because in their minds it has always been the way it is. If you raise the question, people look at you as if you were a fool. What about national defense? you might ask. That is just another way for the government to say, "We need to control people. And we are better at deciding what is good for the world than the people are."

 Throughout history, those opposing immigration have used the same arguments, especially "These immigrants are different from the ones before." Remember how in the mid–nineteenth century Americans complained bitterly that the Irish were "different" from previous immigrants? They were "drunks and outlaws, and they formed gangs." And worse, they were a different religion: Roman Catholic. They could never be loyal Americans because as Papists they would first obey Rome. For 170 years it was inconceivable that a Catholic could be elected president. Then came Jack Kennedy. Later generations said the same thing about Italians, Jews, Chinese, eastern Europeans, Ethiopians, Cubans, Dominicans, and Vietnamese. For decades Asians could not own property because they were "different."

The arguments against all these people sound ludicrous now, just as the current set of "differences" will seem absurd a few years from now. The mayor of Schenectady, New York, is out recruiting Guyanese immigrants now because they add so much to his city.

Closing our doors to outsiders is not going to make the United States any safer. The bombing of the federal building in Oklahoma City reminded us that terrorism is a domestic problem as well as an international one. The McVeigh family had been here for generations, as had the family of John Allen Williams, the alleged leader of the Washington, D.C., sniper attacks, who terrorized the nation for several weeks in the fall of 2002. The Unabomber was an American graduate of Harvard. No war was ever lost because of a lack of visa controls. Mohammed Atta, reputed mastermind of the September 11, 2001, attacks in New York, was in the country legally. The only way to protect the country from outsiders is to close the country completely. Are we all going to quit our jobs to patrol our thousands of miles of borders to keep out foreigners? Under such a system of homeland security, we would admit no foreign businessmen, tourists, sports teams, or entertainers; the Beatles would not have been allowed to tour the United States.

Would you want to live in a country like that? I would not. To achieve the same end, I would recommend as an alternative that we stop making so many enemies.

If ever there was a time when the nation was under serious threat from its enemies, it was Benjamin Franklin's time. The country was full of subversives; a third of the population was in the enemy camp. Even Franklin's only son, William, was a Loyalist (Tory). Furthermore, enemies surrounded the country. The fledgling nation was bordered by warring Indian tribes and by the colonies of England and Spain, two vastly superior military powers—two of the greatest armies in the world at the time. Today, our nearest enemy of consequence is five thousand miles away. Both internal and external threats to the country were greater then than they are now, notwithstanding the existence of weapons of mass destruction. And Ben Franklin's answer to the question of homeland security was this: "They that can give up essential liberty to obtain a little temporary safety deserve neither liberty nor safety."

Of course, if all those foreigners were to come in, they would work for less. Which, contrary to the position your representative in Washington would take, is a good thing. If one country is extremely prosperous, attracting a lot of people, some of those people might hold wages down—or at least work harder, since an immigrant always has to run a bit faster—which in turn would increase productivity. Everybody would be better off as a result; immigrants made us great, and they continue to do so. The guy sitting there with a protected job, corporation, or monopoly would not be better off, but the rest of us would.

Of the legal immigrants living here, 21 percent have at least seventeen years of education, which often includes graduate or professional schools. Among Americans born here, only 8 percent can boast such expertise.

The United States has huge shortages of soldiers, nurses, computer specialists, software and other engineers, veterinarians, doctors, janitors, teachers, clergymen, nannies, housekeepers, and farmworkers. Social Security and Medicare desperately need more young workers to maintain fiscal solvency. We have too many lawyers, too many bureaucrats, and too many people holding protected jobs. They, of course, are the ones trying to close the borders.

Scientists are making huge strides now, especially in genetic research. Someday they will discover that all bureaucrats have the same gene—a defective gene. They are the same worldwide; their eyes glaze or they flinch whenever something new comes along. I have seen thousands of them, everywhere, and their first reaction is always "No."

Having ascertained that one does not just show up and get married in most places around the world—Timbuktu is not Las Vegas—and having discovered that we could marry legally in England, given enough lead time, Paige, by remote control from Siberia, had set about orchestrating our wedding.

Remember, this was January 1, 2000, the turn of the millennium. Baby-sitters in England were charging a thousand pounds, more than $1,500, to baby-sit on New Year's Eve. The Red Lion Hotel in Henley, where we had been hoping to stay and put up our guests—where we had stayed and fallen in love when we attended the regatta—was scheduled to be closed. Most hotels in Henley were going to be closed, simply because they could not afford to pay their help what it would cost to have them work the holiday. The first estimate we received from a wedding planner, for the one hundred or so people we wanted to invite, was $1,500 *a plate* for each sitting.

Our original guest list had already been decimated by other circumstances surrounding the date. Many people had already made plans far in advance to celebrate the turn of the millennium. And of course, a lot of people did not want to travel—thanks to the Y2K software scare, computers everywhere were expected to crash, and airplanes were predicted to come falling out of the sky. Flowers seemed impossible to come by. There was a worldwide shortage of champagne. The difficulties Paige faced planning a wedding for that day would have seemed insurmountable had she been *living* in England. It was not as if she were getting married in her hometown— though her mother did what she could from a distance.

Further complicating matters was that the Anglican church in Henley was overseen by a pastor who would not marry you, or allow you to marry in his church, if you were divorced. I was divorced.

This is only a partial inventory of the obstacles confronting Paige, who, in spite of them, arranged one of the most extraordinary weddings I have ever attended.

Paige found a Catholic monastery in Henley, designed by Christopher Wren and situated right on the river, in a location as drop-dead beautiful as the building itself. In exchange for a contribution to the monastery, Paige managed to secure the use of the site for the wedding reception. Adjoining the Wren building was the small chapel in which we would be married. On what was sure to be a typically English January day, rainy and bleak, there would be no need to transport people any distance between the ceremony and the reception.

Not until the very end did the Red Lion Hotel, at an inflated price, agree to stay open, and not even then, after our prevailing upon him for a full three months, did the manager give us the entire hotel, as we had requested. We had to find another hotel, a small one, and talk it into staying open, also at a jacked-up rate, to take the overflow.

As the date of the wedding approached, much of the hysteria surrounding the date began to subside. The bubble burst. Chiefly due to the reduction in travel thanks to the Y2K scare, people were suddenly available for work, hotel rooms became available, and the idea of paying $1,500 for a baby-sitter or $150,000 to feed a hundred guests per meal became ridiculous. Paige managed to find a professional film crew, flowers, champagne, and a caterer, all at a more or less reasonable price. The Leander Club, an old English rowing club of which I am a member, agreed to open for the party the night before the wedding. And it so happened that in Henley-on-Thames, just as everywhere else in the world, there were New Year's Eve fireworks scheduled for that evening. We told our guests, "We've arranged a giant fireworks display for you to celebrate our wedding."

I had nothing to do with any of this. Paige handled it all.

Later she admitted to me, "Jim, any woman who plans her wedding while traveling across Siberia is nuts." It may have been the fairy-tale wedding that every woman dreams about, but "next time I suggest we elope."

My contribution to the festivities? I provided the preacher.

When I was growing up in Demopolis, Alabama, one of my best friends was a boy named Rusty Goldsmith, who was Jewish. For a southern town—and such a small town—it is surprising, as I look back on it now, how many Jews there were in Demopolis, including the president of the country club and the president of the city council. There was a synagogue in town, as well as a Jewish cemetery. It was not until I went to the North that I found out that Jews were supposed to be different from everybody. In Alabama in the fifties, at least in Demopolis, black and white were the only signifiers—Jewish, Catholic, and Protestant seemed not terribly relevant. I remember being in the army and going through the chow line at Fort Dix, and the guy behind me was asking everybody, "What are you?" And they were all saying Puerto Rican, Italian, Greek. I did not know what to say or even what he meant, so I said, "Episcopalian."

I was in my forties when Rusty called and said, "Guess what I'm going to do?"

Rusty, who had married a Presbyterian woman, was working in finance, and I assumed he was changing jobs.

"I haven't a clue," I said.

He said, "I'm going to the seminary. I'm going to become an Episcopal priest."

I was perplexed. But then, Rusty was probably perplexed by some of the choices I had made regarding my life and career.

By the fall of 1999, when Paige and I were looking around for a preacher, Rusty was the Episcopal pastor of a church in Birmingham. Rusty and I had not seen much of each other in recent years, but when I called him it was as though nothing had changed.

"Look, this could be perfect," I said, "We grew up together, you're my old friend, I grew up an Episcopalian, you're an Episcopal priest . . ."

"And I have a sabbatical coming up," he said.

I was surprised to learn how severe the restrictions on men of the cloth are. The regulations are very complex, and a preacher cannot just go around performing God's work without filling out paperwork. It is a good thing all this madness did not exist until recently, or Christianity would never have made it out of Bethlehem.

At the end of December he flew to Henley-on-Thames to marry us, after obtaining the numerous permissions necessary from the Americans and from the English.

January 1, 2000, at Henley-on-Thames dawned as the kind of beautiful sunny day rarely seen in England at any time of the year, let alone in the middle of winter. If not a summer day, it was as good as

*What a wedding!*
*What a way to start a new life and a new millennium!*

*The Spanish funded Columbus and still claim him*
*(as here in Madrid), though the explorer himself was an Italian*
*who followed Chinese and Viking information and utilized*
*Portuguese technology to reach the New World.*

one—it prompted guests, as they walked the expansive grounds of the monastery and looked out over the river, to remove their coats. Paige traveled the half mile between the hotel and the chapel in a carriage drawn by white horses, clip-clopping through the streets of the town. My dying father, who had traveled to England to serve as my best man, rode with me in the yellow Mercedes.

When he was married, he said, his best man had told him that the obligation of any best man was to provide the groom with a way out. It was his job to tell the groom that it was okay if he had changed his mind and to explain to the assembled masses that there would be no wedding that day. He had known this, he said, since he was a young man. This was the man who had taught me to open doors for women, to hold their chairs. He had taught me everything I knew in the way of chivalry. And in much the same way that he had instructed me in table manners, he was now giving me the advice that it was his obligation to give, both as a father and as a best man.

He also said that if Paige and I had children—the eldest of five boys, I was the only one of his children who had not provided him with grandchildren—he probably would not be around to see them. The end of the trip, shortly after which Paige and I were planning to start a family, was two years away.

"You've made it this far," I said. "Just hold on."

We drove to the chapel with the convertible top down.

And Paige and I got married.

We honeymooned the following night in a five-star luxury resort about fifteen miles away, Le Manoir aux Quat' Saisons, where we slept in over-the-top English country elegance. And dreamed of Africa.

# PART TWO

## 2000

# 8

# INTO AFRICA

WE WERE DRIVING through Madrid with the top down on the Mercedes, looking for our hotel, when a BMW motorcycle pulled up beside us on the passenger side.

The driver looked over and said, "You're Jim Rogers!"

"No," said Paige, "I'm not Jim Rogers. He's Jim Rogers."

The man's name was Gerardo Seeliger, and he was a member of Spain's Olympic sailing team. He had read my book and was spending as much time as he could "driving around the world." After leading us to our hotel, he invited us to dinner, and the next day he introduced us to about a dozen of his friends—one the chairman of a bank, another a Spanish count. Most, like him, were motorcycle enthusiasts. At least one of them was not. She was Chon Gómez-Monche, CEO of González Byass, the huge and venerable Spanish vineyard and spirits manufacturer (its products include Tío Pepe) who invited Paige and me, as we made our way south, to visit her at the company's legendary bodega in Jérez de la Frontera, one of the oldest vineyards in Spain.

Spain, to my utter surprise, with a budget surplus and a balance-of-trade surplus, today boasts one of the best-managed economies in Europe. It has become a very attractive country in every way. We have even discussed living there for a while.

Jérez is the city from which sherry, the fortified Spanish wine, takes its name. "Sherry" means "wine of Jérez." There, with Ms. Gómez, we toured the region's old wine caves. When Ferdinand Magellan set sail to circumnavigate the globe in the sixteenth century, she told us, he had carried sherry produced here.

The feast she and her family hosted we would remember as a highlight of the journey. "That Chon is something else," observed Paige, "a woman running a major bodega and serving the world's best gazpacho." We would fantasize about the cold soup she had prepared when our choices in food were far less tantalizing.

Ms. Gómez presented us with two bottles of the company's millennium sherry to carry with us around the world, just as Magellan had taken the local sherry on his expedition. If we survived the trip, we would keep one bottle to commemorate it and return one to the vineyard to be placed in the company's museum. (Magellan did not take Jerez's product around the world, of course; he drank it en route. And Magellan did not survive the trip; his crew finished it for him.) She also gave us a bottle of the company's sherry bottled in 1968, the year of Paige's birth, so that we modern-day Magellans, in the true tradition of discovery and exploration, would have something to drink on the road.

Since the wedding, I had been calling home to Demopolis regularly to check on my father. When I called from Spain in February, he reported for the first time that he was experiencing chest pains. The cancer was clearly spreading. It was the first time we talked about getting him into a hospice, if for no other reason than to help him manage the pain. I encouraged him to do it. His response was to reiterate to me, with great forcefulness, that I was not to come home or interrupt my trip at all, no matter what. He seemed to be saying that he wanted me to finish the trip not just for me but for him as well—to do it for both of us.

Here I was, driving around the world—we were about three thousand miles apart—and I was reminded that it was he who had provided me with my first car. When I was seventeen, he had bought me a 1948 Plymouth, with the proviso that I pay for all the upkeep on the eleven-year-old car. It was just one of the many ways in which he had helped instill a sense of responsibility into me.

"I'll do it," I promised. "I'll finish the trip."

After traveling for fifty-nine weeks and driving sixty thousand kilometers, we finally reached Gibraltar on the southern tip of Spain. This was the gateway to Africa. We were only fifteen kilometers away, looking across the Strait of Gibraltar at the mighty continent we were about to meet head-on. This promised to be one of the longest legs of our trip, a fascinating journey through the world's second largest continent, a land whose history, culture, and landscape were as diverse and unpredictable as the mind could imagine. I had driven through Africa on my previous, two-year trip, traveling by motorcycle, and the feeling of setting out again was no less overwhelming. Paige and I, as we stood there, were filled with anticipation, both excited by and a little bit fearful of all those things we could not predict.

Until now we had always had a pretty good understanding of every country we were about to visit, each city where we planned to stop. We had always had some sense of where we would be the next day and how we would get there, even driving through Siberia. In Africa, all bets were off. The Western press did a poor job of reporting on events unfolding there, and we had had to do our own research. Our unrealistic hope was to drive down the west coast of the continent, around the Horn, and back up the east coast, toward Egypt. It looked good on paper. But there were wars being waged at various places along our route, from Zaire, Angola, and the Congo to the Sudan, Ethiopia, and Somalia, wars that spilled off in all directions, irrespective of national boundaries. There were border disputes that would make it impossible to cross between certain neighboring nations. The border between Algeria and Morocco, for example, had been closed for six years, and no civilians were allowed to pass. (Natural gas, traveling through the pipeline between the two countries, passed unimpeded.)

Added to the hazards of war were epidemics and natural disasters. Terrible floods the year before had submerged a good part of Mozambique, in the southeast. A story was told of a pregnant woman forced to give birth while caught up in a tree. Antipersonnel mines, deployed in the civil war that had ended a decade before, were floating to the surface.

Whatever plans we made today might be irrelevant tomorrow. No one had driven such a route overland in decades—if ever.

Paige and I had spent hours in consulates and embassies in Europe, from France to Britain to Belgium, trying to get visas for some of the countries we hoped to visit. In the end, it took nearly a month to collect only ten. Unfortunately, most of them were good for only three months, and many would expire before we arrived. We would try to pick up new visas in neighboring countries, though there was no guarantee of success.

Disease was another serious concern. We had been vaccinated for tetanus, typhoid, rabies, and other, more exotic diseases for the first leg, but the biggest concern now was malaria, the largest single killer in Africa. To protect ourselves, we had obtained the drug Larium, which we were instructed to start taking two weeks before entering Africa and to continue taking until two months after leaving the malaria zone. The instructions also clearly stated that the drug was to be used for only three months. We expected to be there at least nine months. The side effects of Larium could be serious; they included things such as delirium. We were warned to discontinue the drug if such symptoms appeared, and we carried a substitute just in case. (The manufacturer later announced an additional risk: suicide.)

We restocked our medical bag with its extensive collection of supplies: hypodermic needles, antibiotics, bandages, medicines for diarrhea and fever. We also checked our water purification kit, which comes with filters and pills, an absolute necessity on such a trip. The water we would find in Africa would certainly need to be purified—there would be no drinking straight from the tap. We tested our camping equipment, everything from tents to sleeping bags to cooking equipment to blankets. We could not count on finding hotels every time we stopped for the night. We bought extras of everything for the car: jacks, tires, tow bars. We had two Iridium satellite phones, one for the car, the other handheld, but were uncertain whether they would work in all parts of Africa. To be safe, we also had two GSM phones. They would certainly work in westernized countries, such as Morocco and South Africa, but would be of questionable value elsewhere; in addition to voice communication, they would allow us to receive data, including e-mail—we hoped.

In London we had purchased a new global positioning system for the car. Our old GPS had been made by Alpine and worked splendidly but unfortunately worked only in Europe. Finally, we had four short-wave radios, three portable and one in the car. These were crucial, for the best way to stay on top of what was really happening on the road in front of us was via the BBC, which produces the definitive broadcasts to and about Africa, and these radios would enable us to pick them up.

When the Berlin Wall fell in 1989, there were about three open markets in all of Africa. Now there were dozens. Many countries wanted to start stock exchanges. Forward-thinking leaders in certain countries wanted to attract Western capital and open their countries to global prosperity. Africa, a continent of 800 million people, was hardly an economic force to be ignored.

I had been investing in African countries such as Ghana, Botswana, Zambia, and Zimbabwe for years—indirectly, I had investments in Nigeria—and much to my delight, the investments had been successful. I believed there was a coming bull market in raw materials, and Africa was extremely rich in such resources. My optimism had been fortified as I saw the former USSR continuing to deteriorate as a future source of natural resources. Botswana was rich in diamonds, Ghana in cocoa and gold, Morocco in phosphates. There were many countries I was eager to visit and revisit, such as Zambia, with its emeralds and copper, and Cameroon, awash in oil. I could not wait to visit some of the places I had been unable to reach on my last trip, such as Malawi in southern Africa, and, of course, in Mali, the city of Timbuktu. I looked forward to my first visit to Ghana and wondered if, when I got there, I would be able to find my broker, a man with whom I had been doing business for a decade from several thousand miles away and had never met.

Most of all, I looked forward to being surprised.

We spent a couple of weeks in Morocco, stopping in Tangiers, Fez, Rabat, Casablanca, and the only Moroccan city that still reflects the exotic, romantic past of French colonial Africa, Marrakech, with its snake charmers in the marketplace. Traversing the Atlas Mountains, passing through Berber country, we moved south, heading for Western Sahara.

Morocco, one of the more fully developed countries in Africa, with

*Legend says Gibraltar will remain British as long as the monkeys remain. London spends a lot keeping them happy. If the young people of the Rock had their way, the monkeys would stay and the British would go.*

*I always wondered what one wore under one's Mauritanian boo-boo.*

*The mosque in Djenné is the largest and most beautiful mud-brick building in the world. It is now closed to nonbelievers, thanks to a European fashion magazine that used it for a lingerie shoot.*

a solid infrastructure and a population of about 27 million, holds roughly two thirds of the world's reserves of phosphate rock—phosphate deposits are to Morocco as oil is to Venezuela—and dominates the world market in this vital ingredient of fertilizers and various chemicals. I figured the newly installed king would be facing numerous difficulties after assuming the throne of his father, who had run a despotic, corrupt regime for decades. He would need more than his father's collection of more than five hundred luxury cars, a dozen secret palaces, and a huge, empty mosque, which had cost the nation hundreds of millions of dollars. Western Sahara, formerly Spanish Sahara, one of the least populated areas of Africa, chiefly desert, was claimed by Morocco's dictator in the 1970s, thanks in large part to the phosphate deposits located there. A guerrilla group, the Polisario Front, has been fighting for the region's independence from Morocco ever since. The United Nations has been trying to hold a referendum on the fate of Western Sahara since 1975 and has spent almost $500 million in the process since it established a physical presence in the early 1990s.

We saw scores of UN fat cats driving air-conditioned four-by-fours, spending government money on elaborate meals in expensive restaurants, filling up the better hotels, living the good life, and foreshadowing a lot of what we would run into in the rest of Africa. These bureaucratic flunkies were everywhere, and many of them had been there for years, international parasites living off the ongoing local conflict, with every reason to sustain the strife rather than end it.

By the end of the trip, repeated experiences like this convinced me that the United Nations was a failure as an institution. The world has spent hundreds of billions of dollars, yet the United Nations has rarely, if ever, prevented a war—its raison d'etre. I am as idealist as anyone, but let's face the reality of the cost and lack of efficiency after sixty years. The execution has been horrible and wildly epensive even for its "humanitarian" missions. I have now met people working as contractors and subcontractors to the United Nations who make more than Wall Street investment bankers.

Once we got south in Western Sahara, where guerrillas were more active, we were not allowed to travel by ourselves but had to travel with a military convoy. The convoy left three days a week from the dusty little Western Sahara port city of Dakhla. There we gathered, waiting in the sun, with numerous people going south, many of them merchants and traders driving large pickup trucks and old automobiles loaded down with merchandise: pots and pans, cooking oil, food, blankets. The convoy left four hours late. It was the strangest convoy I had ever seen in my life.

Everyone just started tearing down the highway, across the desert. The soldiers soon disappeared from sight. It was every man for himself, and that was fine with us, because these military convoys were dangerous. They telegraphed your intentions to the enemy. "Next Thursday at three o'clock, we will all be traveling this route, a hundred of us loaded down with goods, loaded down with valuables, and we may have a few Westerners with us, too, if you want to attack."

By the way, Dakhla was terrific, with wonderful seafood restaurants. One man had the monopoly on selling alcohol, and there were only two restaurants where you could buy it. There is nothing like drinking cold beer and eating wonderful seafood, sitting there on the edge of the Sahara overlooking the Atlantic. I would love to return there—especially if I could get the ice cream and beer franchise.

At the southern border, we were all required to reassemble and set up camp; again, a perfect target. From there we were handed over to the Mauritanian Army and police, whose job was to lead us through the extensive minefields on their side. It was a long haul on the Mauritanian side, and regular checks were made of everybody to make sure that no one had wandered off. We were told stories about hotdogging Europeans driving off into the desert and blowing up. It was hard to know if the stories were true, but you only have to hear one of them to say, "I'll stay with the military."

Eventually, we arrived in Nouadhibou, a major seaport on the north coast of Mauritania, where we were told by a grave young man—we were in serious Muslim country now—that anybody who served beer, helped people to get beer, or touched beer in any way was doomed to damnation. Unless he happened to be Korean. We immediately found a Korean restaurant.

The Koreans, it appeared, had arrived in Mauritania when the government started granting fishing rights to various fleets around the world. (There were some sixty Russian ships and maybe a hundred European ships offshore when we arrived.) And some of the fishermen, including the man who owned the restaurant we patronized, had come ashore and stayed. More may stay in the future as the country ends its decades-old isolation—especially if the new gas discoveries pan out. Koreans had the monopoly on beer in Mauritania. Not that there were that many travelers coming through Nouadhibou, but anybody who wanted a drink or a decent meal had to go to a Korean restaurant. Which served Chinese food. Nobody wanted to eat Korean food.

There are a million Africas, but from a distance one tends to see only two: North Africa and sub-Saharan Africa; that is, white Africa and black. Ordering Chinese food in our Korean restaurant, we were having trouble with our French, and the owners, obligingly, marched out a dishwasher who spoke perfect English, a black African woman from Ghana, a country over one thousand miles to the south, who had been in Mauritania three or four months. She was one of many people in her situation, both men and women, whom we would run across as we traveled the northwest coast of the continent. Part of a pattern of mass immigration in North Africa, she, like many of the laborers in Mauritania, was working her way north, across the Sahara, trying to make it to Europe. Her biggest obstacle would be the Mediterranean, she said. There were stories of hundreds of people, eight or ten every night, who drowned trying to smuggle themselves across the Strait of Gibraltar. In fact, the Spanish Navy patrolled the strait continuously while complaining that it bore the brunt of the effort for all of Europe, where anti-immigration sentiment in many countries was running so deep that it sparked regular outbreaks of violence.

(The Romanian security service would complain of being "invaded by a new generation of musical trash propagated by Yugoslav wedding singers and former circus orchestras from Hungary and Croatia.")

Here was a woman who had made her way from Ghana, through all kinds of trials and hardships, and was willing to persist, going up against the Sahara and the Mediterranean Sea, to make her way to Europe, where opportunity awaited her and where, in truth, she was needed desperately. Considering the current birthrates in places such as Spain and Italy, I would be giving people like her tickets to come across. She is the kind of person America took in for decades and the kind we desperately need again.

From Nouadhibou, in early March, Paige and I headed into the vastness of the Sahara.

There is perfect darkness in the Sahara. At night, there is no light from any source but the heavens. The air is pure, crystal clear; there is no pollution of any kind. There is no moisture in the air. Alone, in silence, Paige and I were drinking this in while drinking the 1968 sherry we had been given in Spain, and because the silence was perfect it took us a moment to identify the sensation on our skin.

"That's the breeze," I said, touching my face.

You always hear the wind. Everywhere else. But here, in the Sahara, there was nothing for the wind to blow through. Here in the desert the silence was absolute.

"My God," said Paige, "it's the breeze."

We were about two hundred miles from Nouadhibou and another two hundred from Nouakchott, Mauritania's capital. It was a day's overland travel in either direction to civilization, hundreds of miles across the Sahara, across nothing but sand, to the nearest road. We were hundreds of miles from electricity. There had never been civilization here, never anything but the sand that surrounded us. Dunes, sculpted by the wind over thousands of years, undulated into infinity. It was impossible to imagine a more romantic place for a honeymoon. You could not dream this up. You could not buy this night. You could not buy the day that had brought us to it.

Tomorrow we would reach the capital, and in a week we would embark on the most eagerly anticipated stretch of the trip. We would cross the Senegal River and enter sub-Saharan Africa.

But before doing that we would drink in this night, sitting here outside our tent, facing into the breeze that came off the Atlantic some unknown distance to the west of us. We would drink our thirty-two-year-old sherry, sitting here in the middle of nowhere, as the ocean wind commenced its 3,500-mile African crossing, traversing the desert to the Red Sea, just as it did thousands of ancient evenings ago when the first caravan passed this way.

Nothing had changed since then but the contour of the dunes.

Before turning in we would download our e-mail.

We had driven all day across the sand. There was no road. We made our own road as we traveled. To the extent that others had preceded us, we tried to follow whatever tracks we could find. But this was not a very well traveled path. At times we would see the imprint of tires—and hope that whoever had left them had known where he was going.

I had always been riveted by the curves of the dunes. No painter could ever capture such sensuality; no sculptor could ever be so erotic. No woman could ever be so delicate and voluptuous at the same time. I was startled but delighted when Paige exclaimed quietly, after her first few glimpses of them, that she had never seen such extraordinary curves on any nude. So spellbinding, yet so remote. We would find them only in parts of the Sahara, the Namib, and the great desert of the Arabian Peninsula.

Once, as night was falling, we came upon about a dozen large tents, as though in a mirage, pitched in the middle of nowhere. It was a band of nomads. There were no men in camp, only women and children. We approached, introduced ourselves, and asked if they minded our camping nearby. They were as surprised to see us as we to see them, and just as excited. They showed us into their tents; they served us tea. A few hours later, after we had eaten our dinner, finished our sherry, and downloaded our e-mail, using a handheld phone and a laptop—we had actually turned in for the night—the women, having worked up their courage, came over and scratched on our tent. They had never seen a two-man pup tent like ours. They asked if they could look inside, and of course we obliged, although we were a little embarrassed after having seen theirs.

Here, in the most romantic place in the world—it is a bitch to get to, but if you can get there, it is the perfect honeymoon spot—we awoke the next morning to a sight even more spectacular than the dunes themselves. We opened the tent, stepped outside, and found ourselves surrounded by a hundred and fifty camels. Some time during the night, the men had returned to camp from wherever it is that nomads go with their camels. Soon the women returned to our tent, offering us breakfast—fresh milk, still warm from the camel.

"Was it pasteurized?" Paige's mother asked when we told her about it later.

The entire episode was one of the more surreal and exotic encounters I had ever experienced, and later that morning, as the sight of the nomads disappeared from the frame of the Mercedes' rearview mirror, I tried to imagine how equally strange it must have seemed to them.

Moving south, our route took us back out along the shoreline. The tide was out, and we drove for a while on the beach, which ran flat, smooth, and wide for a pretty good stretch, speeding along on the hard-packed sand of the Atlantic with ocean spray splashing on one side of the windshield and dry desert sand from the glorious dunes peppering the other.

We were forced back to the desert when the tide came in.

---

On March 21, crossing the Senegal River, we entered sub-Saharan Africa. Here, where black Africa and white Africa meet, the border had never been terribly stable. The whole area was fraught with danger. Things were made worse by the internal situation in Senegal. We had been forced to delay our trip because of the threat of violence surrounding elections there. It was pretty clear, going into the voting, that Abdou Diouf, the president since 1981, was going to be defeated, and the suspicion was that he would not yield power, in which case supporters of his opposition threatened all-out riots. Everybody was being urged to stay away. We delayed our trip for a day, awaiting the outcome. To everybody's astonishment, Diouf stepped aside gracefully following his defeat. The French exert far greater control in "French Africa" than do the English over their former colonies, and no doubt the French Foreign Office had given Diouf the word. I took it as another sign that my optimism over the future of Africa was well founded (especially when the victor, President Abdoulaye Wade, was the only black African president to break ranks with Robert Mugabe, who was pursuing the equivalent of ethnic cleansing in Zimbabwe).

Saint Louis, our first stop in Senegal, is the first French city one comes to in Africa, a phenomenal old French-African town. In most of the French colonies there is a bakery in any town of any size, a pastry shop, a French restaurant or two. Saint Louis was no exception. It provided a touch of France in a place with all the trappings of Africa— sub-Saharan Africa. Coming upon a scene we would run across many times in the months to come, we drove by a huge number of vultures eating a horse by the side of the road. Rarely would you see that in the Sahara. There are not many animals there, certainly not enough to keep vultures hanging around in significant numbers. As we got farther south of the river, the desert would continue to recede, giving way to bush, trees, and a variety of birds.

Senegal, but for a fifty-mile stretch of coastline, surrounds a former English colony, Gambia, a country smaller than Connecticut or Qatar. Driving in, we had to cross the Gambia River. And, thanks to a tie-up

at immigration, we missed the last ferry. I did not want to miss a night
in Gambia, at the luxury resort at which we had booked rooms.

"Listen," I said to the attendant, "you call the captain and tell him
to come back and get me, and I'll give him two hundred dollars U.S."

The attendant's eyes lit up. In the end it cost me $400, but I got my
own private ferry in the middle of the night—transporting two cars
and a trailer—and did not have to spend the night who-knew-where
costing who-knew-what. Of course, when the captain picked us up,
everybody *else* who had missed the ferry piled onto it, too. So I paid
for the whole mob to cross the river, all these other folks sleeping in
their trucks or cars or on the ground.

While we were sitting there, waiting to be picked up, a group of little boys and teenagers came over to talk to Paige. When we had crossed
from Turkey into Georgia and the same thing had happened—people
gathering around the car, staring at her—Paige had been terrified. Now
she was completely comfortable, clowning with the kids. She was having the time of her life, taking pictures with the Polaroid, surrounded by
youngsters singing to her, clapping to the beat.

For many, Africa is a place that you either love or hate in a day or
two. I have met people who fly in only to rush to the next flight home.
I fell in love with Africa instantly. And I have always loved it, every
time. Paige's reaction was mixed. She began what would be a love/hate
relationship that did not completely crystallize until we were leaving
nine months later.

Gambia, 30 miles across at its widest point and 295 miles long,
was carved into being at the end of the nineteenth century out of competing French and British colonial interests. Over the last twenty
years it has concentrated on developing tourism, though not the kind
of vacation travel it has lately become very popular for. Paige and I
noticed that an inordinate number of single women frequented the
many resorts there—English, French, Swiss, German, women in their
twenties and thirties, and it was not long before the reality of their
being there set in.

"Yes," a local reporter confirmed, "all these white women come
down here because they want a black boy. They bring their own condoms."

Taking up with the locals—you see the women arrive all by themselves, and then all are at dinner that same night with dates, picking

up the tab for young men—these European women travel regularly to
Gambia on sex holidays.

We drove northeast from Gambia, back through Senegal—on an excellent road, so new that it was not yet included on the Michelin
maps—headed for Mali, our first stop being the city of Kayes. As
soon as we crossed the border into Mali, the pavement disappeared,
and we found ourselves on the worst road we had yet encountered
anywhere in the world. As we proceeded through Mali, it got worse.
Kayes is on record as being the single hottest city in Africa, known to
reach temperatures as high as 115 degrees Fahrenheit as early as nine
in the morning and as late as seven at night.

It was here in French Equatorial Africa, east of the Senegal-Mali
border, that I first encountered—and this is the best translation I
could come up with—what is locally referred to as the "butt dance."
This regional phenomenon, while calling to mind the belly dancing I
had marveled at in Baku, completely outdistanced the latter for sheer
excitement.

In a little village, in the middle of nowhere, Paige and I stumbled
onto a wedding. It was here that we saw, for the first time, women
butt dancing, moving their bodies, specifically the body part in question, up and down in a way that simply defied the natural laws of
anatomy. As the women danced to the sound of drums, their young
daughters watched and practiced and in turn taught the littlest of the
girls how to do it. Amid the feasting, dancing, and rejoicing, the bride
and groom went off to the wedding chamber, soon to return, followed
by their mothers, who were carrying the bridal sheet, stained with the
evidentiary blood of consummation and virginity. At that point the
celebrating became that much more exuberant. Paige and I took Polaroids of everyone.

I would like to return to that village some day and bring an entire
wedding back to the United States—put the whole wedding on as a
Broadway show, the music, the drums, the dancing. You could take
the best twenty dancers in New York, and they could not do what I
saw those women do.

The women of West Africa wore elaborate, colorful headpieces that
matched the fabric of their dresses; the dresses traditionally extended
to the ankle. Many seemed to be especially tall, and they carried themselves with elegance. Thus it was that much more disheartening to

learn that so many of the women in Mali—50 percent, according to one estimate—make a habit of bleaching their skin. The products they use range from pills, advertised to lighten the complexion, to acid washes, which burn away the outer layer of skin to achieve the same effect temporarily. There is a flourishing market in these products, all of which appear to be manufactured in Europe for shipment down to West Africa, where in some sad sequel to colonialism, apparently, to be black is no longer to be beautiful.

We visited Kayes, Kita, and the capital, Bamako, but Mali in its entirety, when I planned the trip, was of consequence only insofar as within its borders lay a legendary city that I had been extremely disappointed to miss on my previous trip through Africa. There was no way I was going to miss it on this trip. Like legions of people from far and wide, prior to discovery of the New World—everybody had heard the tales told of it—I was determined to journey to the fabled city of Timbuktu.

Timbuktu is located about ten miles north of the Niger River, on high land above the flood plain, at a point in the desert where the ancient camel caravan routes and the Niger converge. Some five hundred miles northeast of the capital, the city of fifteen thousand people is now difficult to reach, but it was once a major crossroad.

At the turn of the last millennium Timbuktu went from being a caravan camp to a permanent settlement on the southern edge of the Sahara, a point of cultural interface between black Africa and the Berber tribes of the northern desert. As recently as the sixteenth century, Timbuktu was a city of 100,000 people, a center of wealth, culture, and education with a world-renowned *madrassa,* an Islamic university with some twenty-five thousand students, whose manuscript collection is still there today. The city was legendary as a commercial center for its abundant trade in salt, gold, and slaves. It was the Africans, not the Europeans, who actually invented slavery, and Timbuktu was a great center of the trade. When the first European showed up there—there are plaques commemorating the arrival of various early Europeans—he himself apparently wound up being enslaved by the Africans.

In the seventeenth century the city began its inexorable decline. In fact, for years I thought that "Timbuktu" was just an expression; I did not realize it was a real place. Gold had been discovered in the New World, and the slave trade became international. By then there was a much greater demand for slaves on the coast than in the interior. In the West African coastal city of Ouidah, the king became so rich from slavery that he was known throughout Europe for his wealth and insatiable desire for imported luxuries, as well as his magnificent palace. Only three of Timbuktu's mud-brick mosques remain. Most of the mosques in this part of the world, like the houses, are made of dried mud, the only building material available in any abundance here in the desert. Protruding from the walls of the structures are small logs or large branches of trees, which serve as ladders so that after the rains come the walls can be scaled for the purpose of repairing them. The United Nations has listed Timbuktu as one of twenty-three endangered World Heritage sites, because many of those walls are being washed away.

In dust-choked, sleepy Timbuktu I saw a town slipping backward into the past, and yet at the same time it made me hopeful for the future. A thousand years ago, camel caravans would arrive here out of the Sahara Desert, laden with salt and gold. I could not find enough water in the vast wastes of the desert to last me a day, and these people were going into the Sahara for weeks at a time. Having seen how difficult it is to get around the world in a Mercedes, I was staggered at how anybody could accomplish what these people did even five hundred years ago, let alone twice that many years in the past. I am not worried about man's survival. I also know that no matter how civilized we think we are, there have been others before us who thought they were just as civilized. A hundred years from now, people will look back at us and say, "Who were those primitive slobs?"

South of Timbuktu, on a tributary of the Niger, lies the town of Djenné with its gigantic mosque, the largest mud-brick building in the world and the most beautiful building of its kind. Foreigners are no longer allowed inside since a European magazine used it as a setting for lingerie models, but if you want a rewarding trip to this part of the world, go to Djenné. And forget Timbuktu. Today there is no reason to go there except to say, "I've been to Timbuktu."

It was on our journey through French colonial Africa that we started running into the baobab tree, my favorite tree in all the world. I suggested we name one of our children Baobab, a thought Paige peremptorily rejected. (By the time we reached the east coast of Africa, Paige had fallen in love with the acacia tree and suggested that Acacia might make a nice name for a daughter. I reminded her of the baobab.) With its thick trunk, up to thirty feet in diameter, growing wider at the top, and its wild upper growth resembling a root system, the baobab tree, the source of a hard-shelled, fleshy fruit called "monkey bread," appears to be growing upside down. Legend has it that the trees were thrown into the ground headfirst by an angry god.

All over Africa, the infrastructure left behind by the colonial powers has disintegrated under the continent's liberators. Driving through Mali, we saw the remains of the old railroad, the unused tracks and the ruins of the old slave stations, through which the traffic in people and gold was moved to the coast. We drove south through Burkina Faso, known as Upper Volta until 1983. The new name means "Land of the Incorruptible," which has proved to be a misnomer many times since. We crossed the border into the Ivory Coast, and, passing through the current political capital of Yamoussoukro we saw how some of these African liberators spent their money. We had seen it coming from twenty kilometers away. Driving down from the north, we were heading for the traditional capital, Abidjan, when suddenly, coming up over a hill, we saw an exact replica of Saint Peter's Basilica in Rome. Paige was convinced she had gone nuts, suffering the delirium promised by the malaria medicine we were taking.

The liberator of the Ivory Coast and its first president was Félix Houphouët-Boigny. In the 1980s, Houphouët-Boigny, a Christian in a country where Christians made up only 12 percent of the population, got it into his head to duplicate the largest Christian building in the world and place it in the village of his birth. He would then make that village the country's capital. (The United States has traditionally recognized Abidjan.) Under Houphouët-Boigny's presidency, the Ivory Coast, a former French colony, enjoyed both political stability and economic prosperity. Whenever the price of cocoa went through the roof, Houphouët-Boigny reaped the benefits in hard currency. He was going to make his country's cathedral *larger* than Saint Peter's—until the pope intervened. In the end, at the pontiff's urging, he made it two centimeters smaller. In addition, he built two bishops' palaces, one measuring 20,000 square feet for use solely by the pope when he visits. The pope has done so twice. The church houses its own *Pietà*.

It was while we were visiting the cathedral in Yamoussoukro that we saw rain for the first time since leaving Europe. The heavens seemed to break open. It poured, the African sky showing us something we had not seen in more than two months, as if to remind us that we were now in the tropics and if we thought the roads had been bad up to now . . .

The former village of Yamoussoukro is now a city of 100,000 people, with wide highways and a cathedral that can hold thousands of churchgoers. Unfortunately there are at most 1.5 million Christians in the whole country, and the place is never full, not even on Christmas and Easter. When we showed up, tour guides were sleeping in the pews. The building is air-conditioned throughout, but the system has been used only three times—twice for the pope and once for Houphouët-Boigny's funeral in 1993. Houphouët-Boigny left a huge endowment to sustain the cathedral after his death, one that will no doubt be stolen by a subsequent government. Will this Saint Peter's exist in 3000? Or will archaeologists be exploring the ruins trying to determine its source and meaning?

In December 1999, just before we arrived, there was a coup, almost certainly engineered by the French. Houphouët-Boigny's successor was not paying attention to the folks in Paris—he was spending a lot of money his country did not have—and suddenly the government was taken over by a general who happened to have been in France the month before. In Abidjan there is a large French paratroop brigade in residence near the airport, providing security and stability for the Ivorian government. The day of the coup, the paratroopers stayed in their barracks.

After cocoa, the commodity produced in greatest abundance in the Ivory Coast is to be found in the commercial capital, Abidjan, one of the more cosmopolitan cities in West Africa: NGO bureaucrats. They grow here in enormously high concentration, even for Africa. They and their like have been directing Africa's destiny for centuries. One might wonder why so many national boundaries in these parts consist of straight lines. In Germany in 1884, at what was called the Congress of Berlin, the European powers came together and divided up Africa. They paid no attention to religious, ethnic, linguistic, tribal, national, or historical differences—the Ivory Coast, for example, is divided between a majority Muslim population in the north and those who hold to indigenous beliefs and Christianity in the south, explaining why peace in Africa may be far away. And why there will always be work for Western bureaucrats.

One of our more delightful African nights was in the Ivory Coast, in the little town of Katiola. Paige and I had not eaten all day, and the hotel restaurant was so barren, dark, and dirty that we had to look elsewhere. Walking down the bustling streets, looking for food, we came upon the Restaurant Chicago. There were eight tables (all of which were empty), a young boy, the owner's son, sitting alone watching the door, and Marvin Gaye singing "Let's Get It On" playing at high volume over a loudspeaker. We had to give the place a try. Clearly excited by the appearance of a customer, the boy hurried over when Paige and I entered. We told him we wanted to eat, and he ran to get his mother, who took Paige into the backyard to show her what was available; chicken seemed to be the specialty of the house. The woman disappeared for a while, and it was only later that we realized that she had gone out to the market to purchase the rice and vegetables. While she slaughtered the chicken and prepared the meal, we drank deliciously cold beer—Flag beer, a West African brand, extracted from a cooler that contained nothing but bottles of it—and eventually we were served fried chicken, steamed rice, and vegetables. Despite its simplicity, it was a meal we remember as one of the best meals we had in Africa.

Before leaving the Ivory Coast we visited various consulates. In Abidjan, we obtained visas for Togo, Benin, Ghana, Gabon, Republic of the Congo, and Cameroon. The startled Angolan ambassador told us to get one as we got closer to his borders. Ghana was formerly known as the Gold Coast, after that which had first attracted Europeans to this stretch of African shoreline. European merchants initially came for gold and ivory, but commerce eventually expanded to include the commodity the Africans had been trying to sell them from the beginning: slaves. There was no market for slaves in Europe—the legacy of feudalism was a class of serfs and peasants—but with the discovery of the Americas a market suddenly materialized on the other side of the Atlantic, first in Brazil and then in other colonies. One of our first stops was the port city of Elmina. There we visited an old fortress, initially a Portuguese castle, around which the government is trying to develop tourism related to the history of slavery. This stronghold, which served as a slave market, is an essential stop on the "Slave Trail," a kind of flip side, if you will, to the Freedom Trail in Boston.

I did not appreciate the severity of the monetary crisis in Ghana until I stopped at the bank shortly after crossing the border from the Ivory Coast. When I asked the teller for $200 worth of cedis, the local currency, he responded by passing an empty black plastic bag through the slot in his window. I was about to blurt out, "What's this?" when I suddenly noticed that everyone around me was carrying black plastic sacks, most of them filled almost to overflowing with cash. I had been to countries where the money had lost so much of its value that it was hardly worth the paper it was printed on. And like everyone I had seen pictures from Weimar, Germany, of people turning over wheelbarrows full of cash just to buy a loaf of bread. It had always struck me as such an extraordinary image that I could hardly believe there had been a time when it had actually happened. Until I experienced it myself in Ghana.

At first Paige and I were worried about carrying so much cash around in plain view. We soon realized, however, that even a large bag full of money did not go very far in Ghana anymore. The largest denomination in which the cedi was printed was worth less than fifty cents U.S. A thief would need a small truck to cart off enough cedis to buy anything of real value.

The seriousness of the currency problem really revealed itself when we tried to do business with local merchants. We wanted to buy some of the kente cloth for which Ghana is famous, the colorful patchwork material woven by craftsmen from the Ashanti region. I asked a local where I could buy the best fabric. "God knows" was the answer I received, which I took to be surprisingly impolite, and asked someone else. "God knows," I was told a second time. Before things degenerated into a dizzying Abbott-and-Costello routine, I realized that "God Knows" was the given name of the man for whom I was looking.

Ghana, especially in the south, is heavily Christian, and everything—certain people being no exception, apparently—went by Christian monikers: Hail Mary Plumbing, the I Love Jesus Service Station, the Holy Mary Dry Cleaners. The best weaver in town of kente cloth was God Knows Setordzi.

God Knows was a smart businessman. When he heard we were looking for him, he took the initiative and tracked us down at our hotel. His kente cloth was beautiful: rich yellows, greens, reds, and blues, finely woven. And we bought some. But when it came time to pay, God Knows did not want anything out of my black plastic bag. He would take only U.S. dollars. Soon Paige and I learned that merchants in Ghana would not take credit cards either. Just like the hotel owners in Yugoslavia, they knew it would be a month or more before they received the credit card company's check, and by then their nation's currency might have dropped far enough to turn profit to loss.

In the case of sound money versus fiat money, Ghana was Exhibit A.

Ghana, first a Portuguese colony, then French, eventually ended up in the hands of the British. Which goes a long way toward explaining why in independent Ghana today, unlike in Senegal, the Ivory Coast, and other former French colonies, the nation's currency is collapsing.

The Ivory Coast, the African nation from which we had just come, though heavily in debt, had one of the strongest economies on the continent. Its gross domestic product had grown by 6 percent annually since 1996. It was the world's largest producer and exporter of cocoa. Abidjan, its capital, was a bustling city. It was one place I might have gone if I were an entrepreneur in Africa intent on making a fortune. In Abidjan there were no problems using a credit card. The local currency was rock solid.

What made the difference? The difference between Britain and France.

In the 1950s and '60s, when Ghana, Nigeria, and Gambia gained their independence, the British pretty much just pulled out and left, leaving the new governments to fend for themselves. Each formed its own central bank and printed its own currency. French colonies, such as the Ivory Coast, by contrast, still maintained strong connections to France. In every city we visited in French colonial Africa, the French influence was quite visible. We met many French businessmen, walked by French militia on the streets, ate in splendid French restaurants, and purchased high-quality French wines and cheeses. In bookstores, just as one can in France, we could buy maps of the world that highlight "French-speaking" countries, the kind used in French schools around the world. The French continued to play a hand in local politics, but, even more important, the fourteen former French colonies in Africa used the "franc de la Communauté Financière Africaine," or CFA franc, as currency.

Tied to the French franc at about a hundred of the latter (and now tied to the euro), the currency, imposed on these countries by the government in Paris, has had a profound impact on their financial stability.

When Jerry Rawlings, Ghana's former dictator, wanted to boost his nation's money supply, he simply instructed Ghana's central bank to print more. He did so for years, and that is what sent the value of the cedi spiraling down. When we were in Ghana, an election was under way, and whenever an election is under way anywhere, governments that are able to do so print money, even the United States. Look at U.S. government expenditures for the last half of the year 2000, and you will see a measurable increase. The French learned the folly of this behavior the hard way. They printed money repeatedly for several decades and suffered the consequences. In 1982 they put a stop to this practice.

If the president of the Ivory Coast wants to inject more cash into the system, he must go to the central bank that governs the money supply for all fourteen CFA countries. All of them are similarly limited and must exercise some fiscal discipline.

All this having been said, these countries are not without their problems. Since their leaders cannot always print more currency, they often borrow quite heavily. The Ivory Coast is one of the more heavily indebted nations in the world, which leads to tensions in what was one of the more stable African countries. In Togo, when we arrived, the border guards were less interested in the trinkets we might give them than in any money we could spare, because they had not been paid in three months. They told us they would rather work for the government and be unpaid than be unemployed with no hope of *ever* being paid.

The former French colonies may have wretched economies at times, but they do have sound currencies. Capital will flow to economies where investors know the currency will not decline in value. Such strict management and the fact that the CFA franc is now tied to the euro have made the African currency stronger, and that strength bodes well for the future of their economies. The fourteen countries are even investigating the possibility of establishing a free-trade zone.

While this is happening, the standard of living in Ghana is dropping. It is hard to attract capital when the country's money always loses value. Soon the country will not be able to import anything, because the cedi will have become worthless. Given Ghana's heavy dependence on foreign oil, the ramifications could be quite serious. Nigeria, another former British colony, with the largest population in Africa, is also in trouble for similar reasons. There, in one of the largest oil-producing nations in the world, I would have trouble getting fuel for my car.

I looked forward to discussing Ghana's policies with my broker in Accra when he and I finally met.

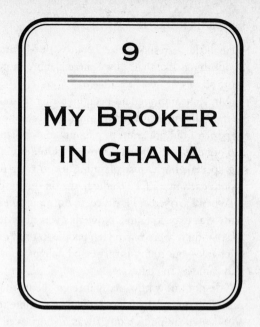

# 9

# MY BROKER
# IN GHANA

IN THE 1960S, '70S, AND '80S, most countries in Africa with stock exchanges would not let foreigners buy shares, a holdover from the "throw out the colonialists" days. During the 1990s, African leaders came to realize that they needed to attract capital, so the rules started changing. At that time I was optimistic about Africa, and I wanted to participate. Through the country's UN representative in the United States, I found the name of a broker in Ghana, Mr. Clarkson Acheampong at Merchant Bank (Ghana) Ltd., contacted him by phone and by fax, opened an account, and bought shares. I did that on the first day it was legal to do so in Ghana. My money was there on day one.

Periodically, over the years, I would make other investments through Mr. Acheampong. We exchanged correspondence, but we never met. In fact, rarely did we even talk, the phone service in Ghana being what it was. Much of our correspondence was written. My shares—in banks and breweries in Ghana—all went up a lot in value, which was to be expected since they were worth virtually nothing when I bought them. Any dividends I received, I would just use to buy more shares. And what little correspondence I had with Mr. Acheampong was mainly about things like that: "I see there is more money. Please buy me some more shares."

Mr. Acheampong had been investing my money for me for several years. I did not know anything about him; he was a name on a sheet of paper. I did not want to pass up an opportunity to go see him, and as I got closer to Ghana, I wrote and told him I was on my way. Nothing special. I was just planning to go over for a cursory hello. We would each put a face to the name on our respective sheets of paper.

When I arrived at his office, to my amazement, everyone in the company was expecting me. Now, this was not Merrill Lynch I was going to see—there were maybe ten people in total on the investment side of the bank—but to my surprise and delight, they all wanted to say hello and came by to chat.

I do not know how many foreign clients they had, but I think I was probably one of the few who had ever come to see them.

Mr. Acheampong himself was a short, well-spoken man in his forties. Like bankers all over the world, he wore a suit that appeared to be tailored in London. He would not have drawn a second look on Wall Street. Nor would the other investment people in the office. Like him, they were all well-educated, well-traveled people. We talked about the market and the elections coming up.

Jerry Rawlings, the country's longtime military dictator, was finally stepping down, which I took as another confirmation of my optimism about Africa. We discussed who was likely to win and what was likely to happen to Ghana. I explained to them that their currency was in free fall because the government was printing money to buy the election. They did not like hearing that, nor did they accept that analysis at the time. (They do now.) I told them I would not be putting more money into Ghana until the government's debasing of the currency had come to an end.

From Ghana we continued east along the Gulf of Guinea, through Togo, Benin, and Nigeria, in the direction of Cameroon. The most striking phenomenon of both Togo and Benin is the practice of voodoo. Both countries support populations that are only 30 percent Christian and Muslim combined. The other 70 percent in each country adheres to what are described there as indigenous beliefs. Indigenous beliefs in

Togo and Benin generally mean voodoo. In Benin we visited the Temple of the Python in the town of Ouidah. The dozen or so snakes in the place—they were mainly sleeping—did not know how successful, rich, and powerful they were. The python being the source of spiritual power in the animistic religion, the snakes had the run of the city, roaming the streets unchallenged, going wherever pythons go, like cattle in India. With the exception of people, one presumes, whom they never seemed to bother, the pythons could eat anything they wanted. Across the street from the Temple of the Python was a much larger Roman Catholic church that paled in importance by comparison to the temple. (Christians of *all* denominations in Benin amounted to 15 percent of the population.) To give the church the stature it needed to compete, the pope had found it necessary to upgrade it to a basilica.

The pythons in Benin were not nearly so frightening as the prospect of entering Nigeria. As we approached the Nigerian border, my apprehension grew. For the first time on the trip I was actually scared. Everything we had heard about Nigeria—riots, corruption, mismanagement, bandits, the mutual slaughter practiced by Muslims and Christians, coup after coup—could pretty much be taken for granted and had been reinforced for me personally on my earlier visit to the country. Though Nigeria, as previously stated, is one of the largest oil-producing nations in the world, its chief export is probably organized crime. When we crossed the border, the first border guard I met said, "Give me some money."

Everybody, all the way down the African coast, kept saying, "You ought to avoid Nigeria; it will ruin your experience of Africa."

The son of the former dictator had testified while on trial that he alone, the son, had taken $750 million in cash out of Nigeria for his family, in boxes and bags from various and sundry bank accounts. The president of Texaco Nigeria, who had been sent there because everybody was stealing from the company, told us that he had been at the central bank one day when the former dictator's wife came in with a lot of friends, all carrying suitcases. About to go to Europe, they cleaned the bank out of all its U.S. dollars.

Nigeria, a member of OPEC, has vast amounts of oil and natural gas, but the resources are of little benefit to Nigerians. (The country's population of some 130 million is the largest in Africa.) All the money is stolen, for the most part. Or was. There are four refineries in Nigeria. When we were there, none of them worked for lack of capital. During our visit, parliamentary elections were under way, and Parliament passed a measure giving itself $200 million so that each of its members could buy a luxury car and partake of a $30,000 furniture allowance.

We did not want to spend much time in Nigeria. We were in and out in a few days, and the border was just as bad as everything else. Trying to leave the country, we had to visit eight separate stations. Few people crossed the border—there was serious trouble between Nigeria and Cameroon—but forty people were employed there. It was not as though there were a big demand for personnel. Looking at the books, I discovered that only three people had crossed the border that day.

Nigeria, like most of Africa, was created by fiat. There is no rhyme or reason to its borders; some European simply said, "This is Nigeria." And its internal strife is particularly hellish. Take the attempted secession of Biafra in the mid-1960s, and the seven thousand people recently slaughtered in Islamic-Christian clashes, and you have a pretty good picture of the country's political viability. Miss World 2002 was Nigerian, but the contest for her successor had to be moved to London because of religious riots. I do not anticipate that Nigeria will survive as a nation.

"Jim Rogers?"

This time it was not a motorcycle but a black Toyota four-by-four, and not Madrid but the wilds of western Cameroon. Paige and I were refueling the Mercedes at a gas station in Kumba and had attracted a pretty large crowd—soon we were surrounded by what could accurately be described as a mob—when I heard my name being called by a man whose local stature was only marginally reflected by his ownership of a new sport-utility vehicle. He was not wearing a suit, but his casual wear would have been acceptable at any London cocktail party, and when he stepped out of the car, the crowd of some three hundred local people, the most prosperous of whom were wearing jeans, grew quiet. When he walked over to introduce himself, all stood aside to let him through.

His name was Mukete Ekale, which did not tell me much about him. His title was Prince, which did. Though long since co-opted by

*The python is the source of spiritual power in the animistic religion practiced by a majority of the people in Benin.*

*My barber in Gabon offered a variety of stylish cuts.*

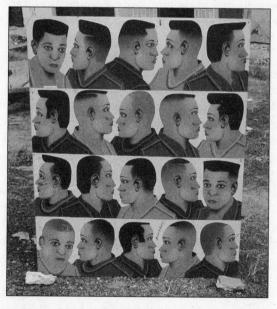

the British and outweighed in actual authority by the country's president, Mukete's father was still titular king of the region surrounding the town of Kumba. Educated in England, Mukete had worked in the City of London, that city's financial district, and had read what I had written over the years, my articles and columns and my book. He remembered with delight that I had been optimistic on Cameroon in the past. Here at a gas pump in the wilds of Africa—here in an equatorial rain forest where I would dine on armadillo, wild boar, and porcupine—I had run across a reader.

I thought the malaria must have been kicking in.

He invited us back to his home, a large colonial plantation house on the outskirts of Kumba, where we had lunch with him and his brother. (We saw them again in the capital, Yaoundé, and had dinner with them a couple of times.) Meeting his brother Godfrey only served to make the episode that much more surreal. Godfrey, also a prince, was an Eli—Yale class of 1975. He was about to head back to the United States to attend a class reunion.

It was just one more improbable encounter in a journey that was rife with them, but informative as they all were. I could see the wonderful opportunities in rubber, pineapples, and other agriculture in Cameroon. Under government direction, progress had been pathetic, so I thought of buying land and reviving production. The brothers quickly informed me that it was illegal for foreigners to buy land in Cameroon. I protested that new capital and expertise would provide jobs and income for everyone's benefit, but they gravely rejected the idea. I then realized that one reason land was so cheap was that most potential buyers were banned. Many Africans complain that land is undervalued in their countries, but they bring it upon themselves. The land could bring great riches for all, but they would rather let it deteriorate than let in "foreigners."

Thank goodness the United States did not take such an approach when the nation was developing. We begged foreigners to come and buy whatever they wanted. We gave them land if they would move west and develop it. And we went from being an insignificant little chaotic country to being the most successful and powerful nation on earth.

One of the reasons for my earlier optimism on Cameroon and Africa had been my conviction that the new group of leaders was different from the previous cast of "liberators" who had become crooked dictators. Here it was a decade later, and Cameroon's president, whom I had regarded with optimism on my last trip through the country, had turned out to be no better than his predecessors. Exploiting linguistic and ethnic differences, he was stealing with the best of them.

I wondered if my earlier enthusiasm for the development of Africa were misplaced.

We left Cameroon on May 10 and, traversing Equatorial Guinea, arrived in Gabon on the same day. Much of the time we spent there was devoted to getting ourselves south, through the war-torn Republic of the Congo—avoiding the even more seriously war-torn Democratic Republic of the Congo (formerly Zaire)—and into war-torn Angola.

In Gabon we crossed the equator, but because almost nobody but local residents followed the route, there was little opportunity to commemorate the event, as there was at crossings in other countries. There was a simple sign in the weeds that said, L'EQUATEUR, and we stopped only long enough to take a snapshot. Gabon was the only country in the world that had the millennium right. It would celebrate the start of the new millennium as January 1, 2001. Other than that, it had gotten little else right. Huge oil wealth had been squandered in the 1970s. The buildings had become seedy and the paved highways have become mud tracks again. Six of the first seven officials we encountered refused us passage in the absence of payoffs. A *cadeau* is one thing, but these were out-and-out bribes.

In Gabon, unlike in Benin, the python is not sacred. I ate both python and boa constrictor before leaving the country. As we traveled south through Gabon, we saw monkeys and parrots for sale. Hanging dead, suspended from sticks by the side of the road, they were not being sold as pets.

In Libreville, the capital, we stopped in at the Congolese Embassy. It was our understanding that the recent civil war in the Congo was winding down, but we wanted all the information we could get. Since buying our visas in Abidjan, we had continued to check with Congolese officials as we headed south, gauging the viability of getting into the country.

"Can we drive through the country?" we asked the consular official in Libreville.

"No problem," he said. "As long as your visas are valid."

"They are."

"May I see them?"

We handed over our visas.

"That's not a visa," he said.

"We bought them at your embassy in Abidjan."

"We don't have an embassy in Abidjan."

The man selling Congolese visas out of an elaborate office in the Ivory Coast, we were told, was a crook. Our visas were fraudulent. So we bought more from the man in Libreville. Who knew which were valid?

"Go on," he said. "You can go south."

And that is what we did.

For purposes of clarification: there are two Congos. There is the Republic of the Congo, where we were headed, which was formerly part of French Equatorial Africa. With its capital at Brazzaville and its strong ties to France, the country was undergoing a difficult transition from civil war to multiparty democracy. But its modern history was not nearly so tumultuous as that of the former Belgian Congo, now called the Democratic Republic of the Congo, which, since independence in 1960, had been giving new meaning to the word "instability." Between 1971 and 1997, under the regime of Mobutu Sese Seko, the country was known as Zaire. At the time Paige and I were traveling, Mobutu, whose regime had been marked by unprecedented corruption, had recently been driven from office, and the civil war that led to his ouster was still under way.

After visiting the Congolese Embassy in Libreville, we inquired at the office of Gabon's minister of transportation and tourism. We were still unsure whether the road was safe and passable. I always made a habit of seeking information from several sources. I found that most people in positions of officialdom preferred to give bad information to no information. Rather than admit that they did not know the answer to a question, they would lie.

"Is the road down there safe?" we wanted to know.

"Absolutely no problem," we were told. "You can drive down there with no worry."

"What do you hear about the condition of the road?"

"The road in Gabon is good, and the road in the Congo is good, too."

It was clear from the way the man said it that he had no idea what he was talking about. And he had absolutely no qualms about winging it.

About 250 miles later, 29 miles north of the border, in a little village called Ndendé, we discovered that the border was closed.

"Don't go down there, you're wasting your time, you're not going to get across it," we were told.

It was the truth, unfortunately, and we finally heard it from a couple of Frenchmen who had a logging operation in Ndendé. They were harvesting exotic hardwoods for export.

"How do you get your trees out of here?" I asked them.

They trucked them over to the coast, they said, to the town of Mayumba, for shipment to Europe. Mayumba seemed to be the only town of any consequence. And if there were ships or even barges there picking up lumber, perhaps we could find a captain who would agree to carry a couple of vehicles and a party of adventurers. We were not about to turn back, so we headed west.

We wound up staying in Mayumba three or four days. We stayed in a beautiful cabin on a cliff overlooking the valley, part of a fading luxury complex (we provided the diesel needed to generate electricity) owned by an aging Frenchman who had been there for forty years. Eventually we arranged for a barge and a tug to take us out into the Atlantic, around the closed border, and into the port city of Pointe-Noire in the Congo.

The only way to load the cars was to drive them right onto the barge, and we could do that only at low tide. But the barge could get out of the harbor only at high tide, so the better part of the afternoon passed between loading and departure. Paige spent the time shopping. She had become very excited when the crew said she could use the kitchen. She bought the best ingredients she could find, and by the time we got under way, she was cooking up a storm. As soon as we hit the Atlantic, she fell flat on the floor, seasick. For the next twenty hours or so she lay on the deck. I did the cooking.

Within a few days of our arrival in Pointe-Noire, we crossed the border into Cabinda, which is separated from Angola proper by the Democratic Republic of the Congo's outlet to the sea, granted to the king of Belgium in 1884 by the Treaty of Berlin. The king of Belgium got the mouth of the Congo River, and the king of Portugal maintained possession of that section of Angola (Portuguese West Africa) currently known as Cabinda, which proved to be flush with vast amounts of oil. I had not told Paige that I had heard on the BBC that secessionists there were kidnapping foreigners that week and holding them hostage. But when we reached the regional capital, the city of Cabinda, it became pretty clear pretty quickly that there was political unrest. We were clearly in a war zone. The hotels had been destroyed; the entire city appeared to have been firebombed. No sooner did we arrive than we started making arrangements to get ourselves farther south.

Anticipating (correctly) the impossibility of traversing the border of the former Zaire, we had asked the Angolan ambassador in Gabon how one got from Cabinda to Luanda, the Angolan capital—from one end of his country to the middle.

"There is a regular ferry two days a week."

"So if we find we can't drive . . ."

"You just take the ferry."

"Have you taken the ferry?" Paige asked, by now suspicious of all official pronouncements.

"I was on it last year. It takes two days to travel from Cabinda to Luanda. It's a nice ferry, don't worry," he said with a smile.

In bombed-out Cabinda, once we found a hotel, we wasted no time investigating the ferry schedule.

"There is no ferry," we were told. "There has not been a ferry for decades."

I went to the "tourism office" in Cabinda, looking for help, and of course the guy there was perplexed, because I said, "How do I get out of here?" He told me there were big plans for Cabinda. There were going to be nightclubs and golf compounds, there would be restaurants, there would be a disco for the oil workers.

"They never come to town, they just stay on their compound," he said, as though he could not understand why.

"The ferry," I said.

"No, there's no ferry."

He knew of no boats. He did not know of any way out.

I continued to make inquiries and ultimately found a young Portuguese businessman, Julio Florida Lopes, who ran a construction company.

"I can maybe get you a barge," he said. "That's how I get my materials in. But it will be two or three weeks at the earliest."

An honest fellow, he could barely bring himself to tell me how much it would cost.

"Five thousand dollars."

It was not so much the price but the two or three weeks that I found troubling.

Here we were in a war zone (the people of Cabinda wanted to take their oil and secede from Angola), and within fifty miles of us there were two other wars (in the former Zaire and in Angola proper) and within a hundred miles, there were three (given the civil strife in the Republic of the Congo). A total of four separate wars, and oddly enough, what I was trying to do (my first choice, to head south) was to drive into one of the more dangerous of them.

We were still driving around, making inquiries and chasing down leads, when passing the airport I saw a gigantic Russian cargo plane on the runway. Banging a turn, I drove the Mercedes out onto the airfield and raced out across the tarmac. The cargo plank was down, and loading was under way. Overseeing the operation was a two-star general in the Angolan Army. He was headed to Luanda.

"Will you fly us out of here?" I asked.

He said he would do it for $400 U.S.

"I'm leaving in forty minutes," he added.

We raced back to the hotel, got our stuff, and, even pausing to deal with a dead battery, we made it back to the airfield on time.

"We're ready to go," I told him.

"Where's the twelve hundred dollars?"

He had a fish, and he knew it. But what could I do? Twelve thousand would have been cheap. I already knew a barge would cost $5,000, if and when. Organizing a charter flight to come pick us up, with a cargo plane large enough to carry the vehicles—what would that have cost? Assuming it could be done. Fifty thousand? More? Who knows how much? I shelled out the $1,200 as fast as I could, before he could change his mind.

Inside the plane when we drove aboard were probably three hundred people. There were soldiers, civilians, old men who looked like lawyers, young people who were clearly students, men and women of all ages, a mass of people sitting on the floor, lying on the floor, standing, every form of humanity you can imagine. And even as the plane was pulling away and the crew members were pulling up the cargo plank, they were pulling people aboard the plane. There were no seats, no safety precautions of any kind. With the exception of the six Russian and Ukrainian aircrew, we were the only outsiders on board. The others were obviously friends of the general, or people who had influence with him. He was without doubt the most powerful man in Cabinda. He was commander of all the troops in the region.

Upon landing forty-five minutes later at an air base in Luanda, we would discover that this cargo plane was one of two on lease from Russia to the Angolan military. While we were airborne, the crew invited Paige and me to visit the cabin. Paige took them up on the offer, and I followed a little later to see what was going on. When I got there, the entire flight crew was drinking vodka. I turned down their offer to join them, figuring somebody had to keep his wits about him.

(Two months later, listening to BBC Africa, I heard that the plane had crashed and that everyone aboard had been killed. Two months after that, the second aircraft went down, likewise leaving no survivors.)

The civil war in Angola had been raging for more than twenty years, not including the warfare that had led to independence in 1975. For many years the war had been financed by the two superpowers and fought with troops contributed by Soviet and U.S. clients, Cuba and South Africa. An ideological battleground until the collapse of the Soviet Union, Angola had put the United States into dubious partnership with an apartheid government fighting to overthrow a government in Angola that was democratically elected. The end of the Cold War and the departure of the two superpowers should have put an end to the conflict. No one on the government side wanted to be a Communist anymore. Then the U.S.-backed side, UNITA, again refused to accept the results of the democratic election. It was another case where our support of a tyrant, Jonas Savimbi, wound up making us more enemies than friends. So much for a war over "democracy and communism" fought by innocent boys from the pariah nations Cuba and South Africa. In the beginning, the public had been rallied to war by appeals to emotion and ideology. Now the conflict took power from more tangible forces: oil and diamonds, the real story all along.

Situated on a large bay in picturesque surroundings, Luanda, in the absence of war, could be Rio or Stockholm. But war has made it a hellhole, seedy and run down, its buildings collapsing, everything in disrepair. Walking streets named for Communist heroes—Avenues Che Guevara, Karl Marx, Fidel Castro, and the like—we shared the sidewalks with a crushing population driven from the countryside by war. Everywhere I looked I could see a strong entrepreneurial spirit at work, enormous amounts of energy and motivation just waiting to be harnessed.

It reinforced an impression from my last trip that had begun to build again in me as I traveled through Africa, whose population has an image in the West of being congenitally lazy or crooked or both. Nothing, I confirmed, could be further from the truth. Throughout Africa I would encounter vast numbers of people with talent and drive willing to labor from dawn to dusk, their work ethic no less powerful than that of the Chinese.

And this only added to the sadness of driving through the battle-fields of southern Angola. As we made our way down the coast, we thought of all the young soldiers, black and white, who had died fighting for communism or apartheid, they and all the innocent civil-ians who had perished in a hopeless civil war, in support of ideologies that had now essentially vanished.

At a checkpoint not far south of Luanda, we had been told, we would be prevented from proceeding without a military convoy. We were prepared for that. We knew now that in many places that was simply how the world worked. Arriving at the checkpoint, we entered the guardhouse and asked when the next convoy was scheduled to depart. Officials in the capital had explained that there were two con-voys a day, morning and afternoon.

"There are not enough people for a convoy," the guard informed us. "You can park over there," he said, pointing to an eighteen-wheeler parked by the side of the road, the only other civilian vehicle in evidence, "and when we get enough people, we will put a convoy together."

"How soon do you think that will be?" I asked.

"I don't know, maybe next week. Maybe next month."

"Jim, we can't sit here like prey," said Paige.

There had been no reports of guerrilla activity for several weeks, I learned after asking around. And so, weighing our options—waiting here, camped on the edge of a war zone for a week or two weeks or who knew how long, or proceeding on our own without a military convoy—we decided to push on. The guard, who had fallen asleep, did not seem to care one way or the other. On nothing more than our assurance that everything would be fine up ahead, he let us pass.

Over the next many miles, we ran into soldiers with regularity, some of them no older than fifteen, stopping us at various intervals, each one more dumbfounded than the next to see us pull up to his checkpoint. We gave out a lot of Marlboros and took a lot of Polaroids over that period. We were heading for Benguela, a port city we had been told was controlled by the government. All along our route we passed bombed-out vehicles, cars, trucks, buses, their charred remains occupying the middle of the road.

"We must be nuts," said Paige. "This is a serious war zone." Noting a complete absence of traffic, she added, "We've seen nothing but soldiers."

About twenty-five kilometers outside the city, as we were coming up to the rise of a hill, a soldier stepped into the road and stopped us. We gave him cigarettes and talked him into letting us proceed. We were delayed, however, by our videographer, who was lagging about three kilometers behind, filming footage of all the carnage in our wake. Ordinarily, we would have raised him on our walkie-talkie to hurry him up, but we worried that pulling out communications equipment might spook the army. Two-way radios and cameras had a way of raising suspicions among even the most sophisticated soldiers.

While we were waiting for the second vehicle to catch up, an officer made his way down the hill and told us we were not allowed to go any farther. We pleaded, we argued, to no avail. We were forced to spend the night by the side of the road.

That night was the only time during the entire trip that Paige actually cried out of fear. She had cried before, but never out of fear, and she had been fearful many times but had never cried. She insisted on sleeping in the car, so we never even pitched the tent. Surrounded by all these soldiers, adolescent boys, laughing and giggling in the dark, she had no idea what they wanted, whether it might be money, her, the car, me. It was unclear why they had stopped us. We spent the night terrified, unable to sleep, and rose very early the next morning.

This was clearly the point installation protecting the city. If the rebels were going to attack, this is where the assault would begin. I had to assume that the soldiers assigned to this post were on edge.

*The only night Paige cried from fear was the night we were*
*forced by an Angolan army general to camp with his soldiers*
*on the front line they were holding in their war*
*with UNITA rebels.*

And for that reason I was very careful, and very slow, as I ingratiated myself that morning with the officer in charge, to raise the possibility of taking Polaroids. He gave me permission, I took a picture of him, and he loved it. He was absolutely thrilled. He gathered all his boys around him, all their guns and artillery and rocket launchers, everything, all their ammunition, and we took picture after picture. Finally he said we could go. And he wanted to travel with us to the top of the hill, so he could introduce us to his general.

It was when we reached the top of the hill that everything was made clear to us. About three hundred meters beyond the hill was a bridge. And the reason we had been refused passage was that by the time we arrived, the bridge, as it was every night, had been mined. They mined the bridge to prevent the rebel forces from either crossing it or mining it themselves. They removed the mines every morning. Had we crossed the night before, as the young soldier had been prepared to let us do before his commanding officer intervened, we would have been blown to pieces.

We met the general—more soldiers, more Polaroids—crossed the bridge, and drove into Benguela, a glorious town, uncluttered by foreigners, where we ate wonderful seafood. (Along this stretch of coast one finds the largest crabs of their kind in the world, and, largely unharvested because of the war, they are available, all you can eat, for a dollar.) As we traveled farther south, we traversed some of the most beautiful countryside we had seen on the whole trip, completely untouched, untrammeled by tourists (as I suppose one would expect of a war zone).

The border crossing into Namibia, the former South-West Africa, took a matter of minutes. The customs agent seemed excited to have us. The immigration agent actually said, "Welcome to Namibia. I hope you will bring investors." He did not know I was an investor; he was simply giving voice to government policy. The country's openness to investment was sincere and had trickled down to the grass roots. Our reception stood in stark contrast to the treatment we received in Mali, for example. There we had come upon a billboard encouraging investment in the country, and our cameraman had been arrested for filming it. We had been subjected to more harassment at the hands of the police in Mali than we had anywhere other than Georgia and Russia. In Namibia, they actually seemed glad to have us there.

*Lesotho*

*Beijing*

*Australia: roadhouse*

*Belize*

*Western China*

*Outback of Australia*

*Namibia*

*Hamburg red light district*

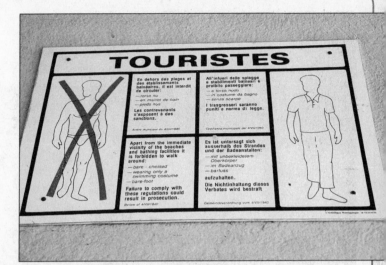

# TOURISTES

En dehors des plages et des établissements balnéaires, il est interdit de circuler:
— torse nu
— en maillot de bain
— pieds nus

**Les contrevenants s'exposent à des sanctions.**

*Arrêté municipal du 4/VII/1940*

All'infuori delle spiagge e stabilimenti balneari è proibito passeggiare:
— a torso nudo
— in costume da bagno
— senza scarpe

**I trasgressori saranno puniti a norma di legge.**

*Ordinanza municipale del 4/VII/1940*

Apart from the immediate vicinity of the beaches and bathing facilities it is forbidden to walk around:
— bare - chested
— wearing only a swimming costume
— bare-foot

**Failure to comply with these regulations could result in prosecution.**

*By-law of 4/VII/1940*

Es ist untersagt sich ausserhalb des Strandes und der Badeanstalten:
— mit unbekleidetem Oberkörper
— im Badeanzug
— barfuss

aufzuhalten.

**Die Nichtinhaltung dieses Verbotes wird bestraft**

*Gemeindeverordnung vom 4/VII/1940*

*Even in Monte Carlo?*

*Iran has a strict dress code even for men at its "resorts."*

*Dangerous Pakistan*

*India*

Persons who dirty public places, are social criminals.

Culprits can be fined and arrested.

Littering, Spitting or Urinating in public places is an offence and culprits can be fined Rs. 100/- to Rs. 2500/- and arrested.

BE AN ALERT CITIZEN. KEEP MUMBAI CLEAN.

BRIHANMUMBAI MAHANAGARPALIKA

*Bangladesh is a dry country.*

# NOTICE

It is notified for information of guests that only foreign nationals are allowed to bring their own alcoholic drinks within the premises of the restaurant.

This is as per the law of the land which is governed by the Liquor and Narcotics control department of the Government of Bangladesh.

By order of
The Management

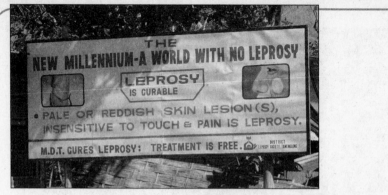

*India*

*Australia: roadhouse*

*Australia: opal-mine shafts*

*Dubai: ladies' beach*

*Mongolian rock group*

Water is rare in Patagonia.

Crossing the equator in Gabon, 10,300 kilometers from New York

*Six-hundred-year-old library in the Sahara*

*Pick your style in Gabon.*

*Isolationism in Australia*

*I should move my office to China.*

*Tanzania*

*Watch for alpaca while crossing the Andes in Bolivia.*

*Watch for koala bears crossing in Australia.*

South Africa

Guatemala

LA HOJA DE COCA

En los momentos en que vuestro espíritu melancólico quiera fingir
un poco de alegría, esas hojas adormecerán vuestra pena y os
darán la ilusión de creeros felices.

*The Valley of the Coca Leaf, Bolivia: "Boost Your Spirits"*

*It's a long way to Alaska from the bottom of South America.*

Parque Nacional
Tierra del Fuego
BAHIA LAPATAIA
República Argentina
Aqui finaliza la Ruta Nac. N° 3
Buenos Aires 3.063 Km.
Alaska 17.848 Km.

*A most descriptive pharmacy in Mali*

Aboubacar Cisse Guerisseur en
PHARMACOPEE

*Forbidden City*

The town just across the border, Ondangwa, was booming. Angolans came here to buy all the goods unavailable at home due to war. There were warehouses, shops, new hotels. In Ondangwa I was approached by a smuggler who was associated with the rebels in Angola and who offered to buy my vehicles and pay me in diamonds. From him I learned that diamonds smuggled out of Angola were sold for an average $500 a carat in Johannesburg, South Africa. He showed me his diamonds, and when I finally got him to accept that neither Mercedes was for sale, he offered to sell me the diamonds for cash. He said they were worth $70,000. I paid him $500. I was very proud of myself. It was just one more skillful deal on the black market by the Indiana Jones of investors.

From a diamond merchant in Tanzania I learned that they were glass.

Now, how many times have I told people that you should never invest in something unless you yourself know an enormous amount about it? It is a mantra of mine: "No, I am not going to give you any hot tips. The only successful way to invest is to know what you are investing in, and to know it cold. If you do not know about an apple orchard in Washington, do not get into the apple business."

So I bought a handful of diamonds that turned out to be glass.

It was my first and last investment in Namibia.

For a variety of reasons, I did not want to drive through Zimbabwe. From all the press reports we received, it was clear that outbreaks of violence were widespread. President Robert Mugabe was, and still is, engaged in his own form of ethnic cleansing. He has been quite up front about his intention to drive all the whites from his country, to take possession of their money and their land. But there was another, equally persuasive argument against our going. From those same press advisories, and from everyone we talked to, we learned that diesel fuel was virtually unobtainable.

Zimbabwe's foreign minister was a man I knew from New York, when he had been the country's ambassador to the United Nations, and I had investments in the country's stock market held over from previous years. But there was virtually no foreign investment now, and with the currency undergoing collapse, money was moving the other way. To the degree that people could get money out, everybody was doing so. As far as looking for opportunities, there was nothing to be gained by a visit.

Furthermore, my professed intention was to circumnavigate most of Africa, to drive down the west coast to the Cape of Good Hope and up the east coast to Cairo, hoping to become the first person ever to do so. Heading into Zimbabwe at this point, and thus erasing South Africa and Mozambique from the itinerary, would undermine the challenge I had set for myself. While we might on the northern leg be able to slip westward into Zimbabwe, there was every reason on earth for us to skip the country altogether.

But there was one reason we had to go: Victoria Falls.

Extending more than a mile across the Zambezi River, half again as wide as Niagara Falls and almost twice as high, the cascade, its roar audible and its steam cloud visible from more than six miles away, was discovered by David Livingstone ("Dr. Livingstone, I presume?") in 1855. I first sighted the falls 136 years later, in March 1991. We dashed over because I just could not let my wife go through life without having seen them. Victoria Falls were revealed in all their awesome glory to Paige Parker on June 14, 2000, nearly six months into our honeymoon.

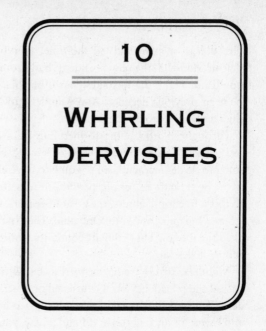

# 10

## WHIRLING DERVISHES

THE LAST TIME I had been in South Africa, it had been controlled by a white minority government under the rules of apartheid. And the death of apartheid in the early 1990s, while of great moral and historical moment, was one of the few good things I was able to record about the country on this trip.

As we drove around a refurbished Cape Town, which had succeeded in becoming a center of culture and commerce with world-class hotels and restaurants, my high expectations were challenged by the ever presence of horrible slums. Even the new residential construction in the city, replacing the earlier shantytown dwellings, created living conditions that were little better. The houses were constructed row upon row, packed tightly together, and in neighborhoods all over the city people were unhappy. Demonstrations were commonplace, and Cape Town's crime rate was escalating dramatically. The police force was unable to cope—although it did find time to waste harassing us a couple of times.

South Africa's troubles were due in great part to dashed expectations, the government's inability to deliver on the optimism that came with defeat of apartheid. At the time, everybody had thought, and Nelson Mandela, the new president, had promised, that South Africa would not make the mistakes that other black African nations had made in previous decades. And Mandela, to the degree that he was able, had delivered on the promise.

Throughout Africa, the former European colonies, imbued with new freedom often bought with oceans of blood, claimed, "We're going to be democracies, we're going to have elections, we're going to create better nations for our people." It was not long, however, before all those freedom fighters, the great liberators, became dictators themselves. One man, one vote. One time. They liked being in power. They liked the money. They ruined economies, entire societies. Capital fled, people fled.

Mandela, to his credit, stepped aside when his term was up and passed the presidency on. He insisted on elections, and his vice president, Thabo Mbeki, was elected to replace him. (If I were Mandela and I were in my eighties and I had a new, young girlfriend and I had spent twenty-seven years in prison, I would not want to be sitting around trying to run things, either.) But, in my opinion, the only thing currently holding South Africa together is the fact that Mandela is alive. As a symbol he is very powerful, everywhere, with everybody. He could walk into a riot, and it would stop immediately. Once he dies, I am much less optimistic about the country's prospects.

In South Africa I saw the same sort of corruption and lack of discipline that ruined other African nations after independence. South Africa, with little to sell the rest of the world—gold and diamonds are its primary exports—had the most extraordinary infrastructure we had seen since leaving Morocco, but it was not being maintained. The new minister of roads acknowledged that the country was spending less than half of what was required for maintenance. Being close to the ground, I could corroborate that, unfortunately. And while we were there, the government, to make matters worse, was debasing the currency. Stories of political corruption were rampant. Mandela and Mbeki, while learning their lessons from the failure of their sub-Saharan neighbors, had been unable to control a government that was responsive to eleven official ethnic groups.

Right now, black South Africans are furious at their lack of economic progress. They expected more of a black government, and what they got was more of the same, bureaucrats as dishonest and incompetent and equally as horrible as those they endured when whites were running the country. They got a government as slipshod as any in the world. (One can obtain professional certification by paying the right price; I was disheartened when I heard about the "special fees" for barbers and lawyers but horrified when I heard even nurse's and pilot's licenses were available.) And to make matters worse, they got foreigners. We met a lot of black Americans who had moved to South Africa, pulling up stakes as people always do when a new frontier opens up. And many of them are resented by black South Africans, who accuse them of being arrogant and patronizing, acting as if they were smarter than the locals, as if they were doing everyone a favor by showing up. The locals kept calling them the new "Ugly Americans."

South Africa has three capital cities, Cape Town, Pretoria, and Bloemfontein, the legislative, executive, and judicial capitals, respectively. We visited all three, and I saw nothing to make me any less pessimistic about the country's future. In Johannesburg, we visited a white South African who had been one of my closest friends at Oxford. He and his wife, who is black, have two children. She took Paige to the black school at which she taught in Alexandra Township, a black enclave left over from apartheid. The all-black school, she explained bitterly, was faring worse under the present government than it had under apartheid. The black government placed less emphasis on, and invested less money in, the education of blacks than had the white government. Her new principal was nothing more than a political hack, concerned only about the security of his job and how he might be able to use the power it gave him to enrich himself. He knew little about education and cared less. Locals of every ethnic group are now leaving the country.

My friend's wife took Paige to an AIDS orphanage in Johannesburg so that she might see firsthand the effects of the disease making front-page headlines around the world. That evening we had dinner with a prominent African consultant, and Paige recounted the heartbreak of seeing so many HIV-positive children facing the same fate as their deceased parents. It was a horrible plague, we all agreed, visited upon Africa and the world, and unfortunately, he reported, it was nearly impossible to compile solid statistics on the extent of it. Despite their apparent precision—and the UN figures were staggering—

the numbers were based not on scientific estimates but on guesswork, extrapolated and promoted, often, by people whose intentions were good. Often they varied according to politics.

His experience, which was extensive—his work took him all over the continent—confirmed our experience on the ground. An absence of roads and infrastructure in Africa, lack of money and expertise made it impossible to compile accurate statistics. Large parts of the continent were cut off, and in many countries little was known about anything outside the capitals. There were no tools for measuring many of those plagues one associates with Africa: TB, AIDS, poverty, slavery, malaria, refugees, casualties of war. Even if there were a will to do so—and there was no payoff for many governments to use their limited resources for such purposes—there was no mechanism for conducting such things as AIDS tests.

In our travels we met nobody out compiling numbers, nor did we see the massive evidence of death reflected by the numbers that were being published. The populations in the countries we visited were not noticeably declining. This is not to understate the nightmare of the plague. In Africa, we would learn, there is never a shortage of statistics; among the hardest things to find, however, are figures that are reliable.

Leaving South Africa, we stopped in the Kingdom of Swaziland. Unlike the Kingdom of Lesotho, which is entirely surrounded by South Africa, Swaziland shares a border with Mozambique. Lesotho, which we had visited earlier, was set up as a black homeland—an enclave of black self-government or a prison camp, depending on who's talking— by racists in South Africa. Invented as a way to keep blacks in their place, it is as poor and hopeless as one might imagine. Swaziland we found to be faring somewhat better. Educated in England, its king, unlike the king of Lesotho, has power and has been more successful in attracting foreign investment. And that is not all he attracts. Every year, in a ritual that is centuries old, he summons all the virgins in the country. They all show up in traditional dress. In a celebration marked by singing and dancing, he selects one, if he finds one worthy, and marries her, adding to his collection of wives. When we were in Swaziland, at which time he was thirty-two years old, he had seven wives, seven children, and two girlfriends. He recently decreed it immoral and illegal for females under eighteen to have sex. Too many of his cabinet members were having sex with schoolgirls. He later selected a seventeen-year-old as his next wife.

While staying in Johannesburg, we had hopped over to Madagascar. The former French colony, now independent, is the largest island nation, the fourth largest island, and among the poorest countries in the world. Having floated away from continental Africa, Madagascar, drifting off into the Indian Ocean, took with it various forms of fauna and flora that are found nowhere else on earth, making it of great scientific interest. Ten years before we arrived, the smallest mammal known to science, the dwarf lemur, was discovered there. We wanted to visit the rain forest and catch a glimpse of the wildlife. We had heard about the raising of the dead in Madagascar. Four to seven years after one dies, it is customary for the family of the deceased to gather at the grave, dig up the body, rearrange the bones, and fill the dearly departed in on all the news. Sadly, like many newly independent countries, Madagascar suffers from rising political instability. Otherwise, it would be a great destination for travelers.

Mozambique, according to the World Bank and the United Nations, was the poorest country in the world by every standard measurement. The former Portuguese colony was the embodiment of just about everything that was wrong with Africa. And therein, I was convinced, lay a lot of opportunities. Everything was dirt cheap, the government had been saying all the right things, a long civil war had ended, and I arrived on a wave of personal expectation and excitement.

All I found was corruption.

Money was pouring into the country in response to the floods of the year before (the damage, while truly devastating, was not so widespread as the world was led to believe), but it was clear to see that the money was not getting very far. Like the money thrown around by numerous NGOs, it was aimed chiefly at the pockets of various politicians and bureaucrats. (Mozambique is the poster child for my campaign to abolish aid to Africa. I have an alternative plan for the development of the continent that I will lay out in detail later.)

We met an employee of an NGO whose mission was malaria control. He was in Mozambique with a team of people.

"Has there been an outbreak as a result of the floods?" I asked.

"No," he replied, "but there will be."

*Local villagers, unless invited by a guest, were banned from this Lake Malawi resort, which had been booked solid for a week by a German NGO. I invited those who are pictured here.*

*We always sought to do what the locals were doing, such as attending this Mozambique football game. Because the NGO bureaucrats who haunt the Third World rarely do as the locals do, ours were often the only Anglo faces in evidence. (Here, because this is sub-Saharan Africa, Paige is one of only three women.)*

The floods had occurred more than a year before. I thought, if malaria were going to break out as a result of the floods, it had better hurry up. But there he was spending money from headquarters, he and his team, driving around in their air-conditioned four-by-fours with the windows up, living the good life.

My objection to people like this is exceeded only by the contempt in which they are held by the locals.

"If doubt persists, ask the NGOists to send their own children to 'schools' they have created for us," wrote one African journalist.

Africans call them the new colonialists. They act the same way. They look upon the countries the same way. They know more than the locals know, and they have better money than the locals. At least the colonialists had to answer to someone. These people have to answer to nobody. They live in compounds with guards and gates and satellite TVs, and they drive around the country telling the poor locals how dumb they are.

"We're waiting for it. The malaria will come."

If not, he would pray for rain.

Later, in Malawi, we got the last two rooms in a Lake Malawi resort because the entire hotel had been taken over by a German NGO for a week. Government ministers were flying in from all over Africa for a conference. The conference agenda constituted the NGO blue plate special: "assessment and evaluation." While we were in South Africa, President Mbeki had joined Malawi's president, Bakili Muluzi, in denouncing such extravagant wastes of money. Neither would henceforth allow their ministers to attend any of the dozens of similar conferences that took place every year.

Instead of *talking* about the new South Africa, we have to *build* the new South Africa, said Mbeki. We have to stop talking. We have talked enough. We spend all our time going to conferences, and nobody is *doing* anything.

The conferences are a complete waste of time, money, and resources, and they are the definition of modern government service. The African ministers all love them—why do anything to improve your country, when you can stay at a five-star resort and *talk* about what you might do?—and the NGOs love them more.

Our last taste of Mozambique said a lot about what Mbeki and Muluzi were up against in trying to drag their countries into the twenty-first century. As we were leaving the country, heading into Malawi, we were held up by a border official, who insisted we buy car insurance for Mozambique.

"We're leaving."

"You have no car insurance," he said.

"We did everything required of us when we entered the country," I told him. "Here are the stamps—the customs stamps, the immigration stamps. We didn't sneak into the country."

"You have to have car insurance."

"For what? We're not driving in Mozambique. We're leaving. We're never coming back."

"I will not allow you to leave the country unless you buy car insurance from that man right there."

We had to buy thirty days' worth of car insurance before he would allow us to leave.

Tanzania, in my opinion, when it comes to tourism, is the single best country in Africa. You could put together any six other countries on the continent, and the result would not present as complete an African experience as Tanzania offers. And you do not have to work hard to enjoy it—closed off to the rest of the world until the 1980s by Julius Nyerere, that great icon of socialist liberators, it has not yet become overrun by foreign visitors. Tanzania's joys are manifold. It has beautiful beaches on the Indian Ocean. It has the exotic, ancient island of Zanzibar, fabled for Arab trade in pearls and spices, whose history is passed down in the kinds of timeless stories that make your eyes light up. It has the legendary city of Dar es Salaam. It has game parks that are unique in the world, teeming with animals. Near the famous Serengeti Plain, it has Ngorongoro Crater, on the edge of which sits Crater Lodge—as Paige describes it, Versace-comes-to-Africa—completely over the top, with rose petals in the bathtub. Tanzania is one of the safest countries in Africa, as far as Paige and I could tell. And it is cheap. And, after everything else, you can climb Mount Kilimanjaro.

Tanzania was the first country in which we visited a game park where we were allowed to drive our own car. They even let us put the top down. There were animals everywhere. And no people. In South Africa, Namibia, and other countries, we had been required to travel with guides in *their* vehicles, and only occasionally had we seen any animals. All of our tours, before arriving in Tanzania, started with a disclaimer: "Game drives are hit or miss. We cannot promise you will see any animals." In Tanzania such disclaimers were unnecessary. There were animals everywhere: elephants, lions, buffalo, hyenas, cheetahs, zebras, gazelles, giraffes, and crocodiles.

Tanzania was formed in 1964 from the union of Tanganyika and Zanzibar, both of which had achieved independence from Britain, which had taken them from Germany. Awakened from its enforced isolation in the 1980s, the country underwent free-market economic reforms. Today the country encourages foreign investment and its economy has great potential, thanks to extensive natural resources, one of Africa's best educational systems, and a very high literacy rate. Despite ethnic and religious tensions that exist between Zanzibar Arabs and mainland Africans—they would be better off splitting up again and getting on with it—the country, thanks to its enlightened economic thinking, is on the verge of a boom. The government claims that in just a couple of years it will open the country's stock market to foreigners. Obvious emphasis is being placed on tourism.

Near Arusha on the Masai Steppe, southeast of the Serengeti, there were at one time well over a hundred, perhaps as many as two hundred, coffee plantations, all but six of which were nationalized by Nyerere. Within a few years of his doing so, none but those six was still producing coffee. All were stripped, cannibalized, and left to stand empty once it was discovered by the lackeys who took them over that raising coffee required competence, expertise, and a willingness to work. One of the plantations still in operation belonged to the Davico brothers, Carrado and Ruggero, whose father had come from Italy and started the business in 1931. Carrado had been following our trip on the Internet, and we had traded several e-mails. Paige and I stopped to visit him and his brother when we were passing through Arusha.

The plantation, the Mondul Coffee Estate, near the village of Monduli, consisted of about 1,200 mountainous acres, and it was a testimony to their work ethic that the brothers had managed to stay in business and hold on to the plantation through such difficult times in Tanzania. They had prevailed with no help from the government, in the absence of any national infrastructure. The plantation was thirty kilometers from the city over very bad roads, which the family itself had maintained for the past forty years. The family permanently employed 120 Masai laborers and put up to a thousand people to work at harvest time.

The Masai, legendary as a tribe of fierce warriors, famous for their fearless hunting of lions, made a poor impression upon Paige, who observed that the women among them did all the work, carrying heavy loads uphill on their heads, with babies strapped to their backs, while the men sat around sipping tea. She had found this to be true in societies throughout Africa, and her opinion was reinforced by the Davico brothers, who cited the macho warrior ethic among the Masai as particularly counterproductive.

Had we not stayed with the Davicos outside Arusha, we would have been unable to stay in Arusha at all, unless we were prepared to sleep in the car. Every hotel room within a hundred-mile radius had been booked, mostly by Americans traveling with, or in advance of, U.S. President Bill Clinton, who was focusing on Africa with the most extensive trip ever by a U.S. president. Having made a big show of praising the democratic credentials of Nigeria's president, Olusegun Obasanjo (whom *The New York Times* now mercilessly lambastes), he had decided to drop in on the signing of a treaty in Arusha that would bring an end to the civil strife in neighboring Burundi. The visit was little more than a photo op. Clinton, part of whose purpose was to galvanize votes for Democrats in the upcoming national election at home, was capitalizing on a chance to share the frame with President Nelson Mandela of South Africa, who had been instrumental in pulling the peace treaty together.

The army of camp followers necessary to such imperial visits—the White House security detail, staff members, hangers-on, and all-around flunkies, not to mention the American press—had locked up everything around Arusha for an entire week, even though the president would not even spend the night. The Secret Service had cut off all the phones in the city except its own and, presumably, those of the presidential press entourage. The African press, not to mention the local citizens of northeastern Tanzania, would just have to put their calls on hold while the American eagle extended its wings.

The fury not just of Tanzanians but of all Africans at this kind of offhand American arrogance, which makes enemies of people everywhere in the world, reached full flower when U.S. Secret Service agents removed Tanzanian President Benjamin Mkapa from his limousine and searched it, shaking him down before allowing him to enter the venue where the signing was to take place. He entered alone. His bodyguards were not allowed in. Nor was anyone allowed into or out of the venue once the Secret Service had locked it down.

Try to imagine a Tanzanian security detail yanking an American president from his limousine outside the White House.

In the end, the refusal of certain factions to sign the treaty rendered the convocation meaningless, and the whole thing took on the effect of a farce. The failure of the effort was reported in the African press but seemed to go unnoticed by the American media. It is probably safe to assume that few members of the White House press corps even know where Burundi is, let alone care. Nonetheless, the episode was memorable for being merely one of several stops on an African tour that garnered as much ill will as diplomatic mileage, at a huge cost to the American taxpayer.

Later, in India, the cost of these adventures in dollars alone came home to us as we read about the scores of cargo planes full of equipment flown into the country for a state visit there by the U.S. president. The people and equipment he moved required twenty-six C-17 and C-5 cargo planes, five C-130 and C-141 cargo planes, seven KC-10 tanker planes, and thirty-nine KC-135s. To support the five-day visit, the U.S. Air Force flew 1,150 sorties, according to the *Air Force Times*. The routine mobilization of all this matériel, not to mention the vast infusion of functionaries into a given location whenever the president travels, unfailingly displaces the local people and disrupts the orderly function of their societies. And unknown to the average American is the negative effect the imperial style of these visits has on the nation's friends overseas. While the American media is covering the crowds of locals in the street waving American flags provided by the U.S. Embassy, the foreign press is asking, "Who do these arrogant SOBs think they are?"

We stayed a couple of days with the Davicos before heading for Serengeti National Park.

Though Tanzania was encouraging tourism, it had yet to address the problem of infrastructure. The road to the park was so horrible that we broke the leaf springs on the trailer (again) trying to get there. We spent eight hours by the side of the road while a "bush mechanic" (as they call themselves) welded the springs back together. A hundred kilometers later we broke them again. We realized why everyone flies in. A truck was dispatched, the trailer was carried off, and while new leaf springs were being made, we checked into Crater Lodge.

Thousands of years ago, the highest peak in Africa was not Mount Kilimanjaro. It was the volcano that erupted to leave behind the Ngorongoro Crater on the edge of the Serengeti Plain. We were bowled over by the luxury of Crater Lodge—the rose petals leading to a drawn bath, the sherry and handmade chocolates in the sitting room, the gourmet food, the location itself—which was striking evidence of Tanzania's move toward development. Managed by a South African hotel chain, it was one of many similar establishments springing up around a country newly hospitable to this kind of business.

Only so many people a day are allowed onto Kilimanjaro. There is a variety of routes one can take to the summit. The one we chose represented the easiest climb, five days and four nights, up and down. Guides, who also act as porters, are not mandatory but might as well be. It is more difficult to get permission to climb the mountain if you go alone, but Wilfred Onyoni helped us. One of our two porters, Zebidiah, who was in his early fifties, had been taking people up and down the mountain for thirty-four years and had made the round-trip at least once a month over that time.

Our route, the Marangu route, is named for a town located about two kilometers from the main gate. The trip begins at the 1,700-meter mark, and there are preassigned stopping places along the way, where small A-frame cabins have been erected for camping overnight. When we made our ascent, in the middle of August, there were several single women making the climb, few single men, and a lot of couples. We walked eighteen kilometers the first day and fifteen kilometers each the second and third days. The last six kilometers of the hike began at midnight on the fourth day.

On day two we got our first really good look at the summit, Kibo Peak, situated 19,565 feet (over 6,000 meters) above sea level. As we ascended, we walked through several microclimates, moving from forest into very thick rain forest, emerging into an alpine desert as we approached the summit and the temperature dropped. The last thousand meters of altitude consisted of nothing but sand and gravel, with snow and ice at the very top.

I had run the three most recent New York Marathons before leaving on this trip. But I had never been so short of breath as I was five hundred meters from the top of Kilimanjaro. I was really sucking wind. Later, of course, it hit me as it would a dunce that I was 19,000 feet above sea level and climbing, and perhaps that had something to do with it. After finishing the climb, I returned to camp exhausted. All in all, it was a rewarding experience but not that much fun, despite the beauty. I would certainly not want to do it again. The best part is being able to say I climbed Kilimanjaro. I have the certificate to prove it.

The Marangu route, the tourist route up Kilimanjaro, is also known as the Coca-Cola route, presumably named for the refreshments available for sale to neophyte climbers at camps along the way. "Coca-Cola" is also employed as an expression by Tanzanians for an entirely different purpose, which I fondly remember. For probably the greatest testament to my enjoyment of their country is that I even like their system of bribery.

The signs on which speed limits were posted in Tanzania appeared to be portable, and not long after arriving in the country I recognized a pattern. I realized that whenever I saw a speed limit sign, I could expect to see a cop with a radar gun not too far away. Eighty kilometers per hour was the speed limit on the road leading out of Dar es Salaam. As I was speeding out of town and saw the limit posted on a portable sign, I immediately slowed down, but too late. Out of the bushes stepped two policewomen, who shared with me the reading on their radar gun—I had been doing ninety-four when they nailed me. The fine was 20,000 shillings, they told me—about $25 U.S.

"Okay," I said. "Of course you will give me a receipt?"

Neither spoke English—they did speak Russian—but both understood the word "receipt." And I understood, from locals I had run into, exactly what to expect when I used the word.

"Coca-Cola," one of them said, smiling.

Which in Tanzania meant "half the price without a receipt."

"Okay," I said obligingly and handed them 10,000 shillings. The policewomen smiled. I smiled back. "Coca-Cola," I said, and off we went.

The whole thing took less than two minutes.

I will say it again: If you are going to Africa, and you want to have the complete African experience, Tanzania is where you will find it.

Tanzania is everything that Kenya is not. There are not nearly so many animals on the Kenyan side of the Serengeti, but far more tourists and too many lodges. The Kenyan side of the preserve is massively overbuilt. In Nairobi, when we arrived, the Kenyan Parliament had just awarded a $5,000-a-month travel allowance to each of its members, this in a country where the annual per capita income is $1,000. Not long before that, they had voted themselves a 200 percent salary increase. A Catholic priest, trying to expose government corruption, had recently been murdered. Carjacking, we were told, had originated in Nairobi, a crime copied all over the world after first being committed in the Kenyan capital. And the Kenyans seemed strangely proud of it. With violence rampant in the north—more criminal than political, apparently—it was not enough that we had to travel with a military escort; we had to pay the soldiers ourselves. This was the single worst road of our trip. We met a trucker who shredded six tires. Before leaving for Ethiopia, we managed to make our visit somewhat memorable. In a wild-game restaurant, we ate a couple of local specialties, crocodile and porcupine—both of which are very bony—just as we had eaten bouillabaisse in Marseilles and spaetzle in Stuttgart.

Before we left Dar es Salaam, we visited the Saudi Arabian Embassy. We had been trying to get permission to enter Saudi Arabia since before leaving New York. In Africa, in those capital cities where they were located, we systematically visited Saudi embassies and tried to get visas, and we were turned down every time. In embassies all over the world, Paris, London, Tokyo, whenever we stopped or called and said, "We are driving around the world and want to go through Saudi Arabia," the conversation usually ended right there. There was no tourism in Saudi Arabia, we were advised, and even if there were, one would never be allowed to drive. Through Mercedes USA, we had been communicating with the Mercedes people in Abu Dhabi and the United Arab Emirates, both of whom were very influential on the Arabian Peninsula, as well as the Mercedes dealer for the whole of Saudi Arabia, who was a member of one of the richest families in the world. All told us it could not be done.

The day I visited the embassy in Dar es Salaam happened to be the day we were leaving town, and we had thought twice about actually going. We knew they were just going to turn us down. We arrived at the embassy in the car, a photo of which (along with us) had appeared that day on the front page of the city's English-language newspaper. The official in charge loved the car, and we took pictures of him and his assistant posing in front of it. Paige, in a show of respect, wore a long skirt and covered her arms and head. The official started writing everything down, all the vehicle numbers, our passport numbers, and assured us he would get us permission to drive into Saudi Arabia. He told us to stay in touch. I did not believe for a minute that he would come through, but what did we have to lose? I figured we would drop him postcards from Nairobi, Addis Ababa, and places along the way north.

When we arrived in Ethiopia, it was September 10 by our calendar and New Year's Day by theirs. Ethiopia is one of the few countries in the world that still uses the Julian calendar, which is named for Julius Caesar and which, in much of the Western world, was supplanted by the Gregorian calendar in the fifteenth century. In Ethiopia, not only was it New Year's Day, but it was New Year's Day 1993. Paige and I were each seven years younger the minute we crossed the border.

Ethiopia has been a Christian nation since the time of the Roman Empire. Islam, as it rose in the seventh century, surrounded but failed to penetrate Ethiopia, thanks in large part to geography. A mountain kingdom—the source of 85 percent of the waters flowing into the Nile—Ethiopia remained isolated not only from Islam but also from the evolution of European Christianity, a much later form of which was carried to Africa by missionaries. Religiously, then, Ethiopians are different from all their neighbors, Christian as well as Muslim.

Ethiopian Christianity is more in keeping with the religion practiced by the earliest Christians, more Judaic and Old Testament than its western European counterpart, which became what is essentially a New Testament religion. The Ethiopian Bible conforms to earlier versions of the standard text. Geez, the Semitic language of ancient Abyssinia, is still used for liturgical purposes and employs an alphabet unique unto itself.

One can also see the Semitic influence in the genetic makeup of the Ethiopian people. After all, we were now entering the land of the Semites, which runs from Ethiopia through Sudan and Egypt, across the Fertile Crescent through Iraq, and down the Arabian Peninsula. We now repeatedly found people who were proud to be Semitic but furious at America's misuse of the term "anti-Semitic." They kept pointing out that there were well over 100 million people in the region. Some of them might be anti-Israel, they insisted, but they were Semites themselves and could hardly be "anti-Semitic."

At one time the largest part of U.S. aid to Africa went to Ethiopia, the Eritrean coast of which held strategic command of the Red Sea. The country's military relationship with the United States ended in 1976, two years after its emperor, Haile Selassie, was deposed in a Communist coup. Hence the U.S. adventure in Somalia in the early 1990s under the guise of a humanitarian gesture. Selassie, who had been driven into exile in 1936, when Italy, under the Fascists, invaded the country, was lionized for having fought with British forces to end the occupation during World War II. His legacy today is that of a ruthless, isolationist dictator, although the Marxist government that replaced him is considered to have been no improvement, initiating a bloodbath and executing thousands of opponents before being overthrown itself in 1991. In 1993, the years of unrest eventually resulted in independence for Eritrea—which promised Ethiopia continued access to the sea—and establishment of the representative government that controls Ethiopia today.

The new constitution, acknowledging Ethiopia's diversity, allows for any of nine separate constituencies to withdraw from the nation. A mechanism for averting civil war, it forces the central government to be responsive to everyone. This enlightened approach I found fascinating and was one of the reasons I was excited to get to Ethiopia. I was equally excited to visit Eritrea, which had announced its intention to develop along the lines of free-market capitalism with no handouts from anyone. Unfortunately, an absurd resumption of hostilities, a boundary dispute, between the two countries had resulted in the closing of the Eritrean border and made a visit to the latter impossible.

Ethiopia, according to the World Bank, is the second poorest country in the world. Many Americans associate the country with drought and famine, and while there is no minimizing the fact that three million people went starving in the 1980s, what went unreported is that

*The single worst road we traveled on the trip was in Kenya. This was one of the better stretches. The Western consultants overseeing its construction had completed their contract, and they and the locals with whom they had worked had long since sent their money to Switzerland.*

*A young Ethiopian priest in Lalibela reading from an eight-hundred-year-old handwritten Bible. We were invited to read, too, but our command of Geez, the Semitic language of ancient Abyssinia, was inadequate to the task.*

some sixty million people were unaffected. There is desert in the north, and the region suffers periodic droughts, horrible and devastating, but most of Ethiopia is high-altitude rain forest—wet enough to provide the Nile with the vast majority of its water—and the country, which is capable of producing much of its own food, has been feeding itself for centuries.

What Ethiopia lacks is the incentives to get food to the people who need it. Seeing leaking water towers all over the country, I was reminded that Indian economist Amartya Sen had won a Nobel Prize for demonstrating that most famines are caused not by a lack of food but by government bungling.

While we were in Addis Ababa, the capital, the U.S. State Department official in charge of aid flew in with her team. They spent four days in one of the most luxurious hotels in the world, one day in the field, and flew back to Washington.

About two hundred miles due north of Addis Ababa is the ancient city of Lalibela, the center of Ethiopian Christianity at the turn of the last millennium. In the twelfth century, in a vision, the monarch for whom the town was named saw Jerusalem, to which Ethiopians were unable to pilgrimage, cut off from it as they were by the Islamic world that surrounded them. He was instructed to replicate the holy city, to build a new Jerusalem, in Lalibela. In the vision, he also saw many churches. And so today in Lalibela, which is home to several twelfth-century, solid stone churches that were hand-carved out of the side of a mountain over a period of forty years, one can find a Mount of Olives, a Jordan River, and other biblical echoes of the Holy Land. The Ethiopians are doing their best to open Lalibela up to the rest of the world. There are now an airport and a paved road providing access to the city.

The market in Lalibela was glorious, run pretty much the way it was run a thousand years ago. There were people making pots, making shoes, selling firewood. We did not know it was market day when we arrived, we just lucked into it, and we were rewarded with a look at the real Ethiopia, the way it was a long, long time ago. The town was still so untouched that we were able to walk into a church where a priest pulled out an eight-hundred-year-old religious text and allowed us to leaf through it and to photograph it. There were many ancient icons, many medieval treasures. Every church had its own cross. We saw a wide variety of crosses, some of them gold, most of them silver, throughout Ethiopia.

Massive amounts of aid in the form of free food have been going to Ethiopia since famine was first reported in the Western press, and we were in Lalibela the day one of the monthly shipments arrived. People from all over the countryside came into town on their donkeys—well, not into town, but near it. The poorer you are, the more food you get, and no one wanted to show off his possessions, so everyone parked his donkeys about three kilometers from town and walked the rest of the way. There were hundreds of donkeys around, waiting on the edge of town, and hundreds of people in the center of town, waiting for the food trucks to arrive. With their arrival, fifty-kilogram sacks of wheat stenciled with the name of the contributing country—some from the United States, some from Germany on this occasion—were distributed.

While this was going on, glorious, lush fields all around Lalibela lay fallow because nobody farmed them anymore. An entire generation of Ethiopians has grown up without learning how to farm. Instead, to put food on the table, they go to town every month, park the donkey, and collect grain. Some recipients, the day we were in Lalibela, carried their ration of wheat directly over to the town market and started selling it. And so, in addition to that generation that has never learned how to farm, there is a generation of farmers who have simply stopped farming because they can no longer sell the fruits of their labor—there is no way to compete with free grain.

Africa could feed itself and export food again, but not when its farmers are up against subsidized Western agriculture and free lunches.

"Let's go down to the market and look at the things your mother's church has sent to Africa," I said to Paige, when we had arrived in Senegal.

"What are you talking about?" she said.

I explained the massive scam involving donations of clothes in the United States—how they were diverted systematically from charity to the black market—and at first Paige did not believe me. Not until I walked her through the markets in sub-Saharan Africa did she realize that charity not only "begins at home" but ends there, too. The practice is continentwide, but in black Africa the evidence jumps off the

page—for the simple reason that not as many Americans, who generally donate through their local churches, give to God-fearing Muslims
as give to God-fearing Christians.

Throughout the continent there are huge markets where one can
find bundle upon bundle of T-shirts spread out for sale, donated by
places such as the YMCA of Cleveland and the First Baptist Church
of Charlotte. These and clothing of all kinds are given as donations in
the United States destined for the poor of Africa, but by the time they
reach the continent, they are sold as a commercial product. Not only
do they enrich the entrepreneurs involved in the traffic, they also put
local tailors out of business. The tailors cannot compete, nor can the
people who weave cloth, spin yarn, or grow cotton, the people whose
costs the tailor incurs. In Africa you used to see tailors everywhere.
You would see them by the side of the road with their sewing ma-
chines. Now you see them only rarely. How can any of them compete
with a product that the entrepreneur gets virtually free?

Charities in the United States—the Baptist Church, for example,
sending goods off to a church in Africa—turn the merchandise over to
consolidators in, say, Brooklyn or Jacksonville, where it is loaded into
containers and shipped overseas. The merchandise is the consolidator's property now. When it gets to Africa, it comes off the boat and
is spread out on the dock, where wholesalers go through it all and bid
on it. The consolidator takes the money. The clothing moves by the
truckload back into the interior, to the local village markets, where it
is retailed. The charity gets nothing. Indeed, the minute the merchandise leaves North Carolina, it is doomed. Almost everything else you
donate to Africa ends up in the same system.

The traffic in charitable goods, which I first became aware of on
my motorcycle trip, has been one of the great growth industries of the
last decade. The fortunes to be made have spawned an army of middlemen who, for no more than the price of going to church—a little
money in the collection plate—procure boatloads of free inventory by
visiting do-good organizations in the United States. Announcing that
they are collecting clothes for Africa, they go from church to church.
Of course, if we were to allow tailors in Africa to stay in business, if
we were to help them become productive and self-sufficient, we might
find ourselves importing the goods they produce. Better to give them
shirts and put them out of business so we can give them *more* shirts

than to threaten the job of a textile worker in North Carolina—who
is donating his used T-shirts to the church and putting the African
weavers and tailors out of work, just as the U.S. government is donating food to the people of Lalibela and driving the skills of the
farmer from their collective memory.

In Addis Ababa, with a new Ethiopian friend, Anina Abbullahi, whom
she had met at the hotel, Paige had gone shopping for an *abaya,* the
traditional head-to-toe covering she would need to wear in Saudi Arabia, should we be granted permission to enter the country. We thought
it might also come in handy in the Sudan. By now Paige had become
quite independent. She had taken to abandoning me frequently, striking out and heading off to pursue interests of her own. She had really
taken to Africa, and by the time we reached Ethiopia, she pretty much
owned the continent.

For most of the trip through Africa, we had been lucky to be running against the rainy season, rather than with it. The rainy season is
pretty much a moving front, and when we had entered Gabon four
months earlier, we had gone through as it was moving north. Now, as
we were traveling through northern Ethiopia heading for the Sudan,
it hit us coming the other way. The road going north was so terrible it
took us almost twelve hours to go a hundred kilometers. Soon the
road became all but impassable, little more than a giant swamp, and
as darkness fell we found ourselves stuck.

We wound up in a tiny village, which I later learned was named Negade Bahir, from which I walked half a mile to reconnoiter the road
ahead, looking for the best way through. I found trucks that had been
stuck there for days, their drivers trying to dig them out. I searched out
the village chief, a tall, thin man whose dark brown safari suit defied
all of Paige's expectations of how an African chief would dress, told
him we were stuck, and asked if there were a place for us to stay. The
best hotel in town was the only hotel in town and consisted of a small
collection of primitive sheds with thatched roofs, dirt floors, and no
plumbing, and none of them was large enough for more than a single
person. Surprisingly, they were relatively clean and well maintained.
Indeed, as Paige observed, the accommodations were far superior to
those of our "four-star" hotel in Georgia.

"The floor is swept, the sheet is clean, the blanket doesn't smell, and there's water to wash my face and brush my teeth. What more could I want?" she said.

She found a rock outside to hold shut her door, which did not even have a latch.

The night we ended up in Negade Bahir was the eve of one of the most important religious festivals in Ethiopia, the celebration of the Finding of the True Cross. According to legend, the Ethiopian monarchy was founded by Menelik I, the son of Israel's King Solomon and the queen of Sheba. Three hundred years after the Crucifixion, one of Menelik's descendants, an empress of Ethiopia, was instructed in a dream to travel to Golgotha and return to Ethiopia with a relic of the Cross, the location of which would be revealed to her by the smoke of a fire she was to build there. Her success was commemorated annually in Ethiopia with bonfires, singing, and dancing.

The people of Negade Bahir were in a celebratory mood in anticipation of the festival and its bonfire, and we were delighted to celebrate with them. That night I met two young priests, who had just finished their novitiate, and I bought them the first beers they had ever drunk. We took a Polaroid of an older priest, who was ecstatic when we gave it to him, not having seen a photo of himself in a very long time. We shared photographs with numerous people, some of whom had never seen a foreigner, let alone an instant camera.

Hostilities had closed the border between Ethiopia and Eritrea, which meant we would not, unfortunately, have an opportunity to visit the latter. It also meant that in moving north, we would have to skirt close to the war zone in Sudan. A seemingly ignored, if not forgotten, conflict, the revolt of the black South against the Muslim North was the longest-running war in Africa. The rebellion waged in the name of a secular Sudan—in reality a war over control of the South's oil reserves—had deteriorated into mutual slaughter among the people of the South along tribal lines.

As we crossed the border, the churches and Bibles and crosses of Ethiopia gave way to fundamentalist Islam. The topography changed as well. It was suddenly dry; we were coming into the desert. And even more dramatic: it was the first border we had crossed at which we saw no money changers. There were always money changers, and you did not have to look for them, they always found you. But nobody crossed this border. Crossing at a village called Gallabat, we were so far off the beaten track that, unable to find a place to stay, we had to sleep that night at the local police station. The police, who were delighted to see us, were very hospitable—despite America's having launched a cruise missile into Khartoum two years before, blowing up a perfectly legitimate pharmaceutical factory. The police set up cots outside the station. That's where *they* slept. They insisted we sleep on their bunks inside.

We arrived in Khartoum on the twenty-ninth of September. Among the first things I did was call the Saudi Arabian Embassy official in Dar es Salaam to check on the visas he had said he would arrange. I was getting anxious now. We were headed for the Indian subcontinent. Things were going to become very complicated very fast if we were not allowed to drive through Saudi Arabia.

"Do not worry," he said. "I told you I would get you a visa."

I had heard this said too many times in too many countries not to worry. I knew it was never true until you had the thing in your hands. And even then it was often not true.

I called my father from Khartoum. I had been trying to get him to join us in various places throughout Africa, but it was clear now that it was not going to happen.

"My traveling days are over," he said.

His traveling days had been mainly limited, I realized, to those he had spent in Europe during the war and to the years he had spent at the University of Oklahoma. His own father had died young, and an uncle, who owned an oil company, had sent him to Oklahoma to study petroleum engineering, with the expectation that my father would work for him when he finished school. The war had intervened, however, during which his uncle had died and the business had been sold. From Europe my father had returned to Demopolis, where he worked as the manager of the Borden chemical plant, the job he held until his retirement.

He was a tough guy, but he was now experiencing a lot of pain. He had boosted the dosage of the painkillers he was taking. The pain medication was his sole treatment for the disease. Having refused chemotherapy, he was merely treating the symptoms. The good news that day was that he had actually gained a pound. Right up to now he had been losing weight steadily.

*Celebrating the Finding of the True Cross in Negade Bahir, I bought these young Ethiopian priests their first beers. They seem to be holding theirs better than I.*

*A wonderfully romantic place for a honeymoon, the Sahara is not easy to get to or from—not even for camels.*

We spent about a week in Khartoum, and among the things we did before we left was witness firsthand the spiritual ardor of the whirling dervish. A dervish is a member of a Muslim order of ascetics who practice the achievement of collective ecstasy through whirling dances and the chanting of religious formulas.

In front of a mosque outside Khartoum one Friday, we watched a group of dervishes dance themselves into a trance. It started with two men, and before it was over, with the music growing more frenzied, there were fifty men dancing. A woman, swept away with the holiness of it all, rushed into the crowd and joined the dancing, and was immediately yanked from the throng. Women are not allowed to dance with men, nor even sway on the periphery to the powerful rhythms invigorating the men, especially not when the men are dancing for the glory of God.

Just outside the circle of dancers, a camel was tethered, crouched on the ground in front of his keeper, who was sharpening a knife. Camels must be the most contented animals on earth. Donkeys may be the most patient, but I have never seen a camel that looked unhappy. There he was sitting down, his legs under him, as content as could be, and all of a sudden, at a certain point amid the religious observance, his keeper cut off his head. Just like that.

Every Friday, as it happened, a camel was sacrificed and given to the poor.

The White Nile, which rises out of Lake Victoria, and the Blue Nile, which originates in the mountains of western Ethiopia, converge in Khartoum to form the Nile proper. You can actually stand and see where the different-colored waters (though not white or blue) come together, which is pretty romantic stuff for a simple boy from Alabama. Like the river, we were headed from Khartoum to Wadi Halfa, where we would cross the border into Egypt.

Where we would go from there was anybody's guess.

# 11

## ARABIAN NIGHTS

IT HAD ALWAYS BEEN my belief that the Indians were the most hopelessly bureaucratic people in the world. But the Egyptians, I found, who like Indians had learned from the British, took it to an even more ridiculous level. Before this trip was over, by the time I was out of Egypt, I came to appreciate the country as a world-class bureaucratic disaster. All my excitement at the prospect of going there, my optimism surrounding the country's plans to open the economy and attract foreign investment, evaporated. I found businessmen who painstakingly met all the requirements for importing raw materials who then saw them impounded for months awaiting more government inspections. We met two tourists whose prescription medicine was impounded while they awaited certification of its contents from their pharmacist in the United States. Even then the medicine still had to be analyzed by Egyptian chemists. The pills were still lost in the bureaucracy by the time the tourists flew home.

More darkly, we learned why the government of Hosni Mubarak is hated in the streets. The government has spies everywhere and strangles any initiative or dissent. Egypt receives more U.S. aid than any

*We were struck by the beauty of the women of Sudan and were delighted to learn that here in Wadi Halfa every (Muslim) girl attended high school.*

*It was hard enough for us to drive around the world at the turn of the third millennium; here is but one of the things the Egyptians managed to accomplish five thousand years ago.*

The vehicles, however, presented a problem. There were a couple of special stamps I needed to prove legitimacy of ownership, and they would have to be picked up in Cairo. The vehicles were allowed off the barge, but only to be placed in impoundage. I would have to pick up the necessary stamps before the cars were released into my possession.

I checked everyone into the Old Cataract Hotel, and then I flew to Cairo to straighten everything out.

While I was running around wrestling with Egyptian bureaucracy, Paige was ensconced happily at this wonderful old hotel in Aswan, which claims to have the most beautiful view of any hotel in the world and is perhaps justified in doing so. It looks out over the Nile to Elephantine Island, which takes its name from the shape of the outcroppings of rock that are visible there. The aging establishment is right out of an Agatha Christie novel. Paige read *Death on the Nile* during our stay. Sitting on the veranda, you could just imagine that Christie's Belgian sleuth, Hercule Poirot, was sitting there with you and somewhere nearby, probably by poison, someone was getting murdered.

After twelve days in Wadi Halfa and five days aboard a barge with nothing but a hole in the deck for a toilet, the experience of being stuck in Aswan at the Old Cataract Hotel, waiting for the cars to be liberated, was just fine with everyone. Nobody was in a hurry to leave.

You cannot argue with the pyramids. Whatever you say about the Egyptians, you have to give them that. They've got 'em and you don't. The pyramids, the Sphinx, Luxor, we saw it all. These ancient wonders are something of a cliché, a kind of shorthand for everything associated with "the grand tour," the definition of exotic travel. And like most clichés, they come by their power honestly.

I reported dutifully to the Saudi Embassy in Cairo, a city that, by the way, surpassed Istanbul in my estimation as the worst city in the world in which to drive. I had called both the Saudi official in Dar es Salaam and the Mercedes dealer in Jeddah, and both had told me that if I went to the embassy in Cairo I would get my Saudi Arabian visas. I will never know which of these two people came through (both inevitably took credit), but I arrived at the embassy to discover, to my astonishment, that the visa request had been honored.

Driving south along the Red Sea, we saw literally thousands of unfinished condominiums and hotels, a result of the collapse of a speculative boom in the late 1990s, one indication among many that Mubarak had butchered the Egyptian economy and things were falling apart.

When we had begun the journey through Africa nine months before, I had been exceedingly optimistic. On my previous trip in 1990–1991, I had discovered a continent poised for change. People were beginning to acknowledge that the old socialist ways no longer worked. Leaders understood that excessive government control stymied growth. Africa had begun to turn the heads of foreign investors. Ten years later, I returned hoping to find new and revitalized countries on the track toward prosperity.

Alas, I was disappointed. The Africa I had discovered on this leg of the journey still had a very long way to go. Certain countries among the thirty-two we visited—Tanzania, Ethiopia, Mauritania—were making some right moves, privatizing industry, loosening bureaucracy, and getting rid of the crooks who had run their economies into the ground. Many other countries, however, had taken steps backward. I had expected to be seduced by investment opportunities in places such as Kenya, Uganda, and Mozambique. There I found only corruption and petty, but violent, disputes, motivated by greed and the lust for power.

I had hoped to find the perennial conflicts winding down, but they were worse and more senseless these days in places such as Western Sahara, Nigeria, both Congos, Angola, Zimbabwe, Uganda, Sudan, and Ivory Coast. The new generation of leaders in whom I had placed such faith proved to be as hopeless as the old. In Angola a formerly ideological war has been exposed for what it was, a naked grab for power between rebels who controlled the country's diamonds and a government that controlled its oil, a bunch of thugs on both sides killing anything that moved.

As I write this, the Angolan madness seems to have ended with the death of the guerrilla Jonas Savimbi. If so, it presents one of the world's great opportunities. One of the best ways to get rich is to get thee to a nation just as a horrible war ends. Angola is gorgeous and lush. It was the largest African producer of coffee before the war. It now imports coffee and much of its food, as the war destroyed most agriculture. The opportunities for tourism, fishing, mining, and infrastructure are everywhere. Still not sold? Angola will soon be Africa's largest producer of oil—larger than Nigeria, Libya, or Gabon. Its diamond production will be among the world's largest. There are only twelve million Angolans, so there will be plenty to go around no matter how much the liberators steal.

I have seen so many success stories following wars that I know this is low-hanging fruit.

Driving through Egypt, an ancient culture rich in history that dates back six thousand years, I saw awe-inspiring monuments and temples and marveled again at how far advanced societies were centuries ago. Nowhere is this more obvious than in Egypt. While the English were still painting themselves blue, the Egyptians were developing arithmetic, astronomy, an alphabet, the 365-day calendar, agriculture, advanced medical practices, and national government. But whereas Egypt stood in the forefront of progress for thousands of years, it now lags hopelessly behind. Following the country's effort in the mid-1990s to deregulate state-run enterprises and privatize industry—earning it the title "Tiger of the Nile"—I figured I would finally find some investment opportunities there.

No such luck. Egypt, like many countries I visited in Africa, has one foot still stuck in the past. The country has been run by the same group for the past thirty years, and when one way of thinking dictates a country's growth, the result is predictably dismal. Democracy, by contrast, brings change, a newness and vibrancy to political thinking. With little change over the past three decades, Egypt is rotting at the core. I found little to invest in there. It was a sober end to my journey through Africa.

That said, I believe Africa still holds promise. And here, I think, is how that promise can be realized.

Forgive all the debt. Right now. African countries, combined, owe some $350 billion plus in foreign debt, according to the International Monetary Fund. While no one really expects these countries to pay back that debt, they are still required to finance it, making annual payments on the loans. If we assume the interest on the loans to be 8 percent, it means that African countries must collectively pay $26 billion a year in interest. That does not include principal payments. If we assume principal payments to be another 2 to 3 percent, annual payments to finance the debt total over $30 billion. Once the debt is forgiven, Africa's leaders will have an additional $30 billion annually that can be put to productive use, plus no debt hanging over them. Call the $350 billion reparations for supposed past sins, if it makes you feel better.

However, part of the deal would be no more foreign aid.

The effects would undoubtedly be profound. Africa would be left to survive on its own. The people of Africa, no longer relying on hand-outs, would learn to fend for themselves. The Ethiopian teenagers I met who had never learned how to farm would have to take up the plow. The madmen fighting on the Horn of Africa would stop receiving arms from around the world. Nigerian leaders would no longer be able to walk into banks and walk out with sacks of U.S. dollars. Those who run Mozambique would no longer be able to solicit flood relief money with which to line their coffers. The IMF and World Bank would go bankrupt, and local NGOs would be forced out of business.

In Ethiopia we ran into a guy who operated an orphanage. There were no orphans around at the time, but we were told that when the foreign inspectors came up from Addis Ababa—"Are the kids getting blankets, are they being well fed?"—the place would be full of "or-phans." It was easy enough to round kids up. When the inspectors left, the kids would go back home. Libraries are another favorite of NGOs. They love to build libraries. And they love to do feasibility studies.

NGOs are big business. Spawned by government corruption—"We won't give that dictator any more aid, we'll give it to an NGO"—these cash cows have succeeded only in inserting numerous middlemen between the foreign aid and the corrupt government. So bureaucrats and local entrepreneurs now take a piece before the money evaporates. If an orphan needs a place to sleep, he can go to the library.

Presently, as we had seen in half the world, most foreign aid winds up with outside consultants, the local military, corrupt bureaucrats, the new NGO administrators, and Mercedes dealers. There are Mercedes dealers in places where there are not even roads.

One Sudanese entrepreneur, applying his talents to making easy money rather than building a productive enterprise, worked the corrupt NGO system perfectly. It was a "known fact" that slavery was rampant in northeast Africa, especially Sudan. He and a Swiss NGO found each other, and he agreed to buy slaves for the charity, which would then set them free. By the time the Swiss figured out what was happening—he was going to his friends and relatives and "buying" them, giving them good stories to tell the charity about their enslavement—the Swiss were out $20 million.

Obviously, some people will suffer once the aid spigot is shut off.

Many Africans will be dislocated from their positions, forced to move and to work where they can live properly. Many others will thrive as their energies are directed toward productive ventures and away from corruption. It is time for Africa to unleash the ambitious, as China did in the late 1970s. That is why I believe that, as a second step, Africans should organize a new continentwide congress. Call it the Congress of Kinshasa, for the city in the Democratic Republic of the Congo. It would be made up of representatives of the countries themselves, not the vestigial colonial powers, many of which still pull the strings in African politics. The new congress could correct the mistakes of the 1884 Congress of Berlin, which divided Africa among the European powers.

This congress should redraw the borders of the various African nations, accounting for religious, linguistic, historic, and ethnic differences. The result might be many more countries than exist now, possibly dozens of small countries—but dozens of nations consisting of people working together, seeking prosperity collectively, collaborating rather than competing as they do now. African history was full of extraordinarily successful countries organized along ancient lines before the Europeans and Arabs arrived. There is a tremendous reservoir of brainpower, energy, and drive among Africans just waiting to be tapped. Freeing Africa from the mistakes of the past and leaving Africans themselves to direct resources toward the building of new societies will lead to what I believe would be a real African Renaissance.

The gift of a $350 billion debt write-off would be one thing, but then the aid would have to be stopped. What our aid buys first is guns to keep thieves in power. Without aid, hopeless leaders would be forced to produce. They would lose power if they did not. Africa would have real liberators and inevitably real liberation. The freedom to organize all that energy and drive and to exploit the continent's massive resources would bring to the people of Africa great prosperity and wealth.

Paige's feelings about Africa, which came into perspective after her nine months on the continent, are shared by many who have spent time there. She loved the people, the markets, the countryside, the unstoppable work ethic, particularly that of women, but deplored the lack of infrastructure, education, and health care, the poor living conditions, and the second-class status of women.

"If I'd flown in and out, visiting a wildlife lodge for a week, certainly I'd say, 'I love Africa,' but nine months was enough to show me the ugly reality that exists for many of the people who live there," she said.

I pondered all this as we were racing to Hurghada, about two hundred miles south of Suez. It was from there that we had been instructed to cross the Red Sea, entering Saudi Arabia at the town of Dubā. The ferry from Hurghada to Dubā did not make the trip every day, and I was hurrying because I did not want to give anyone in the Saudi government an opportunity to change his mind. I was excited to see Saudi Arabia, but I was that much more eager to drive it, which had been especially high on my hit parade because nobody was allowed to do it. My hearing that it was forbidden was like Huck Finn's hearing Miss Watson say, "You cannot go down the Mississippi on a raft."

The only time we had a problem with the first aid supplies was entering Saudi Arabia. We landed in Dubā, very excited and frightened, of course, as usual. All border crossings are anxiety-provoking, but especially this one. Not knowing what to expect, Paige was wearing her black *abaya*. We were not sure at this stage whether it was mandatory for foreigners—it was—but to avert any potential problems, she was covered head to toe. The Saudi official we had met in Tanzania had made it clear that he would expect Paige to be properly covered. He had also insisted on seeing that we were in fact married. I had shown him an article from *The New York Times*, which had covered the wedding, but that was insufficient. He wanted to see the marriage certificate, which I subsequently produced. It was all strict and holy.

We drove up to customs in Dubā, and true to form, just as expected, we were ordered to take everything out of the car. It was one of the most thorough searches of the whole trip. But we had prepared for it. We had double-checked everything. I was hoisting suitcases out of the car when the inspector set the medical bag on the table. And before he opened it, I knew I was in trouble.

The first thing he pulled out, of course, was a bottle of vodka.

The penalties for alcohol possession in Saudi Arabia are imprisonment, exile, or flogging, eighty lashes being what is actually specified in strict Muslim countries. (The penalty for drug trafficking is beheading. No questions, they just chop it off without even notifying your ambassador.) Given a choice, I knew what I would opt for, but the expression on the inspector's face told me that it was probably not going to be up to me.

Before heading across the Red Sea, I had warned everybody to get rid of any alcohol aboard. Even entering Sudan, we had been careful to ditch whatever alcohol we were carrying except the carefully hidden millennium sherry. Clearly, I was very aware that there was absolutely no alcohol allowed in Saudi Arabia. And we knew we would be searched. So before driving onto the ferry, we went through everything three times—not that we carried a lot of liquor, but we might occasionally have received a bottle of brandy as a gift. We had even organized for the González Byass sherry to be transported around Saudi Arabia. We went through everything but the medical bag.

The vodka, which we carried in addition to hydrogen peroxide, had been recommended by one of the doctors as an additional form of sterilization, given its collateral benefit as a means of anesthesia.

"What's this?" the agent said.

"Oh, my God," I said. "We forgot we had it. It's for medical use, but we don't need it. We don't want it. Throw it away."

He was most perplexed. It was clear that we had permission to come into the country. He knew he was supposed to let us in; we hoped he was not supposed to flog us. Earlier in the trip we had met a European who had actually received eighty lashes for possession of alcohol while in Sudan temporarily, so we knew it was a real possibility. Not knowing quite what to do, the agent went off to talk to one of his superiors. And it was an extended consultation. Everyone else was searched and allowed to go on their way, and we were left standing there.

Finally I was summoned into the building, where I was presented to his boss, the head of the station. I was shaking. There were four other people present who spoke only Arabic. His boss handed me a form to sign, a handwritten statement saying that I understood that alcohol was illegal in Saudi Arabia and that he was destroying the bottle with my permission. I signed as fast as I could, the four witnesses signed, we all stepped outside, and in a ceremony memorable for its brevity, he poured the vodka into the sand and threw the bottle onto the ground. I would have expected them to smash it, hide it, or do whatever one does to such unholy containers, but it just lay there in the sand, in full view, as we drove off.

Still terrified but relieved, we entered the Kingdom of Saudi Arabia, an empty bottle of Absolut vanishing in our wake.

The Arabian Peninsula, part of the Ottoman Empire as recently as a century ago, parts of which had never been explored to anyone's knowledge, came under the hegemony of the British after World War I. It was here that T. E. Lawrence, organizing the Arabs to fight the German-allied Turks, achieved immortality as Lawrence of Arabia. Ibn Saud, whose family had risen to leadership in the nineteenth century, consolidated control over the region after the war, and his kingdom was formally recognized by Great Britain in 1927. The kingdom was renamed Saudi Arabia five years later.

With discovery of oil in the 1930s—recognized very quickly, very clearly as big oil, and I mean big, big, big oil—the country went from poverty to enormous wealth virtually overnight. Within a generation, the House of Saud went from traveling by camelback to traveling by Cadillac. The transfer of assets to full Saudi control was completed in the early 1970s. Up to then exploitation of the oil fields had been an exclusive concession of an Arabian-American corporation, Aramco. The price of oil escalated dramatically, and by 1981 Saudi Arabia was by various measures the richest country in the world.

There are now something like twenty thousand princes in the royal family. Polygamy is customary, and having numerous children is the norm. (Osama bin Laden's father had more than fifty children.) And the Saudi government funds all of these princes with six-figure annual salaries. The majority of the actual work done in Saudi Arabia is done by foreigners—Pakistanis, Sudanese, Bangladeshis, predominantly Muslims. Accountants, computer technicians, shopkeepers, janitors, and numerous entrepreneurs, all from overseas, constitute a large percentage of the workforce.

But a Pakistani cannot just show up in Saudi Arabia and open a butcher shop. He has to find a Saudi partner. The Saudi may never show up at the shop, he may never even see it, but the Pakistani must send him a check every month. Overseas corporations that do business in Saudi Arabia must hire a certain number of Saudis. And while the Saudis may not do much, they nonetheless expect to be promoted to executive positions. Most do very little, if they do anything at all, according to foreign businessmen, and their absentee rate is high. (One employee, we were told, had taken off three times, saying his mother had died, before his employer caught on to the scam.) They spend most of their time "being Saudi." That is the expression used. Visiting the mosque, visiting the family, visiting the shopping mall, drinking tea, talking about the horrible foreigners, whatever it happens to be—if they are unable to make it to work, it is because they are busy being Saudi.

We ran into a lot of foreign doctors, dentists, and other professionals in Saudi Arabia, presumably for similar reasons. While there is no shortage of highly educated people in the kingdom, being Saudi makes it impossible for many of them to dedicate the time and energy necessitated by the practice of such professions.

It would not be until the end of our first day in Saudi Arabia that we stopped making fools of ourselves. The evening of our arrival, we checked into a hotel and immediately went looking for something to eat. We found the Saudi equivalent of a fast-food diner. The counter man ignored Paige, so I ordered our food, and we sat down. And noticed everyone staring at us. Nobody said or did anything, we were not hassled by the police, who showed up outside, but we did cause quite a stir. We assumed that it was partly the car—it always prompted curiosity—and the fact that we were clearly foreigners, though Paige was dutifully wearing her *abaya*. But we were mistaken. Later, after eating and returning to the hotel, followed by the police, it was explained to us why we were drawing so much attention.

Innocently, naively, rather stupidly, I have to admit, we had made the mistake of doing just what I described above: walking into the restaurant, ordering food, and sitting down. In Saudi Arabia, if a woman wants to eat in a restaurant, she enters through a separate door to a special family section in the rear, consisting of individual cubicles, closed off from one another, so that nobody but her family can see her. And nobody suffers the uncleanness of having her sit in the same room. Looking back on it later, we realized that everyone else in that room was a man. There had not been a single woman in sight.

Apart from that—apart from life itself—everything in Saudi Arabia is up to date: the infrastructure, the highways, the buildings, the ports.

The country consists almost entirely of desert, with wonderful highways crossing it and the occasional city or village rising up out of the sand. Every gas station has a mosque attached to it. There are numerous shopping centers, no movie houses, very few restaurants, and thousands of mosques. Life is fairly simple: either you shop or you go to the mosque. The mosques and the shopping centers share the same parking lot.

Muslims pray five times a day. And when the muezzin calls the faithful to prayer, everything stops, all businesses close. The hours of prayer, which are listed in the newspaper daily, fluctuate based on the hours of dawn and dusk. The Koran says that dawn arrives when you can discern the difference between a black thread and a white thread. When you can no longer tell the difference, dusk has arrived. Because sunset and sunrise vary from city to city as you move across the country, which is almost four times the size of Texas and more than four times the size of France, the hours of prayer in Jeddah differ from those in Riyadh.

The shopping centers in Saudi Arabia are elegant. Every designer is represented. At night the souks, the old marketplaces, are packed, especially the gold souks. I have seen wealth, riches, and jewelry emporiums all over the world, but I had never seen anything like the gold markets in Saudi Arabia. Almost everything was twenty-four karat. The cheapest gold you could buy was eighteen karat. The merchandise was all highly polished. There were gigantic belts, six inches wide, necklaces, tiaras, bracelets, and rings, many encrusted with diamonds. (Much of the work is done in India and shipped to the Arabian Peninsula. The craftsmen are on the subcontinent, although many Muslim Indians are now residents.) In one shop alone, a shop no bigger than a thousand square feet, I saw more gold than in Tiffany's main store on Fifth Avenue in New York.

None of it, not the designer fashions, not the jewelry, would you ever see on a woman in Saudi Arabia. The souks and the shopping centers are full of women spending fortunes on merchandise—clothing and jewelry—that they are not allowed to wear in public. Only at home are they able to show it off. In the shops there are no dressing rooms. Even in the women's clothing shops, the attendants are all men. And it would not do for these men to see women trying on clothes. If a woman buys a dress, she takes it home to try it on, or she may, if she wishes, try it on in one of the ladies' bathrooms located in the shopping center. In public she must remain covered from head to toe.

When you ask Saudi women how they feel about this, many say the system has its advantages. Whether they are simply rationalizing is hard to know, but comparing their treatment to that of European women, they say, "Nobody ever bothers us, nobody ever approaches us, nobody tries to pick us up or pinch our bottoms. We can do anything we want, we can go anywhere we want without being bothered."

Well, not entirely without being bothered. If a woman's ankle shows in public, the Saudi religious police, the *mutawwa*, officers of the Commission for the Preservation of Virtue and Prevention of Vice, who do nothing but enforce compliance with such laws, will walk up and straighten her out. More than once, Paige's scarf slipped back on her head, exposing her hair, and the *mutawwa* approached and insisted she correct it.

What few outside publications, Western or Arabic, were available in Saudi Arabia were censored. Pages were torn out or photographs of women's exposed skin were blacked out by felt-tipped pen, even photographs of women's tennis matches. We saw this throughout the Gulf States and marveled at how many people—and how many felt-tipped pens—it must take to individually censor every copy of every periodical that enters the region.

Women in Saudi Arabia are not allowed to drive. They must travel in the backseat of a car with a male driver unless the driver is a family member, in which case they may sit in front. Many are not allowed out of the house without their husbands' permission. In November 1990, forty-seven Saudi women staged a protest. They took the keys to their cars and drove themselves through Riyadh in a convoy, albeit fully covered in their *abaya*s. The protest ended very quickly when they were stopped by the police. Their families' passports and livelihoods were threatened. Soon thereafter, driving by women, which up to then had been forbidden by custom, was made illegal by statute.

Paige interviewed three young female journalists at the *Saudi Gazette*. They worked in a separate building from the male reporters. "We do want our freedom. We do want to drive," one of them told her. "Being dependent on men is part of our everyday lives. But things will change one day, I believe. My mother could never have had this job."

In Saudi Arabia the public and private exist in a strange sort of mutual tension. We visited some Saudis in their homes. They served us vodka, champagne, and caviar. They had European butlers and maids and homes decorated in the international style by famous Western designers. The women and children walked around the house in Western clothes the price of which I could not bring myself to imagine, much less pay. The children owned all the most up-to-date videos and CDs, and the entire family, thanks to a satellite dish, was conversant with television programs from around the world.

The kingdom is characterized by seething tensions of all kinds, political and economic as well as cultural.

By the 1990s the Saudis were spending much more money than they had, and the nation's debt began to skyrocket. Today, despite its considerable assets, the country is one of the more indebted countries in the world. If the price of oil drops, the government will ultimately go bankrupt. It will no longer be able to support all its princes, much less its mullahs. Only if oil prices remain high will Saudi Arabia be able to weather the storm—perhaps.

Seventy-one percent of Saudis are under the age of twenty-nine, and the men running the country were all born before the Second World War. Combine this with the political tensions resulting from the rise of fundamentalism, popular dissatisfaction with the stranglehold maintained by the royal family, and falling oil prices, and the kingdom becomes ripe for destabilization. The kingdom's collapse could lead to seizure or closure of the country's oil fields, and oil prices would immediately and dramatically escalate.

One way or another, we are going to be paying a pretty penny for oil for at least the next ten years.

We spent two weeks in Saudi Arabia. We visited the Red Sea city of Jeddah, the country's commercial capital; the political capital, Riyadh; and the oil fields in Al-Khubar, situated on the Persian Gulf. Heading out of Jeddah, just west of the holy city of Mecca, we came upon a highway sign stating that all foreigners and non-Muslims were required to take the next exit. The advisory was printed in three languages and was one of several preceding the turnoff, the signage growing bolder and bolder as we approached. The road we were traveling led to Mecca, one of Islam's two holy cities (Medina, the other, lay to the north). Non-Muslims were not allowed anywhere near Mecca. Even Muslims, if they were foreigners, needed permission to go there.

On the road to Riyadh we passed numerous camels, held back by magnificent fences from roaming out of the desert onto the highway. Riyadh, flashy and modern, was Jeddah all over again, only somewhat duller, as might be expected of any city devoted to bureaucrats. The kingdom's lifeblood flowed from the east, from the oil fields around Al-Khubar. While there we visited the country's oil museum. And to my surprise, I found it to be one of the great museums of the world. Forget the fact that it is an oil museum. It traces the entire development of the region. The history of astronomy, mathematics, pharmacy, geology, and other technological and cultural advances associated with Arabia are all presented in depth and in magnificent fashion. The Saudis have money, and they spent it. Unfortunately nobody goes there, because the country is essentially closed to tourists and has been since its founding, initially a result of a lack of basic infrastructure and today a consequence of xenophobia.

There is no such thing as "the Muslim world," as the Western press likes to call it. The idea of a monolithic Islam is ludicrous, and nobody knows it better than the Saudi royal family, whose hold on power is tenuous. Sunnis and Shiites, just like Catholics and Protestants, have been slaughtering each other for centuries—there have been wars *within* the sects just as there have been within Christian sects—even during the *hajj,* the holiest period in a Muslim's life. The million plus pilgrims allowed into Saudi Arabia for the *hajj* every year are allowed in for only a short visit. And refusing or limiting admittance to so many Muslims makes it impossible for Saudi Arabia to open the doors to many tourists of other faiths.

In Jeddah, in one outdoor restaurant, we did notice about a dozen Frenchmen. They seemed to be tourists, and I assumed their presence represented some sort of experimentation on the part of the Saudis, who need foreign currency. After that, we never saw another tourist all the time we were there.

I think it is safe to say that in all the time we were in the country, we did not run into a single American. Twenty-five years earlier, there had been Americans everywhere. Now the Americans in Saudi Arabia

*Taking a wrong turn here on the road to Mecca could have serious consequences.*

*I would always facetiously answer, "One million dollars," when asked how much for the car. These guys promptly responded by asking, "Cash or electronic transfer?"*

*Many girls in Oman will "cover" themselves when they reach puberty.*

ventured no farther than the walls of their compounds. They, like all foreigners, kept a very low profile and had been doing so since 1996, when terrorists had bombed a complex in Dhahran, killing nineteen American soldiers stationed there and wounding more than three hundred people.

A year before we had celebrated Thanksgiving in Monaco, and the best we could find was an American restaurant that celebrated with Tex-Mex fare and sangria. In Saudi Arabia, given the history of an American presence, we hoped to find a place that served turkey, but in the end we had to settle for going to a Turkish restaurant that served chicken kabobs.

While we were in the country, several Westerners were assassinated. In two separate incidents, cars with Westerners in them were blown up. In the previous ten years, as everyone knew, the United States had made an enormous number of enemies throughout the Middle East. And Saudi Arabia had become a fertile breeding ground of resentment, especially after we stationed troops there in the 1990s. The idea of Christian troops stationed in Islam's holiest country was infuriating to more and more Saudis and devout people elsewhere. They kept asking me how we would feel if Muslim troops were stationed in Rome. (My answer was, and is: if Saudi Arabia needs protection, substitute U.S. troops with troops from Turkey or Morocco, both of which are Muslim countries, the first of which is a member of NATO.) Less than a year later, manifestation of their resentment would reverberate around the world from the World Trade Center in New York.

Before leaving the Arabian Peninsula, we visited Qatar, Bahrain, Oman, and the United Arab Emirates. The Emirates, which have won awards from environmental groups worldwide, are greener than New York, Paris, or London, lush with forests, exotic parks, and gardens, all irrigated with water drawn from the Persian Gulf and desalinated. Dubai features the world's richest horse race, the world's richest tennis and golf tournaments, and the world's only seven-star hotel. The last, designed to resemble a vast sailing ship, is owned by Dubai's royal family. The cheapest room goes for $1,000 a night, the most expensive for $8,000. (We stayed at the Hyatt.) The wealth here is staggering, even when compared to that of the richest areas in the rest of the world. In nearly all matters the Emirates can pursue their independent policies. It is no wonder they were being overrun by outsiders. In Abu Dhabi, the wealthiest of the emirates—first among equals thanks to its possession of most of the oil—so overwhelmed was the country by foreigners that $75,000 grants were being offered to Emirian men who married native women. Similar payments were being awarded in Qatar, where some two thirds of the population was non-Qatari.

I kept marveling at the buildings, infrastructure, palaces, markets, mosques, and life. Someday the oil will be gone or barbarians will arrive, and it will all fade back into the desert. We had repeatedly seen extraordinary civilizations that had inevitably declined and many that had crumbled, even in Europe and Japan. Entire cities in China, Central Asia, and Africa had disappeared over the centuries. The fabled Timbuktu will someday be reduced to ruins resembling those of Carthage. The Arabian Peninsula has always been a sparsely populated wasteland and will be again. What will remain of this in a thousand years? Will archaeologists even be able to find it?

We ended our tour of the Arabian Peninsula in Oman, and there, every day, we visited the Iranian Embassy in Muscat, hoping for a visa to drive through Iran. Every day we called New York, we were told our Iranian visas were ready, and every day we reported to the local embassy to find they were not.

(From Dubai, we had gone over to Kish Island, little more than a duty-free shopping destination, and all in all a waste of time—we did it to see what little we could of Iran, which owns the island and requires no visa to visit, since the local government is trying to develop tourism. It was once the shah's private playground. The beaches are segregated by gender and nationality; there is no alcohol and little nightlife; a strict dress code is enforced for both men and women. I doubt Kish Island will be the next vacation hot spot—we met plenty of Muslims around the world who drink, dance, and go to nightclubs, and they are unlikely to be beating a path there.)

Meanwhile, I had been doing research, and discovered that in season, Pakistani onion boats plied the waters of the Arabian Sea between Karachi and Muscat. Christmas was approaching, but, more important, the Eid holiday marking the end of Ramadan was approaching, during which time transportation would be impossible to arrange. If we did not organize something soon, we were going to be stuck in Oman for another two weeks. Having obtained our visas for

*The first night in our tent on the deck of the dhow crossing the*
*Gulf of Oman was romantic. After five days at sea, things*
*on the Indian Ocean got old.*

Pakistan while we were in Cairo, we gave up on Iran and booked passage on the last onion boat out of Oman, a wooden dhow about forty feet long returning empty to Karachi.

With the celebration of our first wedding anniversary approaching and coming to the end of our second full year on the road, we put the mysteries of Arabia behind us and set sail for the Indian subcontinent.

# PART THREE

# 2001

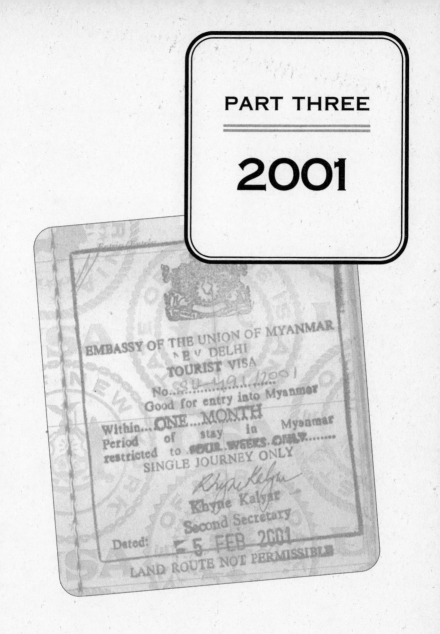

EMBASSY OF THE UNION OF MYANMAR
NEW DELHI
TOURIST VISA
No....SU-491/2001
Good for entry into Myanmar
Within....ONE....MONTH
Period of stay in Myanmar
restricted to....FOUR WEEKS ONLY......
SINGLE JOURNEY ONLY

Khyne Kalyar
Second Secretary

Dated:....5 FEB 2001
LAND ROUTE NOT PERMISSIBLE

# 12

## SIXTY MILLION OF US WASH AWAY OUR SINS

CROSSING THE ARABIAN SEA in a dhow, we spread our sleeping bags on the open deck, and beside them we pitched our tent. During the day, I studied up on Southwest Asia and Paige read the Koran, while members of the Pakistani crew—there were six including the captain—caught fish, which they cleaned and cooked for us on the spot. At night we tuned in the BBC, and there under the stars, in the bow of the boat, we sang Christmas carols to the accompaniment of the King's College Choir. We drifted off to sleep, counting the stars in the belt of Orion. The sunsets on the Indian Ocean, of which the Arabian Sea is a part, were magnificent, the sunrises as red and vibrant as any I had seen in the desert. Christmas morning we woke to discover a school of dolphins swimming along with the boat. Traveling really did not get much better than this, despite the squalor of the vessel and the lingering smell of the onions unloaded in Oman.

Karachi was closed when we arrived. Yes, the largest port in the country, the principal port, the only port to speak of, a port for thousands of years. Not only was it closing for the holiday—celebrating the end of Ramadan—but, as we were told by the government functionaries there, who were shocked to see us, foreigners were not allowed to enter the country by sea. By land or air was fine. It was illegal, they said, for foreigners other than merchant seamen to enter by way of the port. And a car? To bring that in legally required a visit to something like ninety-four offices even with all our documents in order.

It was a couple of days before they let us off the boat, and only after they had impounded the car and confiscated our passports. When I had told various people about Egypt and Turkey and the idiotic bureaucracy of both, they had responded, "You think that's bad? Wait till you get to India." And Pakistan, they said, would be much the same. It was here in the port of Karachi that I learned the concept of "speed money." Nobody ever asked for a bribe, but there was a way to hurry things up. In the end, we visited maybe a dozen offices, and six days later, on New Year's Day, we were allowed in.

With regard to geopolitics and Pakistan: any notions I had going in, any insights I might have come away with, are all rendered moot by the fact that I was there before September 11, 2001. Shortly before we arrived, President Clinton had paid a state visit to India, with which Pakistan has essentially enjoyed a condition of alternately cold and hot war since 1947. Clinton had spent several days sightseeing in India with his daughter. The most he was willing to grant Pakistan, by contrast, was a stopover at the airport for some brief, and not entirely friendly, remarks. So bad were U.S. relations with Pakistan that the president's wife, who was running for the U.S. Senate in New York, had returned a $50,000 campaign contribution from a group of Pakistani-American doctors. Exacerbating Pakistani anti-American sentiment at the time of our arrival: the United States, having sold a large number of fighter planes to Pakistan, had recently refused to deliver them but had kept the money. This was the state of U.S.-Pakistan relations when Paige and I were there in early January, and it prevailed until September 11, 2001. On September 12, Pakistan was America's great ally and longtime friend.

Naturally that infuriated even more Pakistanis, with positions within the politically divided country hardening on both sides. Today anti-Americanism characterizes *all* political opinion in Pakistan.

*Cotton is to Pakistan as oil is to Nigeria.*

Pakistan is one of those countries that I believe will not survive as such, irrespective of its irreconcilable differences with India. The regional differences and shared animosities within Pakistan itself are so dramatic as to threaten its viability. This is a country rushed together by way of a mass migration of Muslims in the wake of Indian independence. (Muslims who came to Pakistan in 1947 are still considered different from those who were already there at the time. Their children and their grandchildren are still "inferior." Class distinctions parallel those now expressed in Germany, where former East Germans are discriminated against.) A nation hopelessly conceived by frenetic English bureaucrats, it is one whose center will not hold. The farmers of the Punjab have nothing in common with the tribesmen of Baluchistan. The inhabitants of the North-West Frontier are descendants of Caucasians who came down centuries ago. Many still have blue eyes. The various places meshed together after World War II have rarely had much in common. The country is unstable (and especially dangerous since it has nuclear weapons). In time it will be several countries.

In Karachi, looking in the newspaper to check out the events of the day, as was our habit wherever we went, we found a horse race, admission a dollar. Paige was allowed in for free, and immediately we found out why. Inside, there were five thousand men, all in traditional dress, and no women. Paige was instantly the focus of attention, drawing eyes away from the horses. With one of the numerous bookies competing with one another for business, we placed bets, and after three or four losses we left.

Paige and I traveled from Karachi, up through the Indus River Valley, to Lahore. India and Pakistan share a border of some two thousand kilometers, and just outside the city of Lahore, Pakistan's second largest, is the only place you can cross from one country to the other. Tensions had cooled somewhat by the time we arrived: the border was open daily; a few years before it had been open only three nights a month.

Heading north to Lahore, we followed a pretty good four-lane highway most of the way. And we had to make adjustments to the international rankings we were keeping. Pakistan, we decided rather quickly, was home to the worst drivers in the world. They were thus far the hands-down winners. They just drove wherever they wanted, sticking to no particular side of the road, traveling on whichever side was in better condition. Inbound, outbound, there was no such thing as far as they were concerned. Donkey carts, oxcarts, and the occasional camel cart all shared the road with vehicular traffic, and all used whichever side of the road happened to be handy.

Traffic in Pakistan is handled far less efficiently than laundry. The laundry system in Karachi is one of those things that defy understanding. You cannot see how it could possibly work, but it does. Men fan out all over the city collecting laundry, picking it up without benefit of receipts, laundry marks, or any apparent system of identification. Nothing is written down. Carrying huge bundles of laundry on their backs or by donkey cart, they deliver it to a central facility that covers maybe fifteen acres and contains hundreds of sinks.

There the laundry is hand-washed and placed in the sun to dry. One man washes colors (most of the employees are men) and another handles whites; various people handle various tasks. If the laundry needs ironing, it is ironed. The iron used is heated by hot coals, held in a receptacle built into the iron itself. There is no electricity. Once dry, the laundry is folded and returned to its owner.

I had come upon the facility by accident on one of my previous trips; I had just happened to be driving by. I was determined to see if it still existed. Paige and I could not take enough pictures. It was the most astonishing enterprise. I kept trying to figure out how it worked. I saw no bookkeeping, I saw no paper of any kind, I saw no money change hands. It was like the market in Lagos, where the streets were absolute chaos. In its own way, each was as marvelous a product of human resourcefulness as the underground cities of Cappadocia. No matter how far I traveled, human ingenuity never failed to astonish me.

Dhobi Ghat, the laundry in Mumbai, is even larger and more chaotic than the facility in Karachi.

The people of the Indus Valley thousands of years ago developed the number system we use today. We call the numerals "Arabic," but the conquering Muslims merely adopted this efficient system and spread it to the world.

The civilization did not stop at mathematics. It proved extraordinarily adept at controlling the vast amounts of water that flowed out of the Himalayas. Today, the country's predominantly agricultural economy owes much to an ingenious system of dams and interchanges known as the Sukkur Barrage, which controls nearly fifty thousand miles of canals. It is a marvel of engineering that we were not allowed to photograph, given its strategic sensitivity. The United States, for example, has nothing on which it so singularly depends. Much like that of the Aswan Dam in Egypt, its destruction would effectively mean the destruction of the country.

The food in Pakistan was consistently good. Often we selected our own food, as we did in China, only here the animals were bigger. Rather than pick a snake or a turtle, we would step outdoors and choose a chicken or a goat, which would be beheaded and served to us fresh. Everywhere we went, we ran across armed soldiers. In every restaurant there were at least ten guys sitting around with submachine guns.

The border crossing east of Lahore, in the town of Wagah, is the scene of one of the goofiest, yet somehow most sophisticated, military ceremonies on earth. There, at five every afternoon, on either side of the international border, the soldiers of Pakistan and India, respectively, in elaborate costumes, enact a changing-of-the-guard ritual, in which they aggressively posture and strut and stare one another down as a substitute for actually going to war, or at least in the forestalling of it. It smacks of nothing so accurately as a Monty Python routine, specifically John Cleese's portrayal of a bureaucrat in the Ministry of Silly Walks. That the participants themselves take the drama so seriously, that they have so ritualized it, speaks well of the whole thing. The simple notion of mock warfare itself is a very sophisticated concept. If all conflicts around the globe could be handled in this fashion, the world would be a much nicer place. It sure beats lobbing nukes back and forth across the border, as these two countries seem perpetually poised to do and may very well do any day now.

We did not want to stick around until five and therefore passed on the ceremony. One basic rule of crossing borders is to get going as fast as possible. Otherwise, someone may change his mind.

Once in India, we headed straight for the city of Amritsar, just east of Wagah. Amritsar, in the heart of the Punjab, is the holy city of the Sikhs. Founded by Guru Nānak in the sixteenth century, the Sikh re-

*The milkman on his rounds in India.*

*A motor vehicle accident in India, one of many accidents around the world
that left us baffled at just how they had ever managed to happen.
Never underestimate mankind's ingenuity at achieving the
seemingly impossible behind the wheel.*

ligion is a hybrid of Hindu and Islamic beliefs, and its followers adhere to a sacred text known as Guru Granth Singh, or the Collection of Sacred Wisdom. There are about twenty million Sikhs in the world, and almost all of them live in the Punjab.

The Punjab, home to one of the chief separatist movements in India, was put under direct control of the federal government in 1984 after Prime Minister Indira Gandhi was assassinated by her Sikh bodyguards following an army attack on the Sikhs' Golden Temple in Amritsar. When I had last visited the region in 1988, one could travel only with a military convoy. Things had cooled down somewhat since then, but almost simultaneously the long-running Muslim separatist movement in Kashmir had grown more violent.

India is a country defined by violence and political instability. Its viability as a nation is threatened not only by the separatist movements of various minorities but also by violent Hindu extremists within the majority population itself. Savagery has been a way of life here since 1947. Immediately after independence, hundreds of thousands of Hindus in Pakistan and Muslims in India were slaughtered by the majority populations in each country, and at least twelve million refugees fled across the border in either direction.

Over the past thirty years India has also been very aggressive toward neighboring countries. It has been at war with China, Pakistan, Bangladesh, and by proxy with Sri Lanka. Indians have marched into and occupied several islands in the Indian Ocean. Not since independence have they had stable relations with any of their neighbors. Nor have they yet proved that they can get along with themselves. Half of the country has no idea what the other half is actually doing. The people in Calcutta have nothing to do with the people in Madras. In Parliament, ministers from Bengal will not have anything to do with ministers from the Punjab, who will have little to do with ministers from the South, who will have little to do with ministers in the North.

Notwithstanding all this, India was one of those countries I visited expecting to find exciting investment opportunities. Having been allied with Russia during the Cold War and pretty much socialist in its outlook, the country had found itself bankrupt by 1991, with no more than three weeks of foreign currency reserves left in its account. So the government started deregulating and opening the economy.

India, it seemed, had learned its lesson. And it was a country with a large middle class, so great things were possible.

Unfortunately, by the time I left India, I found just the opposite to be true. Yes, I did see some signs of a liberalizing economy and a realization on the government's part that it needed outside capital and expertise. But an anticolonial, anticapitalist spirit prevails. The country epitomizes bureaucracy, chauvinism, and protectionism run amok. A recent industry study into the approvals process required for a foreign investment project revealed that it would take an entrepreneur ten man-years to get the approvals necessary. We could not even collect a replacement mirror for our car since we did not have an "import license"—for a one-of-a-kind mirror useful to no one else in India—not even to take it out of the country. It was still in Calcutta Airport as we headed to Bangladesh. "We are smarter than everybody else simply because we are Indians" is the theme of the day. The information technology boom just served to persuade them of that.

In India, self-described as a great incubator of information technology, we could not even use mobile phones universally. We had to buy a different phone for almost every city. A mobile phone in China works everywhere in the country. The Indians are extraordinarily resentful and jealous of the Chinese, especially since India was richer than China as recently as the 1980s. They will tell you that China is not a democracy, that they, in India, are citizens of the largest democracy in the world. Indeed, they do have a large middle class, about 200 million people. But that leaves about 800 million who are not middle class. (And taking the high ground on democracy only casts the abysmal performance of India as a country into starker light; in failing its people, it does not have the excuse that Communist and other totalitarian governments do.) China has grown far more than India in the last twenty years, and China has infrastructure—highways, telephones, mobile phones. India has virtually none of these.

In Mumbai and Delhi, where we went shopping, the most recent computer equipment available in the shops was three-year-old American technology. India, overprotected, will not let in the newest technology. We drove from coast to coast, from Mumbai to Calcutta, and it took us almost a week. Those cities are no more than two thousand miles apart. We drove all day, every day, and we were lucky to average thirty miles an hour. The road, which was paved all the way, was only two lanes wide and used by everybody—trucks, camels, donkeys. Truck drivers average about twelve miles an hour getting across India. How can they be competitive with China, where a trucker can whip across the country at four times the speed?

All of this is a holdover from the days of Jawaharlal Nehru and his daughter, Indira Gandhi, whose Congress Party has controlled the country virtually uninterrupted since independence. Only bureaucrats, politicians, and a small elite of protected businessmen have flourished. Nehru was the poster boy for liberation movements around the globe. A leader in the world movement of nonaligned nations, he was bitterly anticolonialist and anti-West. He considered all foreign capital and expertise to be exploitation and led the nonaligned nations in swearing allegiance to socialism. By now most countries have chosen privatization. When I was in India, people there talked about it, yet in ten years they had privatized only one company, and it was a bakery.

There are some huge companies in India, but it became very clear very quickly that they cannot be competitive in the world market. The country ranks second in the world in number of acres of arable land, but its crop yields per acre are only 30 percent of world averages. China, by comparison, is beginning to export various goods and agricultural products. As you drive around the world, you do not find many Indian products, notwithstanding the country's massive economies of scale—its internal, protected market is one billion people—because it has not developed the concentration of capital, the expertise, or the quality that is required to compete beyond its borders. Like all countries with protected economies, India has no concept of quality. The Soviet Union never exported anything either.

According to a survey conducted by the Delhi School of Economics and the Indian Social Institute, only about 35 million of the nation's 165 million children aged six to ten finish primary school. University in India is for the elite and well connected. The reason one sees so many Indian college students studying abroad is that the government has spent so little money on building places for them to study at home, despite the growing population and demand.

Almost immediately upon entering India, we noticed that there were pigs. Which is not as weird as it sounds. For, having seen livestock of

Many people in the world have never seen pictures of themselves. Our instant camera was an icebreaker—and frequently a lifesaver.

With some sixty million other people in Allahabad, we washed away our sins in the Ganges during the holiest of Hindu festivals, the Kumbh Mela, the largest ever gathering of mankind, not to be matched in importance until 2145. We were given beds by the Hare Krishnas.

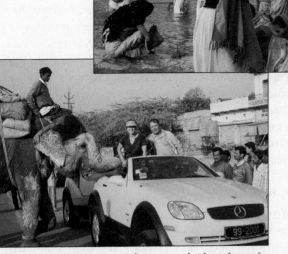

They were on their way to pick up a new bride and transfer her to the groom's home when we distracted them on the street in Jaipur. The smaller of the two could tell we were not from around there.

all kinds every day for three months, the truth is that we had not seen a pig since leaving Ethiopia in September. Muslims, of course, do not eat pork, so there is no reason to have them around. Hindus, to whom the cow is sacred, do not eat beef. They do eat pork, hence the pigs. But because they worship the cow, there are cows all over the place. Cows have the run of the country.

(India, paradoxically, is one of the largest Muslim countries in the world, just by sheer force of population. It has ten million more Muslims than Pakistan and only forty million fewer than Indonesia, which is the largest Muslim country in the world. With only 3 percent of its population speaking English, India, for similar reasons, for what it is worth, is the third largest English-speaking nation in the world, after the United States and the United Kingdom.)

Hinduism, the oldest of the world's major religions, is a blend of polytheistic religious belief and philosophy that dates to the second millennium B.C. With almost 800 million adherents, it is found in few places outside India, where it originated. It comprises numerous religious cults and various schools of philosophy. Ask seven hundred Hindus to define their beliefs, and you might get seven hundred different answers. Different sects rely on different sacred texts, and worship is largely an individual or family matter. Accepted by virtually all Hindus, however, is the belief that the waters of the Ganges River are sacred.

Every twelve years, in the greatest and holiest of Hindu festivals, Kumbh Mela, millions of Hindus meet in the city of Allahabad, where the Ganges and Yamuna Rivers converge with the mythical River of Enlightenment, and bathe in especially holy stretches of the Ganges to wash away their sins. Celebrated since the second century B.C., the Allahabad Kumbh Mela is one of a cycle of pilgrimages—lesser Kumbh Melas alternate among three other holy cities during the intervening years—and is the largest gathering of humanity on earth.

The twelve-year interval is stipulated by the Hindu calendar, based on astrological readings of planetary alignments. The most powerful alignment, and the most propitious period for immersing oneself in the holy waters, occurs every 144 years. Paige and I arrived in India during such a period in January 2001. Not until the year 2145 would the heavens align themselves in such an auspicious way. As a result, Allahabad would host a human convergence that over a period of a few weeks would amount to some sixty million people. If this was not the largest gathering of human beings in history, it was certain to be the largest in 144 years and was unlikely to be exceeded for another 144.

Obviously, one cannot be in India during this period of time and not hear about it. Paige and I heard about it, and of course we made our way to Allahabad.

There were tents up all over the place, there were dancing and music, gurus were leading their flocks into the water. There were holy men everywhere, many of them naked, some being carried to the waterside by their acolytes, some smoking holy stuff. In the water at any one time there were as many as five million people.

Think of Woodstock and multiply it by ten.

We were first made aware of the Kumbh Mela in a series of e-mails we received on the Web site. One of our correspondents, encouraging us to go, advised us to make our way to what he referred to as the ISKCON educational camp. Mention his name, he said, and the people there would provide us with accommodation. We did, and nobody recognized his name, but they gave us accommodation anyway. ISKCON, we discovered, is the International Society for Krishna Consciousness. These were the people who, in my sole experience of them, danced down the street in orange robes with their heads shaved, chanting "Hare Krishna." Most Americans see them as a bunch of lunatics. If I had told my mother I was staying with the Hare Krishnas, she would have been horrified. Lord Krishna, of course, is a major Hindu deity. As it happened, they could not have been more hospitable. In a large communal tent that accommodated about two hundred people and featured running water and electricity, Paige and I were each given a bed and fell asleep to the rhythmic chanting outside of "Hare Krishna." And it was in the Krishna compound, where we spent only one night, that I experienced a convergence as rare in its way as that which brought the planets into alignment for the Kumbh Mela itself.

"Jim Rogers," said a black African Hare Krishna, a great big guy, walking up to me and introducing himself. "I met you in the Central African Republic in 1991. You were on a motorcycle, going around the world."

I was speechless. I remembered him well. We had been in Bangui,

*In a small village in Jabalpur, we stopped to take her picture.*
*While I was taking a second picture, an instant photo to give her,*
*Paige was assuring a male villager of several reincarnations of ridicule.*

the capital of the Central African Republic. He had been there doing missionary work, as he had explained it at the time—proselytizing Krishna consciousness, no doubt. His name was Bali, and he was a Nigerian. He had had a walking stick that I liked and that he had sold me when we met in Bangui. I still owned it. That our paths would cross again, that we would just stumble upon each other in a crowd of maybe seven million people that day, at the Kumbh Mela in India, was absolutely astonishing.

A small world? So small as to be beyond comprehension.

The next day Paige and I washed away our sins in the Ganges.

After Allahabad we drove to Agra, so I could show Paige the Taj Mahal and to see it again myself. No matter how often you go, it knocks you over with its majesty every time. Foreigners pay forty-seven times what it costs Indians to visit the site—or admission—or ninety-four times, if you factor in the tax foreigners are required to pay. By way of helping you swallow your outrage, the Indians label the difference an environmental tax.

This mixture of annoyance and wonder was characteristic of our visit to India. It is a glorious place in which to travel, a picturesque country with beautiful people and exquisite cuisines, its temples and peasant villages a reflection of thousands of years of culture. But the infrastructure is a nightmare—the phones, electricity, water, and roads are hopeless—and bureaucracy has a choke hold on the country.

Before seeing the Taj Mahal, we had visited the Golden Temple of the Sikhs at Amritsar. We traveled east from Agra to see the temples of Khajuraho, over a thousand years old and mathematically precise, and probably most famous for the erotic sculptures that adorn them. Had we not detoured to visit the temples of Khajuraho—our intention had been to drive from Agra directly to Mumbai—we would have found ourselves asleep in Ahmadabad at the center of an earthquake that took the lives of tens of thousands of people.

We were traveling through a small village in Jabalpur State, south of Khajuraho, when Paige left an indelible mark on the people of the Indian countryside. They do not see many foreigners out in such little villages, and rarely do they see people with fair complexions and light hair. Paige always drew attention in such places, and on a couple of occasions she had actually been pawed by local men.

*This lady of the night awaits clients in her three-by-three-by-six-foot cubby. Her new labor union in Calcutta has met with some success in promoting the use of condoms.*

*Space is scarce in densely populated Bangladesh, so cow pies are dried on trees. They will later be used for fuel.*

*Martial law was in force in Bangladesh after an opposition political party declared a hartel—a state of protest during which anyone who ventures out is considered an enemy and subject to murder.*

We had stopped in the village to film a villager we had spotted, a young woman carrying large jugs of water on her head. As usual we attracted a crowd. A local man walked up behind Paige and put his hand on her bottom. She spun around, and there he stood, making no attempt to disassociate himself from the offense, assuming, it seemed, that he had every right to do what he had done.

To appreciate what happened next, one must remember that in India women are the lowest of the low. To call them second class does not come close. They are treated more as property than as human beings. Out in the villages, just to take one example, women are not allowed to leave their homes without the permission of their fathers or husbands.

Paige turned on this particular man, grabbed him by the shirtfront, and started smacking him. She hit him three times, slapping him around the way Humphrey Bogart slapped Peter Lorre in *The Maltese Falcon*. Startled and clearly horrified, he scurried off as soon as he could extricate himself. It was probably the most humiliating thing that could ever happen to the man, being beaten by a woman in public, in front of all the men and women of the village. Hindus, of course, believe in reincarnation, and this poor fellow, in all of his lives, would no doubt be cursed because of the day he was slapped in Jabalpur, put in his place by the petite Paige Parker.

Traveling across India from Mumbai through Bengal to Calcutta, we entered yet another civilization. Calcutta gets horrible press, but it became one of our favorite Indian cities, proving once again that the conventional wisdom is rarely correct. We happened to meet a professor who was helping organize the local prostitutes into a union, and he organized a tour for us of Calcutta's red-light district, led by a group of madams.

We entered Bangladesh toward the end of February, looking forward to learning about an Islamic country where the leaders of both major political parties were women. Among the many things we found there (statistically and by personal experience) is that the capital, Dhaka, is the most polluted city in the world. The country is the world's most densely populated, though the United Nations and other organizations may be helping to solve that problem.

The Bangladesh International Network (BIAN), while we were

there, filed suit against UNICEF, WHO, the World Bank, the Islamic Development Bank, NGO Forum, and other groups that were responsible for funding the sinking of wells contaminated by arsenic and other poisons. Studies done in the 1980s had shown the appalling state of the water in Bangladesh, so the groups cited in the suit had instituted a policy of digging shallow tube wells throughout the country.

In the words of BIAN, "In our globalized world many decisions that affect Bangladesh's future are made outside the country by international agencies, creditor governments, and multinational companies." As a local newspaper reported, "The short and long term effect of arsenic poisoning is lethal. Research has proved beyond doubt that the source of arsenic poisoning is the shallow tube wells from which ninety-seven percent of the rural population receives its drinking water. People are drinking poisonous water every day from shallow tube wells while policymakers and their implementing agencies continue to sink these. While World Bank's own figures claim 20 million people are currently at risk and 75 million are potentially at risk of arsenic poisoning from tube wells, donors continue funding to sink tube wells."

Rather than stop digging wells, international agencies were conducting the Third International Symposium on Reducing the Impact of Toxic Chemicals on Bengal Basin's Economies—the *third*—in the midst of what may be the largest mass poisoning in history.

We reentered India as we moved east, headed for Myanmar (formerly Burma). Traversing Tripura State in the far eastern part of India, we traveled with a military convoy. Not the first convoy with which we traveled on our trip around the world, this was one of the more serious. All the soldiers wore flak jackets, and all the trucks were mounted with machine guns. Leaving at seven in the morning after sharing Polaroids with many of the troops, we traveled as part of the convoy for about seventy kilometers, in the direction of neighboring Assam State, and every hundred meters along the road we passed more soldiers in full battle gear.

In the relative safety of Assam, we got hung up for four days, bivouacked in the city of Silchar, stymied in several attempts to enter the State of Manipur, which alone was undergoing twenty-four different armed insurrections. Kashmir gets the press, but people in Manipur go there for R and R. The eastern states of India are much more chaotic and separatist. It was in Silchar that we learned that our convoy, the day after our leaving it, had been ambushed and eleven of the soldiers with whom we had traveled had been killed. No doubt we had photographs of some of them. Had we traveled with them a day later, we might have been killed along with them.

We were turned back at the border of Manipur, told we could not drive through the state without permission from Delhi, which I was convinced we had already received. As we found in numerous places, people do not even know their own country.

After returning to Silchar and receiving the permission we needed, we returned to the border and were turned back again. This went on for four days, as we jumped through every hoop the border official told us to jump through.

Meanwhile, the state police chief in Silchar, who was helping me, was trying to talk me out of making the trip.

"I can't stop you from getting permission," he said, "but don't do it. Please don't go. My policemen are always getting killed up there. For your own sake, stay away."

He had lost nine policemen in the previous twelve months, he said.

But I was determined to get to Myanmar. When finally I found someone in Delhi who was able to give me the permission I needed and the border official allowed us to cross, I was instantly terrified, more frightened than I had been at any other point in the trip. I was as fearful as Paige had been the night she had cried in Angola, so fearful that I told Paige of the police warnings only a month later. We were traveling through mountainous jungle, and driving around every turn I anticipated an ambush. Everyone knew we were coming. With all our back-and-forth at the border, word had to have spread throughout Manipur that these crazy foreigners—not many ever come through—were trying to get permission to enter the territory. Every time I saw three or four young men beside the road, I became terrified. Was this an ambush? I wondered.

When we reached the international border safely, we were greeted with great excitement. The guards in Myanmar were expecting us, having been notified in advance that we had received permission to enter the country. Their delight, which we shared, was mixed with amazement—we understood why when they explained to us that we

*We always tried street food, as here in Silchar,
although often we could not identify
what we were eating.*

*They were on their way home from working in the forest in Myanmar
when they ran across us. The astonishment was mutual.*

were the first nonlocals to drive across the Myanmar border from India since the Second World War. But our drama with the bureaucrats of Manipur had not yet come to an end. Whoever had stamped us out of India had obviously not consulted his boss, the subinspector of the station, for the latter came running across the border to tell us that we could not leave India.

My first response was to point out the obvious: we already *had* left India.

No, he said, you cannot leave, because you do not have permission to be in Manipur.

He was telling us—I am not making this up—that we had to return to Manipur, because we were not allowed to *be* in Manipur, and thus we could not leave it.

We were not *in* Manipur (where we were not allowed to be), I told him, and the reason was that we had *left* it. I asked how we could go back to Manipur if we did not have permission to be there. The subinspector insisted we come back to India (although we did not have visas anymore) and drive through the war zones in Manipur (where we did not have permission to be, according to him) to the state capital to gain permission to be in Manipur so we could leave Manipur and India—even though we were already out of both.

Though we never considered acceding to this man's hallucinatory illogic—we were not about to go back to India—the argument nonetheless continued for almost two hours. The Myanmar border officials, rather than simply ignoring him, tried to reason with him, and it appeared they wanted us to do the same. They had to deal with this guy on a regular basis. We were their first foreigners, and they did not want to make this maiden crossing a particularly difficult experience for us, but neither did they want to make it impossible for anyone ever to enter again. In the end, somebody made a phone call and took the subinspector off the hook, and we were free to proceed.

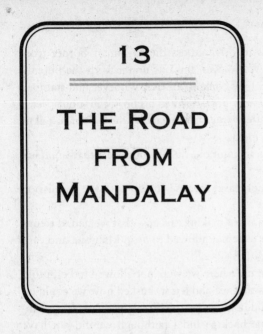

# 13

# THE ROAD
# FROM
# MANDALAY

RULED AS PART OF the British Raj of India since the late nineteenth century, Myanmar, then known as Burma, became a self-
governing protectorate in 1937. It was occupied by Japan in 1942
and was a major theater of military action during the Second World
War. Burma achieved independence in 1948, and, having failed to deliver on autonomy for certain ethnic minorities, the country has been
plagued by various armed separatist movements, including some that
are currently spilling over its various borders.

Burma, now one of the ten poorest countries in the world, was the
richest country in Asia in 1962. That year, in a military coup, General
Ne Win put an end to democratic government, establishing a one-
party state and instituting the party's "Burmese Path to Socialism."
Guided by astrology and numerology and driven by xenophobia,
chauvinism, and arrogance, he cut the country off from the rest of the
world and ushered in the era of economic stagnation that persists
today despite Myanmar's potential wealth in raw materials and agriculture and its large force of cheap labor.

*Nearly everyone in Myanmar protects his skin with thanaka. A sunscreen and skin softener, the wood-bark paste is known as the "Myanmar Max Factor."*

*On the road to Mandalay: one of many reclining Buddhas in pious Myanmar.*

Direct military control of the country came in 1988, when popular pressure forced Ne Win to resign. In 1989 the country's name was changed back to Myanmar. The British started calling Myanmar Burma, after the largest ethnic group, 150 years ago. Outsiders opposing the generals insist on calling the country Burma—a fairly new colonial name. The anticolonialist people of Myanmar and the generals insist on the historical name. I decided to stay neutral on the political situation until I had done my homework, but on the matter of the country's name I did take the side of history and the people in the street: Myanmar. In 1990, for the first time in thirty years, the country held multiparty free elections, but the results were nullified when the opposition party headed by Aung San Suu Kyi, the daughter of one of the country's founders, won a decisive victory. In 1991, Myanmar became the focus of international attention and the target of U.S. sanctions when Aung, who had been placed under house arrest along with other leaders of the elected government, was awarded the Nobel Peace Prize.

Under General Than Shwe, who assumed leadership of the ruling junta in 1992, the political repression diminished somewhat. A convention was called to draft a new Burmese constitution in 1996. (Aung San Suu Kyi's father had been instrumental in liberating Burma from the British, and the constitution whose drafting he oversaw stipulated that Burma could not be placed under the leadership of someone married to a foreigner. Aung San Suu Kyi, educated at Oxford, who had been living in England before the election, was married to an Englishman when she ran for prime minister, making her ineligible for the position, according to the country's military rulers.)

At the same time, the country began to emerge from its international isolation. In 1997, in the face of U.S. trade sanctions, Myanmar was made a full member of the Association of Southeast Asian Nations (ASEAN), the region's powerful trading group. Twenty years ago, there weren't tourists in Myanmar. Fifteen years ago, tourists could spend a week there. In the mid-1990s things loosened up even more. Around the country, tourist hotels started appearing. The government declared 1997 the Year of the Tourist.

When I started posting reports from Myanmar on the Web site, I received numerous e-mails from people who were furious that I was there, insisting that I was merely supporting the rule of the evil generals in charge. I should have been boycotting the country along with all good people, they said. But *not* all good people were boycotting the country. Numerous nations were engaging Myanmar and doing business there: Japan, China, India, Malaysia, Russia, Singapore. These countries were poised to exploit a variety of natural resources—timber, natural gas, gold, and other minerals—and to capitalize on the inevitable growth of tourism.

I would submit that the best way to change a country is to engage that country. Isolation rarely brings change. You want to put an end to Fidel Castro's hold over Cuba? The pope's visit in the late 1990s did wonders—the Cubans have openly celebrated Christmas ever since, not having done so in more than thirty-five years. Send Jennifer Lopez next. Castro will not live forever, and while the U.S. State Department is sitting around waiting for him to depart this vale of tears, the Europeans, the Mexicans, the Canadians, and everybody else are flooding into Cuba, buying up all the good stuff. By the time Castro is gone, there are not going to be any decent deals left for Americans. If it were legal to do so, you can bet I would be putting money there now.

In Delhi I had visited Indian friends, Ajay and Aodiiti Mehta, who had studied in the United States. With them was an American woman who talked about her upcoming trip to Myanmar. When I told her I would be there the following month, she grew indignant, claiming that U.S. sanctions prohibited my going.

"Why can you go and I can't?" I asked.

"Because I work for an NGO," she said.

Terrific.

"I'm going to Myanmar to examine the situation," she said.

"So am I," was my answer. "Why should I let you go to Myanmar, examine the situation, and make a judgment for me?"

Did I mention that we did not get along?

The road to Mandalay, to which we were heading, was no road at all; it was the Manipur and Chindwin Rivers. (The great river of commerce, of course, was the Irrawaddy.) We had to find our own roads, winding through the jungle. And many of the roads were horrible. Myanmar is a primitive country, and thus it was all the more striking to observe that all the houses, however modest, were made of teak.

Men and women in Myanmar retreat to monasteries at various times in their lives for study and reflection, but cars, it seems, never cease to fascinate young men the world over.

On the way to her ear-piercing ceremony, this six-year-old will participate in a rite of passage somewhat analogous to baptism in the West.

But, of course, teak is the country's major export. What would have been really surprising, once we thought about it, would have been to see a building constructed of pine.

One of the first things we noticed about Myanmar was how pious the Burmese people are. Everywhere we turned we saw another Buddhist temple. Every day in Mandalay at four A.M., at a shrine to Living Buddha, the monks wash Living Buddha's face and brush his teeth, preparing the statue for a busy day. For the next twelve hours, as they have every day since 1784, the faithful, lining up and awaiting their turn, walk up to the figure and apply gold leaf to its surface.

The leaf is procured from goldsmiths who work nearby. Wielding heavy sledgehammers, unpackaging gold as it is delivered, they pound for hours, flattening it out. They work all day, taking breaks only when indicated by a variation on the hourglass: a hollow coconut, with a hole punched in the bottom, floating in water. When the coconut fills with water and sinks, it is time to take a break. I bought leaf from one of them—only men, no women, are allowed to approach the statue—joined the queue outside the temple, and added gold to the two hundred years' worth that had been applied to Living Buddha.

There are huge temple complexes in Myanmar. Some are new—the wealthy Asian industrialists whose fortunes stem, respectively, from the Kikkoman and Tiger Balm trademarks have built temples there—and some were constructed hundreds of years ago. Western Myanmar is home to one of the largest temple pagoda complexes in the world. In the city of Bagan, now a UN World Heritage Site, there were once four thousand extraordinary temples dating back to the tenth and eleventh centuries, about a thousand of which have been saved. Breathtaking in the architectural achievement perfected nine hundred years ago, overwhelming in their beauty and significance, they cover the horizon, perhaps the single most impressive collection of buildings and man-made structures that we had seen since leaving Europe. When we were there, hundreds of people were completing pilgrimages to Bagan, making offerings of food and flowers and saying their prayers.

In the countryside we stumbled upon a cheroot factory, where one of the women rolling cigars asked if we could send her some perfume when we got to Yangon. Paige sent her some Chantilly. I suspect that the NGO woman, with her concern about sanctions, would not have approved.

In the past decade sanctions have become a favorite tool of the United States. Wherever we went, however, we found that they were not effective, because competing products swept in or American products were smuggled in. Either way, American workers, businesses, and taxpayers, not the "offending" countries, were the losers. Sanctions resulted only in more enemies for the United States.

We left Myanmar with a certain amount of regret. All in all, it was an exquisite country to visit. The people were gentle, religious, hard-working, and disciplined. While I predict that the country will become more prosperous and more open to the outside world, I do not see a great future for Myanmar within the confines of its British-drawn borders. It is unlikely to survive the next fifty years intact. Already parts of the Shan State are practically autonomous, controlled by warlords empowered by the opium trade. Nor will violent separatist movements in other parts of the country be put down easily. Perhaps the Burmese ethnic group will have its own country eventually. Nonetheless, if you want to see a country that is untouched and pure, if you enjoy noodle soup and fried dough for breakfast—you will get plantains for dessert and a vegetable stew made with fish paste, called *ngapi*, at all other times—I recommend Myanmar as one of the great places to visit, and I suggest traveling there soon before the rest of the world arrives. Entrepreneurs should be especially quick, as the rest of Asia is rushing in.

Myanmar shares a long peninsula with Thailand, and, due to international tensions, we were unable to drive the length of it or across the border. To make our way south—we were headed in the direction of Indonesia—we took a slow boat to the tip of Myanmar, stopping in various ports. From there we made a quick run across the southern tip of Thailand, where an Islamic separatist movement—Thailand is over 95 percent Buddhist—is gaining strength. We headed south to the relative safety of Malaysia.

The Federation of Malaya, now circumscribed by what is known as Peninsular Malaysia, achieved independence from Great Britain in 1957. The country expanded in 1963, incorporating Singapore and the British colonies of North Borneo, which lay about four hundred miles across the South China Sea, and changed its name to Malaysia. In 1965 Singapore, a predominantly Chinese city on the southern tip of the Malay Peninsula, seceded, declaring its independence. Ethnic Malays (Muslims) constitute a small majority of Malaysia's population. Chinese (Buddhists) are a large minority. About 10 percent of the population is Indian (Hindus).

A constitutional monarchy, Malaysia has been run since 1981 by Prime Minister Datuk Seri Mahathir bin Mohamad, now in his late seventies, who has transformed the country from an agriculture-based economy to one of the fastest-growing economies in Asia. The discovery of oil did not hurt the country's progress. Mahathir, in consolidating his power, capitalized on the majority Malays' fear of exploitation by the far more successful Chinese and Indians, instituting incentives and quotas in commerce and education that favor the former. He instituted a policy of Malay as the language of teaching and gave everyone the option of pursuing degrees in Islamic studies without bothering with math, science, economics, or other useful subjects. Most of these graduates, with little marketability in the private sector, have ended up working for the government. Internal opposition to Mahathir's government has increased over the years as he has assumed more and more dictatorial power, which he is certainly going to need if the price of oil goes down. History is replete with evidence that revolutions do not stem from political suppression as much as aroused expectations that go unmet.

A contributing factor to the Asian crisis of 1997 was the fact that the currencies of several Asian nations were tied to the U.S. dollar. The Malaysian ringgit was one of them. Other nations, following the collapse, acknowledged the mistake and cut their currencies free, allowing them to float on the international market. Mahathir, screaming about evil international financiers, blocked his nation's currency, making it inconvertible. He said, if you have money here, you cannot take it out. It remained pegged to the dollar. Horrible economics, but he had the guns.

Rarely do politicians respond to failures by saying, "Oh, I made a mistake, I resign." Usually they do what Mahathir did. He insisted that the collapse was not his problem and blamed it on foreign speculators, rather than on the huge debts he had incurred in pursuit of certain projects aimed more at prestige than prosperity.

Sustaining this delusion carried the price tag of even more repression, as dissension on the part of a very unhappy population became more vocal. When you tell people they cannot take their money out of the country, especially when they have grown rich or even moderately successful, they tend to react poorly. I have a few investments in Malaysia, because it is a huge natural resource economy, and I see all the signs of a bull market in natural resources. But I am not terribly happy because I realize that when Mahathir leaves office, whether he dies or is deposed or resigns, as he says he will do, the country is in for trouble. History has shown that when a strong dictatorial leader departs after a long period—whether from a country, a company, or a family—a period of instability always follows. You can see the signs of it already in political demonstrations, turmoil, and emigration from the country.

What I found in Malaysia was an extremely rich nation with modern highways, hotels, restaurants, and shopping malls. At least some of its borrowing had not been completely squandered. The two tallest buildings in the world are located in Kuala Lumpur. Arriving in the Malaysian capital, Paige was dumbfounded—she ascertained that we had not seen shopping like this in a long time, certainly not since Dubai. At Cartier she found the wedding band of her dreams—to replace the one we had picked up in Antwerp to get us through the wedding. The country's multiyear period of prosperity and development was especially noticeable to us, because what Malaysia meant to Paige and me mostly, as far as the trip was concerned—besides an examination of Mahathir's madness—was comfort and ease of travel. The country was a kind of rest stop.

An even greater economic success than Malaysia is Singapore. The city is strategically located on the Strait of Malacca, probably the single most important waterway in the world—virtually all Asian trade passes through—but even as recently as the 1960s, it was little more than a mosquito-ridden backwater. It is now one of the largest ports in the world, and its broad-based economy draws strength from international finance, banking, communications, high-technology manufacturing, and tourism. With an enormously high living standard, Singapore is perhaps the greatest success story of the developed world in the past forty years.

And the entire story played out under the absolute, authoritarian rule of the country's first, and long-serving, prime minister, Lee Kuan Yew.

Plato argued in *The Republic* that there are four stages in the evolution of nations: from dictatorship to oligarchy to democracy to chaos, and back again. The Chinese, whether or not they have read Plato, operate on the same principle. They see it as the Asian way. A strong central government will lead to prosperity, and the first few who become successful will maintain the stability of society until the government of the few gives way to democracy. But an unfettered democracy, as they see it—and as Plato argued—will inevitably give way to chaos. Until, of course, a new dictator emerges.

We all know the horror stories about Singapore, how you have to have a particular haircut, how you cannot spit on the sidewalk, how chewing gum and smoking are seriously discouraged, and how you can be caned for a variety of minor offenses, such as scribbling graffiti on walls. We can debate what many see as Lee's horribly repressive approach to government. But no matter how horrible you think he might be, there are a lot of dictators around the world far more repressive than he and who do not have anything to show for it. Mobutu Sese Seko of Zaire was one.

You will not find another city in the world that is as rich and as safe as Singapore. Paige and I attended a concert in the park performed by the Singapore Orchestra. The park, like everything in Singapore, was immaculate. The concert was free. There were children running all over the place. People were drinking wine, picnicking, listening to Beethoven. There were thousands of people, and there was not a policeman in sight. Can you imagine that happening in Central Park?

Singapore did not become successful because its government was evil but because its government was disciplined and smart and played by sound economic rules. A well-educated man, Lee, who is now retired but remains a powerful force in the nation's politics, went to work every day literally asking how he could make Singapore better, and not simply that, but how he could ensure it would be better in forty years. With a grounding in serious economics, he understood that developing a sound economy required high savings and high investment. He instituted the mandatory retirement funds that account for Singapore's current savings rate of more than 40 percent.

That is not a typo. Forty percent. Every citizen was required to invest and save huge amounts of his money for the future. Singapore has the highest savings and investment rate of any country in the world. (In the United States, by contrast, there was actually a period in the 1990s when we had a negative savings rate. We had spent whatever accumulated savings we had and were living off credit cards.) Lee also understood that success lay in addressing the country's strengths, the most obvious of which was the port, soon to be one of the world's busiest. As all his neighbors began discovering oil, he began developing refineries. He spent a huge amount of money on education. With an educated workforce, the best educated in the region and perhaps the world, the country was able to ascend to a position of power in the electronics industry when the boom came.

Singapore has the third highest foreign currency reserves in the world. With a population of less than four million, its reserves are third only to those of Japan and China, whose populations are 125 million and 1.2 billion respectively. The people of Singapore have a lot of the other people's money in the bank—per capita, they have more than anybody else.

The downside? Well, freedom of expression is not the only thing that commands a high price in Singapore. The country's very success has escalated the cost of doing business. The costs of production and labor are now very high, and the cost of living has gone through the roof. And thanks to regulation and protectionism, the financial industry is showing signs of rot.

In the beginning, Singapore, capitalizing on its comparative advantage—it had a lot of money, it understood money, and furthermore, it was Chinese—offered incentives to financial companies, especially those in Hong Kong. When Hong Kong, which was the financial center of Asia, reverted to Communist China, Singapore proved a natural place for many companies to set up business. And Lee understood the future. While the Irish were making sure everybody learned to speak Gaelic and Iceland was mandating that its schoolchildren learn Danish, Lee was insisting that everyone speak Chinese or English. But with time inertia set in. The country was rich, the financial industry was protected, and the lack of competition led to complacency.

I had an account in Singapore's largest bank, and while I was there

I wanted to undertake some financial transactions. I deposited a check and started doing business a few days later, only to be informed that it would be five weeks before the check cleared. The check was drawn on Merrill Lynch, which had an office around the corner.

"Do you actually believe," I asked the banker, "that in the year 2001 it takes five weeks to clear a check to the largest bank in Singapore from the largest stockbroker in the world?"

"I don't know why it is," he said, "but that's the way it works."

"I do business all over the world," I told him. "I know how long it takes to clear a check, even an international check. World commerce and finance would come to an end if that were really the case."

"There's nothing I can do," he answered. "I have gone to my boss and my boss's boss, and they say that is how it works."

I let a week pass and returned to the bank.

"I called Merrill Lynch," I said. "They cleared the check. The funds are good. They have given your agent the money."

Nothing doing.

Singapore has since established a high-powered financial services committee to recommend proposals to open the industry. However, as a foreign official was quoted as saying in the *Financial Times:* "I think Singapore has already missed the boat on becoming an international financial center. They should have liberalized when times were good."

Singapore conceivably could become the Venice or the Florence of the digital age. The people have the brains, the money, and the motivation. The problem is that while you can impose discipline, you cannot impose creativity, and the leaders in Singapore now realize that all the guys wearing pink hair, criticizing the government, and spitting on the sidewalk are the new wave of IT experts, so they have loosened up somewhat. Lee, because he is smart, has come to realize that conformity has its drawbacks, and is trying to figure out a way to make his country hospitable to the next crop of innovators.

Every cabinet minister in Singapore is paid the equivalent of more than $600,000 U.S. a year. It is Lee's way of attracting talent and discouraging corruption. A civil servant in Zimbabwe makes the equivalent of maybe $18,000 a year, so every cabinet minister and bureaucrat is likely to be on the take. Lee says that he sees it all over the world, whether in Washington, D.C., or Moscow, and he does not want his guys making decisions based on anything but merit and what is best for the country. And he does not want them leaving government and going off to run a company.

Singapore: one of the largest, most magnificent ports in the world, one of the most efficient container operations on the planet. Indonesia: the world's fourth largest population with more than 200 million people, sixty miles away across the Strait of Malacca, the most heavily traveled trade route in the world. And there was no way to get from one to the other—no car ferry, no scheduled, simple shipping directly across the divide. The best I could come up with was a container ship that would deliver the cars in Jakarta eight days later.

I did not want to spend more than a week getting my car out of the country, so I sought out alternatives and came up with a barge and a tugboat returning to Sumatra. Local guys, Indonesians, traveling virtually empty. Mine were the only cars aboard the barge, and they were the only cargo to speak of. I was the only human aboard. Officials in Singapore would allow only one of us to travel with the cars. Paige and the others took the high-speed passengers-only ferry that makes the Singapore-to-Dumai run regularly. There were a few crewmen aboard the tug, but I was alone aboard the barge for the duration of the trip.

The small-time nature of the enterprise worked to my advantage in one way. This was the most important artery of commerce in the world, and huge numbers of pirates had figured that out. They were organized and ubiquitous. Sometimes they offloaded the cargo to their own ships, but sometimes they went further: killed the crew, sold the cargo, then sold the repainted ship to wreckers. I had heard all the stories and slept uneasily the two nights I spent aboard.

Indonesian bribery is pretty straightforward—corruption there is a way of life—and the bright young police commander I dealt with upon arriving in Dumai was well spoken and well educated. He named a price, and we worked things out pretty quickly. He stamped my papers, let me and the cars into the country, I met up with Paige and the others, and off we went across Sumatra.

We stopped in Minangkabau, whose inhabitants live in huge homes built with roofs shaped like buffalo horns. They claim to be descendants of Alexander the Great's armies. An ethnic group of three million people who dominate much of Indonesian culture, they are a matriarchal society. Property is owned by and passed down through the mother. Bridegrooms move in with the wife's family.

Indonesia, a former Dutch colony, is the largest Islamic nation in the world (87 percent of the population is Muslim) and one of the largest countries in the world geographically. It comprises over fourteen thousand islands that stretch from the Malay Peninsula to New Guinea, about six thousand of which are inhabited, most of which would prefer to be independent. Internal political tension has colored life in Indonesia since colonial times and will continue to do so until the country splits into a dozen or so rational entities. When we arrived, there were serious insurrections everywhere, and much of the time we spent there was devoted to getting across the islands of Sumatra and Java as safely as we could. By 2002 the violence would spread even to Bali. Two percent of Indonesians are Hindus, and most of them live on the island of Bali, the great upmarket tourist destination, which we visited. But precisely because it was what it was—our hotel was full of IBM salesmen on a corporate junket—Bali was not for us. It was just not our style. Making short work of that visit, we headed for the only island in the archipelago that, for my purposes, could not be ignored: the newly liberated island of East Timor.

Indonesia invaded predominantly Christian East Timor, a former Portuguese colony, in 1975. West Timor, formerly Dutch, was already part of Indonesia. Annexation, which was not internationally recognized, followed in 1976, and more than 100,000 East Timorese were killed over the ensuing years in the struggle for liberation. In 1999, when East Timor voted to be independent, the slaughter escalated with the arrival of Indonesian militia. The United Nations, chiefly Australian troops, intervened and was a big presence there when we arrived.

The place was little more than a bomb site when we were there. All the buildings were burned out, there was virtually no electricity, and the only vehicles we saw on the road belonged to the United Nations. Not having paid much attention to what was happening in East Timor except to follow what had been reported in the press, I was unaware until I arrived of the real story behind the war there. It was not about democracy versus dictatorship, Christianity versus Islam, or self-determination versus aggression. Think petroleum deposits. The war between Indonesia and East Timor was about gigantic amounts of natural gas that had been discovered offshore.

On boats in Asia, every inch is exploited.

Newly independent East Timor, with vast riches and a small population—around 800,000—is on the verge of becoming the next Kuwait. Which is why Australia was so willing to send troops. The Australians now have a contract to develop and process East Timor's natural gas. The United Nations is pouring money into the country to help complete its path to independence—and insisting upon a democratic path—but the real money in East Timor is below ground.

I had traveled much of coastal Australia—all but the south—on my motorcycle trip in 1991 and had written about it in *Investment Biker*. On this trip Paige and I would take a different, more inland route, north from Perth to Darwin. We would drive from there, south through the middle of the country, to Alice Springs, then cover new ground, continuing south to Adelaide, east along the coast to Melbourne, and then inland to Sydney.

In 1991, I had spent six weeks traveling Australia, a country the size of our lower forty-eight states (with a population no larger than that of our third largest, New York). Paige and I would complete our visit in five.

In Perth, it became very apparent very quickly how provincial Australia can be. All the shops closed at five P.M. and did not open on Sundays. (There may be one supermarket in the whole state of Western Australia that opens on Sunday.) The practice is explained as being in support of family values, with the limited hours allowing Australian families to spend time together. But it is in no small part a function of protectionism. For example, any newly arrived entrepreneur—or, say, a large chain, such as Wal-Mart—in an attempt to compete, might wisely institute a policy of longer shopping hours, opening his place of business at night and on weekends. But local shop owners—and if given the chance, why not?—resist such competition.

We stumbled on a May Day demonstration against globalization, the WTO, the IMF, and the World Bank. The demonstrators had not a clue that these institutions had little in common. I have made my feelings about the IMF and the World Bank clear—I agree with the protestors that they should be abolished, but for very different reasons, I suppose—but abolishing the WTO would lead to depression and war.

The Australian city I was most eager to visit was Darwin, a frontier town of the first order. I had previously picked it as a wonderful place to invest in and was curious to see if my prediction had come true. On my last trip, traveling from Perth to Darwin, I had hugged the shoreline. To get there this time, Paige and I would drive across the outback.

The Australian outback, of course, is legendary, a vast, nearly empty expanse of gigantic cattle and sheep ranches, wild mining towns, and, after that, little else but kangaroos. As you drive across the outback, you have to be careful of the kangaroos, especially at dusk and dawn. They are so fast, they will hit you before you know they're there. They think they're faster than the cars they see coming. We saw a lot of dead kangaroos on our trip (including the kangaroo that provided the meat I ordered in an Australian restaurant), most often the victim of trucks that could not stop if they tried—so-called road trains are up to 150 feet long. A road train, a cab with three tractor-trailers attached, performs as its name suggests, a locomotive on wheels barreling down long stretches of asphalt at a high rate of speed because there was no reason not to.

The Australian outback is for loners, mavericks, and drifters. The towns of the outback are like the cow towns and mining towns of the American West before barbed wire closed the frontier. Two hundred, three hundred people. The first place we walked into when we stopped for the night, a hotel/restaurant/bar, was reminiscent of such an establishment in old Dodge City. The first thing I saw as I swung open the door was a young woman tending bar who appeared to be in her underwear. I was disoriented and embarrassed when I realized she was only half dressed. It was not until we walked into a second establishment—there were no rooms at the inn at our first stop—and found that it featured a similar dress code that we understood what was meant by all the signs we had been passing: SKIMPY BETWEEN 5 AND 7 . . . SKIMPY ON WEEKENDS . . . SKIMPY ALL WEEK.

The owners of these places, whose patrons were miners and ranch hands, paid young women very good money to wait tables and tend bar half naked. Many of the women flew in from places like Perth and Melbourne, commuting, to take the jobs part-time. It was perfectly in keeping with what one might expect from a rough-and-tumble place like the Australian outback.

We learned this from a woman named Trish who looked down on

such behavior, a prospector we met in the outback community of Cue, population 250. Short and somewhat weathered despite being in her thirties, Trish had been working the area for several months, during which she had managed to discover some gold. We happily spent $150 Australian to buy one of her gold nuggets to use as a pendant. Trish went on to explain that many of the people who lived in the towns out here had, like her, left behind their old lives, moving from one town to another, one mining operation or cattle ranch to another, like the characters in American cowboy lore.

We saw them in the roadhouses I wrote about in my last book. Collectively a wonderful institution, Australian roadhouses are separated by a hundred miles or more. NEXT FUEL . . . NEXT SERVICE . . . 200 MILES is how a sign outside a typical roadhouse might read; it might just as well add NEXT ELECTRICITY . . . NEXT MAILBOX . . . NEXT DOG.

Darwin had developed as I had anticipated it would. A wonderful melting pot of races and religions, it had grown and prospered since I had last been there. In addition to the reasons I had articulated earlier—Darwin's proximity to the emerging Asian markets to the north, a labor/natural resources equation similar to that of China/Siberia—there was another factor driving the city's growth: the military was moving into the region, building bases. Any serious threat to Australia was likely to come from the north, but the buildup's more immediate purpose was to support the country's forces in East Timor. And processing plants were obviously soon to come since Darwin was perfectly suited geographically to receive the new nation's natural gas. The decades-old dream of a railroad connecting Darwin to the south was becoming a reality, and that would support and contribute to the growth.

This time, I decided, instead of just talking, that I was going to buy property in Darwin—buy an old house, fix it up, and have it as a place to visit once or twice a year, maybe rent it out when I was not there. I dropped in on one of the area's larger real estate agents and told him what I wanted to do.

"You can't," he said.

"What?"

"You can't. You're not Australian. Foreigners cannot buy houses in Australia."

"Wait a minute," I said. "This is a capitalist country. This is the land of the free. What are you talking about?"

"Listen," he said, "no one hates it more than I do."

It was a new law, he explained, and then I remembered—One Nation, the right-wing political party headed by M.P. Pauline Hanson. Some new anti-immigration movement had recently taken hold of the country. It was the natural swing of a pendulum that had been in motion for a century.

As recently as 1973, Australia had a whites-only immigration policy. As racist as it sounds, it was initiated out of antiracist sentiment. At the time the White Australia Policy (WAP) was instituted, many nonwhites in Australia were not typical immigrants; they had been brought there from the outlying islands as indentured servants to work the mines and farms, no better than slaves. A movement developed within various Christian churches, especially among devout Presbyterians, to put an end to the practice, and eventually the relevant laws were passed with the enthusiastic support of labor during the country's worst-ever depression. But like many other laws in history, the well-intentioned laws had unintended consequences. Originally intended to put the kidnappers and slavers out of business, the laws making it illegal to *bring* nonwhites into the country became the racist, anti-immigration mechanism used to *keep* foreigners, especially nonwhites, out.

Everybody forgot why the laws had been passed. And until the laws were reversed in the 1970s, it was very difficult to get into Australia if you were not a white European Christian. By then the laws were no longer working. Australia needed to expand its ties to Asia and the Pacific Rim, and it needed to attract capital. Indeed, exploitation of mineral resources in Australia was achieved largely with Japanese investment and long-term export contracts with Japan. Considerable industrial development followed reversal of the discriminatory and protectionist laws.

By the end of the century, a predictable reaction to their reversal had set in. Australian Christians could not afford to buy houses because "rich Chinese and Japanese were driving up prices." Australia's economic problems were not the fault of her lackluster politicians, her high spending and high taxes; they were all the fault of the evil outsiders. So guys like me could not buy a house. Isolationism had won the day.

Before leaving, we attended a performance of the Darwin Symphony Orchestra. Among the night's offerings was the Northern Territory's first-ever symphony performance of Beethoven's Ninth. It made me cry, because the twelve-year-old orchestra was virtually all volunteer. The guest conductor and four professional vocalists had been flown in from out of town. Darwin, a city far more sophisticated than when I had first paid it a visit, was bordering on the downright cosmopolitan. I kept thinking of Denver and other frontier cities and what they were like a hundred years ago. The next day we attended the V8 Super Car races, which reminded us of NASCAR races back home, down to the beer, bikinis, and country music.

It was in Darwin, after having broken them a total of eleven times by that point, that we found a man who made us leaf springs that would last the rest of the trip. By the time we found him, the wheel bearings in the trailer had also collapsed. He took care of those, too. In Australia, especially in the outback, mechanics had much more experience with serious off-road equipment than Metalcrafters in California.

Heading south through Alice Springs, where Paige's parents joined us again, with a side trip to see Ayers Rock—the world's largest monolith, holy to the Aborigines and now the national symbol of Australia—we made our way to Adelaide in South Australia, a state I had never visited. On the way we stopped in a place called Coober Pedy.

Coober Pedy, South Australia, did not exist one hundred years ago. The Europeans who first crossed this vast, flat empty desert came looking for gold and whatever other minerals they could find—and discovered opals. Today, Coober Pedy, a town of about thirty-five hundred people, is the opal capital of the world. Fully 95 percent of the world's opals come from here. I was surprised to discover that opals come in a variety of colors—blues, greens, and various earth tones, in addition to the milky white with which we are all familiar. The name of the town is a corruption of Aboriginal words that, loosely translated, mean "white men in a hole." To mine opals, you dig straight down, scooping out the earth and sifting it for gems. The cylindrical holes, about the size of a fifty-five-gallon drum, dug today by equipment mounted on special trucks, are visible everywhere in Coober Pedy, signified by mounds of the dirt that have been removed.

In the summer, the temperature in Coober Pedy rises to well over

110 degrees Fahrenheit, and the early prospectors spent as much time looking for water as looking for minerals. Much of the water here, as in other parts of Australia, is saline and must be purified. Modern technology means there is now enough water for more than a few hundred people. Here it is desalinated by a process of reverse osmosis. To stay cool, settlers began building their homes underground, digging into the indigenous sandstone and carving rooms out of the rock. And it is not only homes that are built that way. We stayed in a hotel that was similarly constructed. Our hotel room was carved straight into the rock.

Once from Coober Pedy and twice from Adelaide, once a day for three days in a row, I wrote letters to my father. In phone calls home, I learned he was getting worse. I had been calling every day to talk to him, but I also wanted to write down exactly how I felt, to let him know how proud I was of him, how much I loved him, and how important he was, and had been, in my life. I was caught in a three-day holiday in South Australia and was up against a three-day weekend in the States. I just kept writing, hoping one of the letters would get through in time. I knew he was fading. The postal services in both countries got the job done. My mother told me that the letters that I had so desperately worried about all week had arrived. I do not think he was able to read them himself. When I talked to him, he was not very communicative. He had held them and looked at them, my mother said. She had read them to him.

Between Adelaide and Sydney I enjoyed a couple of enlightening dinner conversations. In Melbourne, Paige and I dined with an Australian M.P., a motorcyclist, and his wife. He had read my book and discussed it with people in Darwin, and he and they had marveled, he said, at how accurate my prediction had been.

"Yeah, I wanted to buy a house in Darwin, and I couldn't."

"Why not?"

A member of Parliament. I figured he knew. I told him why not.

"You're dead wrong," he said.

He became argumentative, not hostile but clearly adamant that I was mistaken.

"Well, okay, I'm delighted to hear it," I said. "I was unable to buy a house through the real estate agent there, and I'm happy to hear that *he* was wrong."

The next day I received a phone call.

"My God," said the M.P., "I'm embarrassed."

The opposition party was responsible, he said, the party in power, and most people in Australia were unaware of the law.

Yeah, tell me about it, I thought. Not even their representatives in Parliament, who passed the law, seem to be aware of it.

The most passionate expression of Australian anti-immigration sentiment came on the occasion of another dinner one evening from what at first seemed like a very unlikely source. Paige and I were dining with a very well educated couple who offered an inventory of spurious "scientific" reasons for why the country should ban all outsiders. What made their argument especially ironic was that the man and his wife were immigrants themselves.

"Wait a minute," I said, "didn't you immigrate here from New Zealand?"

"That was before," he said. "Now it's different."

Oh.

Australia, he claimed, due to climate, water conditions, vegetation, and other natural factors, was capable of supporting only between eleven and thirteen million people.

What a ludicrous argument, I said. Coober Pedy was desert. Nobody lived there a hundred years ago. And now there was enough water there to support a population of some thirty-five hundred and growing—people responsible, I pointed out, for mining virtually all the opals in the world.

"Well, that's an exception," he replied.

"We should keep people out," said the wife. "In fact, we should let the population decline. Our seventeen million people are too many."

Australia's currency had plummeted some 40 percent in the previous year. The country's economy was a raw-materials economy based on agriculture, mining, oil, and the like—Australians did not sit around making a lot of cars or TVs, but they did mine a lot of zinc. Commodities, unfortunately, had been in a bear market for twenty years. Further, the country had been borrowing huge amounts of money—propping up the economy, buying votes, shelling out for the 2000 Summer Olympic Games. The debt had risen astronomically. Which was all the more reason, as I saw it, why the country needed more people, outside investors, expertise, and capital. I would have opened the gates.

As we have seen, whenever there are hard times, people look for somebody to blame. Politicians in Australia, pandering to voters, had stirred up anti-immigrant sentiment, and, in doing so, not only had they made things worse, they had guaranteed that things would *continue* to get worse. In the process, those same politicians had given people like our two silly dinner companions a voice. Theirs was the same kind of argument I had often run into from certain Americans whose families had immigrated: "We're in! Close the border!" It was duplicity of the highest order. They always claim, "It was different before. The immigrants were different back then."

In one way, I am high on Australia's prospects, regarding raw materials. The bull market in commodities has already begun, and I have shares in natural resources there.

I had been very optimistic about New Zealand on my last trip. Effectively socialist during the 1960s and '70s and flirting with bankruptcy, the country, with the election of a new Labour government in 1984, had turned itself around. It went from a protected agrarian economy to an open free-market economy virtually overnight, and in 1994 it announced its first budget surplus in eighteen years. I, and a lot of other people, invested there. The currency went up. The stock market went up. But as frequently happens among handheld societies, certain constituencies found it difficult to cope. Rising out of the ashes came the New Zealand First Party—populist, xenophobic, and powerful in the coalition government that emerged in the 1996 elections. Soon the currency dropped by almost 70 percent. The government borrowed vast amounts of money. And the huge immigration into New Zealand that had characterized the 1990s was brought to a halt. There is now a net emigration *out* of New Zealand.

The nation's nonwhite population is growing much faster than its white population, and government studies show that if current trends continue, New Zealand, which was virtually all white fifty years ago (less than 10 percent of the population is indigenous Maori), will eventually be a brown country. Add to these dynamics the affirmative action policies and subsidies aimed at the country's indigenous nonwhites—Maoris in New Zealand enjoy the same kind of special benefits enjoyed by Aborigines in Australia—and race becomes a political card that is very easy to play.

*New technology had brought sufficient fresh water to Coober Pedy, Australia, to enable the desert town to grow, but there is still little to do after work.*

*Easter Island was rich and prosperous until it diverted vast treasure and effort to nonproductive uses. These extraordinary statues drained the civilization.*

Paige fell in love with New Zealand—its volcanoes, its mountains, its beaches, its wild animals and sea lions. She sheared a sheep one afternoon and decided that we should move to New Zealand and open a sheep farm and vineyard. She had the whole idyllic concept down. I, on the other hand, came away discouraged. What I saw in New Zealand was another country closing itself off to the world and borrowing lots of money. I kept some money in New Zealand raw materials but sold many of my investments there.

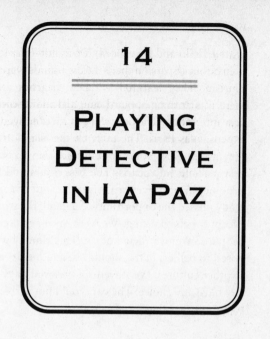

# 14

# PLAYING DETECTIVE IN LA PAZ

ON SUNDAY, JUNE 10, 2001, while Paige and I were in New Zealand—it was June 9 in the States—I received the news that my father had died. The phone rang at five A.M., and we both knew what it was. A week or so before, he had gone into a coma. Had I returned home then, I would have seen him that way, and I am not sure if I am glad that I did not. I had last seen him as the best man at my wedding. For the next several days, my mind was consumed with memories of him. Every time I turned around, I would think of something he had taught me, something he had said, something I had first heard from him. Whatever I happened to be doing, it seemed, I needed skills I had learned from him, whether something as mechanical as changing a tire or as intangible as navigating a simple interpersonal impasse. Using electrical tape or jumper cables, reading a map—driving a car itself—all began with my father. I often wound up crying.

We put the car aboard a container ship headed for South America and killed time in French Polynesia waiting for the car to reach Chile. We visited Tahiti and Bora-Bora. It was not *Tales of the South Pacific,* not even a tourist version thereof. The islands were devoted exclusively to tourism. They featured beautiful beaches and luxury resorts, but there was nothing about them particularly enticing, exciting, or even very interesting. The only thing surprising were the prices. Tahiti is as expensive as Paris. The taxis on the island are more expensive than they are in New York. And despite our expectations, it was not the best place to buy pearls. The best pearls and the best prices were in Broome, in northwestern Australia, but thank goodness we had already missed the opportunity. All in all, the trip was a disappointment except for the dancing. We were once again enthralled by how some people can move their bodies. This time it was mainly hips, as opposed to bellies, butts, shoulders, and heads, which had stupefied me in other cultures. We stayed six or seven days because we did not really have any choice. The car would not arrive in Chile until July 2, a two-week crossing.

When we arrived in Santiago, the fate of the country's former dictator and now Chilean senator for life, Augusto Pinochet, was being decided. Pinochet had been returned from England, where he was being held under house arrest at the request of the Spanish. The agreement that had resulted in his release stipulated that Chile bring him up on charges for the crimes against humanity of which he was unquestionably guilty. The Chilean government was in a difficult position. Passions were high on both sides of the issue. Pinochet, eighty-five, was still the power behind the throne in Chile, and was in fact seen by some as the savior of the country. Chile's has been the best-managed economy in South America for a couple of decades. In opposition were all those Chileans who held him responsible for the brutal murder of thousands during his seventeen-year dictatorship.

While we were there, demonstrations were under way on both sides. It felt as if civil war might break out whichever way the government moved. The decision came down shortly after we arrived, and the Supreme Court, to my mind, exercised the wisdom of Solomon. The court decided he was too sick to be tried, saying it would put him on trial if he showed signs of recovery. It effectively put him under house arrest. If he tried to reclaim his seat in the Senate or showed any signs of reasserting his influence, he would be tried and almost certainly imprisoned. As long as he stayed home in bed, he was a free man. It completely neutralized him. And at the same time it appeased both his supporters and his detractors.

For almost twenty years Pinochet and his murderously repressive government ran a sound economic ship. Under his rule, and thus at enormous cost, Chileans learned something that their neighbors did not, and they know it. Today, looking at the Argentines, looking at the Brazilians, they see national economies in ruins.

Chile's is a natural resources–based economy. Spectacular infrastructure has been built to serve it. You can now tear down the center of Chile—essentially, one long, narrow stretch of mountain—on a four-lane highway, a toll road. The road, among other things, has opened the South, which I had not visited before, to trade and tourism. Driving it reminded me of driving in China. Infrastructure has drawn the Norwegians into Chile, and the country is now the second largest exporter of salmon in the world. It is the same old story: you build a highway, a railroad, or a canal and something is going to happen.

The legendary haze in Santiago, combined with the snow of the mountains, had the salutary effect of providing one of the most beautiful sunrises we had seen on the trip. From Santiago we headed for Tierra del Fuego at the southern tip of the continent. Paige drove us across the snow-covered Andes.

We crossed into Argentina heading for the ski resort at San Carlos de Bariloche, spent a couple of days there, where Paige did some downhill skiing for the first time in many years, and from there we set off for Ushuaia, the southernmost city in the world, on the island of Tierra del Fuego. Crossing into Argentina in the dead of winter was difficult in ways it should not have been. Why, I asked myself, was the principal east-west artery across the center of the country not cleared of ice and snow? This, taken with other signs that I was soon to pick up, was the first evidence that Argentina was in serious trouble.

To reach Tierra del Fuego—an archipelago whose largest island is also so named and is divided between Chile and Argentina—we had to cross the Strait of Magellan. It would be my second crossing of the waterway, and once again my heart skipped a beat. Here I was, a guy from Demopolis, Alabama, crossing the channel named for the Portuguese navigator who passed through here in 1520, commander of the Spanish expedition that was first to circumnavigate the globe.

The flat, windswept, snow-covered plain of Tierra del Fuego gave way as we approached the Andean foothills surrounding Ushuaia, situated not far from Cape Horn. The Argentine government had made a tax haven of Ushuaia, granting a variety of incentives for its citizens to populate Tierra del Fuego. The island lies just north of the Antarctic Circle. Such incentives were undoubtedly necessary, and they have been effective as they are all over the world.

On our way north to Buenos Aires, we detoured at Río Gallegos, heading northwest to see the Moreno Glacier at Lake Argentino, one of the great natural wonders of the world, which I had visited on my last trip. I really wanted to see if it was as extraordinary as I remembered. Paige, who resisted traveling six hundred miles out of our way and into the Andes in the dead of winter to visit the site, was transfixed once she saw it—and heard it. Over 150 miles long and one of the few glaciers in the world still moving, it was visibly and audibly alive, groaning and cracking as it inched its way between the mountains. Vast icebergs crashed into the lake as they broke away from the 160-foot-high wall of ice that was its face. It was the dead of winter, we were all alone, and it was an extraordinary thing to see, more impressive than any man-made thing I had ever encountered. I had had trouble getting Paige to come; now I had trouble getting her to leave. We promised ourselves we would return someday.

We persuaded my mother to join us in Buenos Aires. It had been six or seven weeks since my father had died, they had been married for sixty years, and I was not sure how she might be dealing with it. It does not take a lot to persuade my mother to fly anywhere, so I said to come join us in Argentina, which I remembered as a beautiful, exciting place, especially Buenos Aires. At eighty-two, she was getting frail, and could not travel alone, so one of her granddaughters, one of my nieces, Katie Bee, accompanied her. She spent a week with us in Buenos Aires, during which time we flew up to Iguaçu Falls. The trip did wonders for her spirit.

On my last trip, I had come away from Argentina wildly bullish. I was so excited about the country, I had thought about moving to Buenos Aires, one of my favorite cities in the world. In the mid-1990s I had sold my Argentine shares when I saw the country begin to borrow a lot. But I kept my money there. And I kept it in pesos. The cur-

*The Bank of Argentina guaranteed that pesos and dollars would be equal forever. Skeptics like me took their dollars and ran, despite the central bank's promises. The currency, the economy, and the government collapsed in a matter of months.*

rency, which was tied to the dollar, was completely convertible, one peso for one dollar, and the government gave every indication that it would remain that way. A peso account paid higher interest, so I maintained the account in pesos rather than dollars over the years, waiting to reinvest some day.

Driving through Argentina on this trip, growing fed up with the numerous police checks, which I did not remember from before— sometimes we were stopped every few miles—I came to the conclusion that the country was in the throes of collapse. In Buenos Aires everything was enormously expensive—hotel and restaurant prices were astronomical—especially so compared to what the same thing would cost in neighboring countries, whose currencies were allowed to float and find their value in the market. The dollar had been going up for years and had been dragging the peso up with it. Argentina could not print money and refused to live within its means, so to keep the peso stable, it had borrowed heavily to keep the economy going, to buy votes. An expensive place to live (too expensive to keep the major highways clear of snow) is an expensive place to do business. The country could not remain competitive for long.

While I was there I wrote an article for a Latin American magazine advising readers to get their money out of Argentina. I predicted that the country would default on its foreign loans, freeze bank accounts, block funds, and devalue its currency.

Not that I am so clever. Ben Franklin noted that experience is the fool's best teacher. And I have seen it repeatedly throughout the world: politicians get a country in trouble but swear everything is okay in the face of overwhelming evidence to the contrary. New York- ers may remember the 1970s, when the city got into fiscal trouble. Mayor Abe Beame stood on the steps of City Hall, promising that his salary would be eliminated before New York City would default. Shortly thereafter, creditors took big hits, but the mayor never missed a paycheck.

In Buenos Aires I went to the bank, changed all my pesos into dol- lars, and got them out of the country. The banker handling the trans- action scoffed at me, as did several politicians. The president of the stock exchange, having heard my views, did "not have time" to see me. But not very long thereafter—in three months the collapse of the Argentine economy led the news all over the world—I received letters from Argentines, asking, "What do I do now?" I told them to get whatever foreign currency they could get on the black market at whatever the exchange rate and get their money out of the country. I also suggested they move to Chile or Bolivia.

The Argentine collapse was a horrible shame. The country was heading in the right direction. But like politicians everywhere, Argentina's just started borrowing when things got tight. They had opted for a stable currency, because hyperinflation had destroyed their currencies several times over the previous decades, but then it got to hurting—maintaining a sound currency is always going to hurt, periodically—and what happened is what usually happens. The rest of the world loaned them gigantic amounts of money; Wall Street was in there hand over fist. Indeed, Argentina borrowed so much, it became the single largest force in the international bond market. The country kept things going for five more years. And then it went under. Wall Street did not return its commissions, apologizing for having given bad advice, but several politicians were forced out of office.

In the 1970s and '80s, much of South America was ravaged by military dictatorships and poorly run economies. It was not a great place to be. In the 1990s, South Americans bought into globalization and opened their economies to the miracles of international trade. But once these were implemented and succeeding, politicians began taking shortcuts to keep themselves in power, borrowing or printing huge amounts of money, leading to disaster. Globalization was not the enemy; it was the corrupt and/or inept execution of globalization that led to the backlash that we saw take root in the streets of Seattle, Genoa, and other cities around the world. The nineteenth-century era of growth and expansion ended with events leading to World War I in 1914. Is the world going to repeat the mistakes and close off in our lifetime?

Uruguay, South America's answer to Monaco, bank secrecy laws and all, had boomed during the liberalization of trade. A bull market and several years of prosperity had led to the development of numerous hotels, restaurants, and apartment buildings. Punta del Este, Uruguay's Saint-Tropez, is a gem. Paige fell in love with the city and suggested we buy a place there. I was, and am, sorely tempted to do so. Now that Argentina and Brazil have collapsed, dragging down

Uruguay with them, prices on Uruguay's Riviera are reasonable again. We may have already bought our second home when you read this.

In Brazil, a country I predict will separate into two countries, north and south, we visited Pôrto Alegre, the largest city in the southernmost state, Rio Grande do Sul. South American football, especially Brazilian football, was not to be missed, and we managed to get our hands on tickets when we heard that Brazil was meeting neighboring Paraguay in a World Cup qualifying match. To assure ourselves of good seats, we arrived at the stadium two hours early, only to find the place already mobbed. There were people sitting in the aisles; we stood the entire game. Two hours before game time, the air was absolutely electric. I have never experienced such a constant throb at any event—sporting or otherwise. The hum and buzz of emotional energy continued through the night, across the city, in the wake of Brazil's victory.

With the conquest of the New World, the Catholic Church played an influential role in the Americas through the religious conversion of indigenous peoples and the maintenance of Spanish political authority. Preserving and extending Spanish control was assigned to various religious orders, among them the Jesuits, as official agencies of the Crown. The Church achieved vast wealth and privilege, and at the close of the colonial period the Church is estimated to have controlled half the productive real estate of the Indies. The Jesuit mission system in Paraguay and central South America was one of the most important in the New World. From early in the seventeenth century until their expulsion in 1767, the Jesuits established and maintained an extensive network of missions along the upper Paraná River, the ruins of which cover the territory today.

It is still inconceivable to me how a few priests just showed up in the wilds and organized the entire area, driving the production of manufactured goods, works of art, vast crops, and enormous buildings. The Jesuits became so powerful and self-sufficient that the Spanish Crown finally expelled the entire order from the New World. Equally astonishing to me was that it all just then vanished—the local tribes left the missions, returning to their hand-to-mouth existence and the tribal religions of their ancestors.

In 1813, forty-six years after the Jesuits left, Paraguay became in-

dependent of Spain. But for a stretch of about sixty-five years, it has
been run by dictators absurd even by Latin standards ever since. History abounds with the folly of politicians and leaders: How could the
Japanese have attacked the United States in 1941? How could Sad-
dam Hussein take on much of the world in 1991? In 1865, Francisco
Solano López, Paraguay's dictator, went to war with Brazil, Argentina, and Uruguay in the catastrophic War of the Triple Alliance.
It would be as if Belgium suddenly declared war on Germany, France,
and the Netherlands. Half of the population of 450,000 was lost, and
nearly all the males in the country were killed. Never, ever blindly believe that leaders will not act like madmen. History is replete with
episodes in which the real patriots were the ones who defied their governments.

My chief impression of Paraguay today is that it should not exist.
It has been a succession of disasters since the Jesuits left. The place
should be dismantled and sold for parts. The parts, which are worth
more than the whole, would be snatched up by its neighbors. The citizens could divide the proceeds and move to Punta del Este. Paraguay
does not really operate as a nation; it functions more as an ongoing
criminal enterprise. It is just one huge black market, a place where
anything goes, and serves as a willing anchorage for bad guys. It came
as no surprise to hear recently that Al Qaeda might be conducting
business from there.

Given Paraguay's place in the world, it was fascinating to discover
that vast tracts of the country's western wasteland, the Chaco, were
being bought up by thousands of immigrant Amish from the United
States and Canada. (German Mennonite settlers had been a fixture in
the area since the 1930s.) Those whom Paige and I met explained that
they had immigrated to escape religious persecution in North America and increasing encroachment on their way of life. I had to admit it
made perfect sense. Nothing was forbidden in Paraguay. In a country
that had provided a haven for Dr. Josef Mengele, the Nazi "Angel of
Death," certainly the last thing for which anyone would be persecuted was his beliefs.

Passing once more through Argentina, we headed for Bolivia, entering the country at the border town of Yacuiba. The town was one
bustling market, and with very good reason. Thousands of people

from overpriced Argentina flooded across the border to shop there. In Bolivia, where the currency was allowed to float, goods and services were cheap, and the market that was Yacuiba boomed late into the night.

In Yacuiba I took my mobile phone into a shop, and ten minutes and eight dollars later the phone was adjusted, geared up to operate on the Bolivian system. It worked immediately. Never, all the time we were in Argentina, could we get our phones to work properly. And the Bolivian telephone system was not the only sign of a surprisingly sound national infrastructure. Leaving town, I was impressed by the impending changes to the highway system. All the roads going north were toll roads, even the bad ones. I discovered later that there was a new plan under way to make Bolivia a major transportation cross-roads servicing the continent.

Our next surprise was Cochabamba, of which we had never heard, despite its being the third largest city in Bolivia. Situated in the mountains with a year-round temperature of 70 degrees Fahrenheit, it was sophisticated and at the same time maintained a certain measure of purity. It would be the perfect place to which to return to perfect our Spanish. The gym at which we worked out could easily have been on the Upper West Side of Manhattan, both for its equipment and for the level of flirtation among its clientele.

My expectations of Bolivia had been not so much pessimistic as nonexistent. Not until we reached Paraguay had Paige and I been really sure we would be traversing the country. And when we finally decided to do so, we were looking at Bolivia as little more than a shortcut to Peru. I did want to see Potosí—and the mountain of silver that had made that city one of the most famous in the world at the time of the Spanish conquest. And I figured that if we stopped in La Paz, I might devote a little time to some detective work, trying to find the broker there who had vanished with the investment money I had given him on my previous trip around the world.

What had happened was this:

When I had visited Bolivia ten years before, as a side trip, I went over to La Paz from Lima—the Bolivian stock market did not yet exist. But I thought I saw good things happening there. Other countries in South America were opening up; I predicted that Bolivia would soon have an exchange and figured I would try to get in early.

The country was another in the line of developing markets where things were extremely cheap. I decided to purchase shares—or attempt to—in one of the country's larger banks. I walked into the bank, asked around, and was directed to the institution's president. He gave me the name of an investment company that had recently been established in anticipation of Bolivia's development of a stock market and said that if anyone could help me, it would be the director of that company.

Doing some homework, I learned that the company's director, its founder and principal shareholder, was from a prominent and quite reputable family and that the operation was legit. He happened to be out of the country at the time, and I ended up doing business with his partner. Yes, the partner told me, a stock market was coming, there would be publicly traded companies soon, the government was behind privatization, but as yet there was nothing available. He was sure he could find me some of the bank shares I wanted from a private seller in the street, but I should not expect him to find a lot of them. I said I preferred to start off small. I gave him a token sum, told him to buy the shares, and said that if everything worked, I would send him a little more and we would start investing in Bolivia.

Later, after he had succeeded in rounding up the shares, I sent him another small check from New York. A little time passed, Bolivia developed a stock exchange, I tried reaching him to buy more shares, and my correspondence went unanswered. I finally got a guy at the company on the phone, and asked what was going on.

"Oh, he's dead," he said of my broker.

"Dead? He was young. He was in perfect health."

"He died of AIDS."

"Well, who do I talk to?"

"He died. We can't help you anymore."

"What happened to my money?"

Click.

A cardinal rule of mine when it comes to investing internationally, especially in emerging markets, is always to have the brokerage account with the largest bank in the country. If the bank gets in trouble, you do not lose everything because the government will take it over. Your shares do not disappear. This was the only time in my life that I had not done that—for the obvious reason that I could not. All I had were two canceled checks. I called the Bolivian Embassy in Washington, and it told me to work through the country's new stock exchange. I called the exchange and explained my problem. I did not believe the story of my broker's death, I said, and in any case, these people still had my money. The stock exchange was unable to help me.

I was determined that if I ever got to Bolivia, I would go to La Paz, track these guys down, and get my money. It was not much money, but it was principle as well as principal.

In the middle of the sixteenth century, Potosí, about fifty miles south of Sucre, the judicial capital of Bolivia, and almost three hundred miles southeast of La Paz, the country's administrative capital, was the largest and most famous city in the Western Hemisphere and probably the wealthiest city in the world. At its peak, the population of the city reached 160,000. As the story goes, a local Bolivian, herding sheep on one of the mountains, built a fire to camp for the night. Then the ground beneath the fire started melting. The molten runoff was silver. Subsequent investigation showed that the entire 1,600-foot mountain, in effect, was one solid chunk of pure silver. It became known as Cerro Rico, Rich Mountain, and for the next hundred years or so it was a windfall that kept a declining Spain afloat economically, among other things financing all her wars. It was a bit like the huge oil discoveries that have kept Indonesia alive today. The government mint that was built at Potosí is the source of many of those famous pieces of eight that served as the coin of the realm in the days of the Spanish Main.

The mountain has not yet played out. After more than four hundred years, there are still several hundred miners who continue to work the strike. They are bringing out lead, zinc, tin, and copper, the usual finds associated with silver deposits, and they are still bringing out silver. They are mining the mountain the old-fashioned way, with dynamite and pickaxes, crawling through low, narrow tunnels, and it is not a very healthy environment. The average life expectancy of a Potosí miner is forty-two years. The miners consider all the minerals to be the property of the Devil. They call the mine the Devil's Mouth. They make regular blood offerings to the mountain and to the Devil, whom they refer to as El Tío. They keep little effigies of him around. Every Friday they sacrifice llamas. And just as their forebears have for centuries, they chew coca leaves to give them energy and stamina.

As any student of history knows, many places have had their day in the sun, only to fall into decline. Potosí is pretty seedy now. The city's ornate cathedral, a symbol of her former eminence, has fallen into disrepair. The gilt work is still intact, but the cathedral is missing large sections of its glorious stained-glass windows. There are beautiful churches all over the city, testifying to the city's illustrious past. I had long wanted to see Potosí for the unique nature of its historic ascendancy, rising out of nothing from a single source of wealth. I had to go to Potosí the way I had to go to Timbuktu. One always learns from history in the flesh.


The stock exchange in La Paz was very small and open only an hour and a half a day, but it was located in a new, gleaming, three-story office building. Inside were real people doing real things, maybe fifteen young men and women, all smartly dressed, walking around, buying and selling, the men sporting suits that looked as though they had been made in London. I walked in and introduced myself.

"I've come from New York, and I'm here to find who has my money."

Not a lot had been happening on the stock exchange, which was understandable given its brief history, and I guess I must have been the only person who was currently complaining. Because there I was, much to their amazement, standing before all these people, and they all knew who I was: the guy from New York with the problem.

And they could not have been more helpful.

"I think we should be able to help you find the man you are looking for," said a young woman, consulting a file.

"He's dead," I said.

"Excuse me?"

"He died of AIDS."

She opened the file again:

"He works at the energy ministry."

Son of a bitch!

"I'll write down the address," she said.

This was going to be fun.

"Hello," I said, walking into his office. "I'm Jim Rogers. Remember me?"

"It's not my fault," he said, starting right in. "It was my partner, he took the money."

"Number one," I said, "I didn't give my money to your partner. I gave it to you. As far as I'm concerned, you're the one who is going to jail if I don't get it back. I'm going to the government about you. I've already been to the stock exchange."

It was his partner, he said, babbling on. His partner owned the company. And his partner had never bought the shares I had been charged for. He had taken the money. The company had folded. He was gone; he had left the country.

"And number two," I said, "what is all this about your dying of AIDS?"

"What!"

There was obviously bad blood between these two guys. This one claimed he had quit, he had left the company, before the other one had taken it down. He was prepared to be helpful. When he found out that his partner was blaming it on him and telling people he had died of AIDS, he became *extremely* helpful. The partner's father, he told me, was the former head of the Bolivian office of a famous international accounting firm, one of the largest in the world. The partner's brother now had the job. Both, I discovered, had been shareholders in the now-dissolved company. And both, being well respected, with well-earned reputations in the local financial community, had a lot to lose. Thus it was his own family who led me to the man who had absconded with my money. I found him in Peru and got him on the phone.

"I'm going to sue your brother, and I'm going to sue your father; both of them were shareholders in the company," I told him. "One of you guys has my money, and I want it back."

It was the smallest investment I had ever made in a foreign country, $3,000. You always start small, because you have to make sure everything works. Even with the largest banks—you have to be sure it gets into the right account and that the bank knows what to do with it. I always start small to make sure the mechanics work. And in this case the investment had been that much smaller because there were just not that many shares available. So it was not the money. While I was tracking down my money, I was actually learning a whole lot about the government and the financial workings of Bolivia. As it happened, the Bolivian government and the country's equivalent of the SEC were very diligent in helping me, because they were purposefully trying to attract foreign investors.

"I'm quite serious," I told the thief. "I want my money. I'll come to Peru to get it."

He had no idea I was driving around the world and was headed to Peru. He must have been astounded that I had chased him this far. What really scared him was my threat to go after his father and to bring the government and the stock exchange down on the family.

"I mean it. I will come to Peru. I'll be there in three weeks," I told him.

"Okay," he said. "Come to Peru, and I'll give you the money."

I found him in Lima. And I charged him interest. He paid me 20 percent of what he owed and signed a written agreement to pay me the rest over the next three years, an installment every six months.

Bolivia, along with Ecuador, is the prototypical banana republic, which is basically a South American republic where the government is ever changing, there is a coup every couple of years, the currency is constantly in collapse. Bolivia holds the record for the most governments per annum of any country in history. It had something like 150 coups or attempted coups in one two-year period. Its history has been chaotic, characterized by the madness of a bunch of white guys fighting among themselves to control a lot of indigenous people. The country has been badly managed since its independence from Spain in 1825. (Formerly known as Alta, or Upper Peru, it was the last Spanish possession in South America to achieve independence.) Bolivia has lost every war it has fought, losing a large share of its territory to its neighbors over the course of its history.

Since 1982 there has not been a coup and the government has been more or less democratic and stable. Economically, as a result, things are looking up, but I also had thought that in 1991, on my first trip through—by 1993 the country experienced very high inflation again, but the currency has been comparatively stable for nearly two decades. So I am as gullible, but I am not that gullible. I am impressed by what I see in the way of infrastructure changes. I see that tourism is picking up; there were virtually no tourists in 1991. Metals are still very big. Agriculture is being developed in the east. The Japanese are investing (as are the Amish, who are moving into Bolivia just as they are in Paraguay). And, of course, there is nothing like trillions of cubic feet of natural gas to transform a country.

Bolivia's new reserves of natural gas are gigantic, greater than anybody imagined when they were initially discovered. The country's proven reserves have gone up ten times since 1996, when exports were worth $150 million a year. By the year 2004, exports of natural gas will amount to $500 million annually. And the sky is the limit. They are finding more and more all the time. The geology is perfect for it, apparently.

So I am optimistic, but cautiously so. I cannot help but recall others who have been wildly bullish on Bolivia, three of whom immediately come to mind: Che Guevara, Butch Cassidy, and the Sundance Kid—all of whom lost their enthusiasm quite suddenly, in dramatic fashion, and were buried there.

Since my last visit to Peru (which I wrote about rather extensively in *Investment Biker*), the Shining Path had been effectively destroyed and the president responsible for suppressing the violent insurgency of the Maoist guerrillas, Alberto Fujimori, had been run out of the country. Before he was corrupted by power, Fujimori had turned the Peruvian economy around, pursuing a free-market policy and privatizing major state-run industries. Inflation fell from 7,600 percent in 1990, the year of his election, to 57 percent in 1992. In 1994 the economy grew by 12 percent, the highest rate in the world.

With the Shining Path waging open war, Peru was a very dangerous place to be when I was there in 1991. It was rare for me to bump into another traveler. Now, the country was flush with tourists. There were thousands of people crowding the shops and restaurants around all the country's major tourist attractions. Machu Picchu is now the continent's largest tourist attraction and Cuzco one of its trendiest cities. Lima was bustling, morning, noon, and night. The beaches were mobbed. Tourists had started spilling over into neighboring countries such as Bolivia—especially the backpackers, who are always first.

The lesson that one should get to a country when a long war ends became vividly clear again. I added to my investments in Peru, but I wish I had jumped on the first plane back as soon as the war ended.

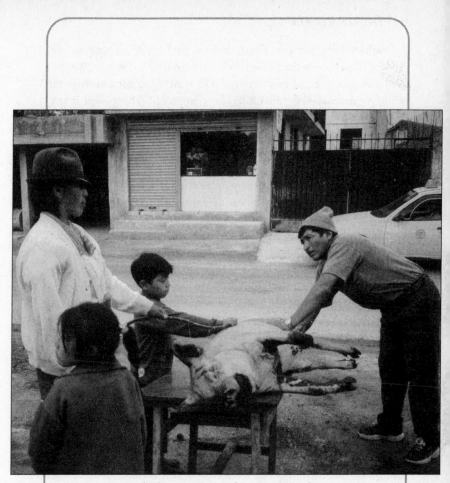

*A barbecue getting under way in Ecuador*

Southern Peru, western Brazil, Bolivia, and northern Chile are exploding now that peace has arrived. Western Brazil, for example, has been a huge source of raw material and agriculture for centuries but has never developed because it has been impractical to transport anything thousands of miles to Brazil's Atlantic coast. New highways and infrastructure are being built to open the various frontiers to the much closer ports on the Pacific. Peru has even ceded part of the Pacific port of Ilo to landlocked Bolivia to ensure open trade and transit in the region. Can you imagine having moved to Omaha or Denver or Salt Lake as the Union Pacific was opening the United States' interior to the sea? This will be one of the great boom areas for the twenty-first century. And it is reality. We drove on splendid new roads already in place as we headed from the interior toward the newly paved, coastal Pan-American Highway for the last lap home.

The hotel at which we stayed in Puno, on Lake Titicaca, was relatively quiet. There were not many people in residence, and we had gotten to know the manager soon after we checked in. I was having breakfast when the manager rushed in, saying, "I'm sorry, I'm so sorry, it is terrible, I'm so very sorry." I had no idea what he was talking about, but he was so clearly distraught that I tried to calm him down before asking what had happened. All I could figure was that somebody must have smashed into the car and the trip was suddenly over. Of course, it was worse than that.

"What are you talking about?" I asked.

He hurried me down to his office, we grabbed Paige on the way, and there, on his television, we watched as a second plane crashed into the World Trade Center in New York City. It was September 11, 2001. We were nine weeks away from crossing the Arizona border. We were about three and a half months from home.

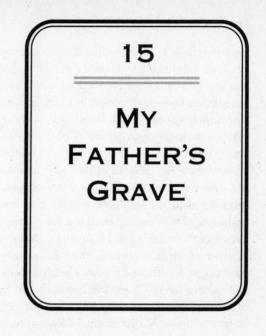

# 15

## MY FATHER'S GRAVE

WE WOULD SPEND ABOUT THREE WEEKS in Central America, which is slightly smaller than California in size and in population. I was eager to see how things had changed since my last trip. The Canal had reverted to Panama, the three wars that had terrified and limited me had ended, new areas would now be open to us. We wanted to see all of the seven countries that make up the route, the only overland passage between North and South America.

In the two weeks that passed between our leaving Peru and our arrival in Panama, where our crossing of Central America began, we visited Ecuador, Venezuela, and Colombia. Ecuador, the other of the original banana republics—there are banana plantations everywhere, by the way—had been living up to its reputation, featuring numerous governments in the ten years since I had been there. But things appeared to be about to improve. The current president had dollarized the economy (the U.S. dollar is the legal currency), and he had done it at an opportune time: when the price of oil happened to be high. Ecuador sits on huge petroleum deposits. A lot of dollars started rolling in almost immediately, and he was perceived, accurately or not, to be a brilliant economist and politician. The true test of Ecuador's new political prowess will come when the price of oil goes down. If it does not run a tight ship, there will be problems. The nation happens to be in a good position right now; a second pipeline is under construction that will double the country's petroleum exports.

We spent a fair amount of time in Ecuador, a beautiful, mountainous country with a cultural richness dating back to the dawn of recorded history. Mankind flourished here long before the arrival of the Incas, whose empire stretched for thousands of miles along the Pacific coast, reaching as far north as Quito, until it was toppled by Francisco Pizarro in 1534. From Quito, crossing the equator for what we thought was the last time, we headed north to San Pablo del Lago and the Hacienda Cusin, which was owned by a friend, an Englishman from New York named Nik Millhouse. Having bought it in rundown condition, Nik has spent a decade restoring the hotel, turning it into a tourist attraction in its own right.

It was Nik who confirmed for us that the Colombian border, thanks to chronic guerrilla activity, was closed. The only way to get north was to head south. We made our way back to Guayaquil, crossing the equator one more time. Even had we been allowed to drive north through Colombia, we would have been unable to drive from there into Panama. Sooner or later we would have hit a dead end.

There is no road through the Darién Gap, which stretches between Colombia and Panama. The only way to make the journey is on foot. More than a hundred miles of swamp, raging river, and jungle, the Darién Gap, named for the region of southern Panama with which it is contiguous, is the only unfinished stretch of the Pan-American Highway between Alaska and Tierra del Fuego. One way or another, it would have been necessary to ship the vehicles to Panama, just as all travelers must do. Had we made Colombia, we would have done so most likely from Buenaventura. As it was, we shipped them from Guayaquil.

In Guayaquil, at the dock, putting the cars aboard a boat headed for Panama, we were subjected to a thorough drug inspection. They put the dogs on *us* as well as the cars. Later, passing through Nicaragua, we would run into the U.S. Drug Enforcement Administration station chief, spend a delightful evening with him and his wife, and he would give us the fascinating lowdown on the latest drug-sniffing dog technology.

While the cars made their way to Panama—it would take about a week—Paige and I went off to see Bogotá and Caracas. The former is a city under siege. Thousands of people in town were wearing body armor. Colombia is a beautiful country, the people are lovely, they are very well educated, and, alas, they are wearing bulletproof vests. A woman in the gym told Paige, "Unless you're rich or a politician, you really don't have to worry about being shot down or kidnapped." Venezuela is a country run by a madman, a nation that should be enormously wealthy but has suffered endemically from bad politicians. After petroleum—Venezuela is a member of OPEC—the country's most visible export is beauty contestants. An entire industry has developed around the winning of international beauty pageants. Just as the Soviets used to cultivate chess players and gymnasts, the Venezuelans take pretty girls at a young age and, going as far as to get them plastic surgery if necessary, groom them to be crowned Miss Universe.

I wanted Paige to see the Panama Canal. Standing by a sign that welcomed us to it, we discovered, much to our surprise, that we were allowed to see the sign but not to photograph its "Welcome." A guard came running over, screaming. It was not the first time in our journey around the world that our brandishing a camera spooked a man in uniform, but if military security were the issue, one would never know it by this character. He and his compatriots, who joined in, wanted us to know that the Panamanian people—or so we gathered from their use of the word "we"—notwithstanding their ownership of a welcome sign, did not particularly like tourists, and did not like American tourists especially. He did let us photograph the Canal but not the sign off to the side of the road. The anti-Americanism was disappointing, because I saw great opportunities for investing in the areas near the presidential palace, which had been bombed out when the United States invaded Panama to seize Manuel Noriega during the administration of the first President Bush.

In Costa Rica, on my last trip through, I had opened a brokerage account. The country goes a long way to create the impression that it is hospitable not only to North American retirees—many U.S. and Canadian citizens have moved there, taking advantage of the climate and the low cost of living—but to foreign investment as well. My experience of the country is quite the opposite. My Costa Rican shares were paying dividends, but I had been told that in order to have them paid into my brokerage account, I would have to show up in San José personally. I was living in New York, and for me to fly to Costa Rica to collect a few dividends was the height of madness. I thought things were bad in Singapore, where it took five weeks to clear a check, but in Costa Rica things were worse. When Paige and I were passing through, I spent a day sorting it out, making all the appearances I was required to make, and the only reason I have not closed the account is that some of the transactions are still bound up in red tape. I will find another place to retire.

When I returned home, I realized I had closed as many accounts on this trip as I had opened, in contrast to my previous trip, when I had opened several and closed none.

Since my last trip to Nicaragua, things had changed dramatically. Back then the war had just been winding down, police and soldiers were everywhere, and military checkpoints dotted the country. This time there was none of that. In Managua, we were at a filling station refueling when an eight-year-old boy, speaking perfect English, walked over and started going on about the car. His father, who followed him over, introduced himself as the American DEA station chief. It was he who wised us up to the latest in drug-sniffing dogs. Over dinner, regaling us with true tales of high adventure in the world of cops and smugglers—it was one of the most entertaining nights of my life—he explained that the dogs lose their training very quickly. They are not as accurate as most people believe, and all the really good dogs are owned by the drug dealers. The dealers buy the best dogs available; they conceal the dope, put a dog on the case, and if the dog finds the dope, they repack it.

In Honduras we stopped at the ruins of ancient Copán, one of a series of rich and powerful Mayan city-states that flourished at approximately the same time as the famous city-states of Italy: Venice, Genoa, Florence, Siena, and others. Once again I was astounded at

the heights to which people rose hundreds of years ago. In San Salvador we tracked down the very same restaurant where I had eaten
my first iguana ten years before. There I ate my second and was reminded that it tasted like fish, though somewhat more chewy. While
in El Salvador, I liquidated the investment I had made in the country
during its civil war on my last trip through. Now that there was
peace and prosperity—and no longer blood in the streets—I decided
to take the profit and move my money elsewhere. (Later President
Bush proposed a free-trade plan for Central America and the United
States; I may wind up wishing I had left my money there.) Located in
Guatemala City is Jean Francois, the only restaurant on the globe to
which we voluntarily returned after eating there to order the very
same meal—a tender steak with a fiery chipotle pepper sauce—the
following night. The food and the wine were that good. (Trapped
in the Sudanese desert for twelve days, we ate the same *ful* [beans]
at the same place all the time, but only because we had no other
choice.) In Guatemala we learned of the unbelievable mistakes the
old United Fruit Company management had made as it retreated in
the 1990s and drove itself into bankruptcy. Perhaps it was retribu-
tion for its earlier sins in Guatemala; more likely it is just another
proof that nothing lasts forever.

We were told that if we were going to be killed in Central America,
it would be in Belize, the former British Honduras, due to violence
along the border arising out of Guatemala's claim on the country.
Four people had been killed there the month before we arrived, but
we safely made it through our last war zone. Since its independence
from the United Kingdom in 1981, Belize has become a passport
haven—if you want a second passport or want actually to escape your
own country, Belize will give you a passport in exchange for a certain
level of investment.

*The Times Atlas of the World,* which weighs in at about eleven
pounds, has been a staple of my library through several editions over
the years. This authoritative vade mecum is the most comprehensive
single-volume collection of maps available outside the Situation
Room of the White House, and if you look at Plate 115 in the 1967
edition of the atlas, you will find that thirty-six years ago the city of
Cancún, Mexico, did not exist. Situated on the northeast tip of the

Yucatán Peninsula, the city was virtually manufactured by Mexico as a tourist destination, a beach resort on the Gulf of Mexico given over almost entirely to hotels, condominiums, restaurants, and retail stores. A place that offers little more than the opportunity to swim or sit on the beach sipping margaritas, it is not our kind of place. But I am glad we passed through just to marvel at the oceanside city as a successful, effectively executed artificial construct. After all, we wanted to see the world from every aspect at the turn of the millennium. I suspect the city will not be there in 3000 or even 2500. The Mayan ruins are more likely to survive than the ruins of Cancún.

We spent two weeks driving north through Mexico, stopping in Mérida, Villahermosa, and Puebla before reaching Mexico City, where I ate tequila worms for the first time, an expensive delicacy, named for the fact that they thrive on the agave plant, from which tequila is made. From Mexico City, we moved up the coast, making for the Arizona border, stopping in Guadalajara, Mazatlán, Los Mochis, and Hermosillo. (In Los Mochis, we chartered a small plane to fly us over Barranca del Cobre [Copper Canyon]. We even agreed to pay extra to ensure good service. Despite repeated promises and guarantees, there was no pilot after two hours. We later heard he was indignant that we had left.) In the course of the journey I formed some pretty serious views of the country, having arrived with great expectations, chiefly because of NAFTA's implementation and the recent election to the presidency of businessman Vicente Fox, which had put an end to some seventy years of one-party rule in Mexico.

I had been eager to travel the country's new toll roads. On my previous trip through, I had found decent roads to be quite scarce, and I expected privatization to change that. Indeed, toll roads were numerous, they were practically brand new, and they were among the most expensive to drive in the world, more so than those in Japan. But I could not help but notice that they were all crumbling. Their rapid deterioration, whether due to incompetence or corruption—graft and bribery are a way of life in Mexico—was only the first sign that my expectations for the country had been overly optimistic.

We were driving a flat stretch of highway along Mexico's west coast when something happened that was extremely rare over the course of our three-year trip: we nearly ran out of fuel. Fortunately, as mentioned earlier, we carried an emergency supply in a jerry can, fig-

How could we not visit Mexico's holiest site, the Basilica of
Guadalupe, where the Virgin Mary is said to have appeared
in a visitation before a peasant in 1531? Skeptics claim the
story was concocted by the Spanish to help subdue the
locals, but Mexicans defy them to disprove the miracle.

Gusanos de maguey—grilled tequila worms—
in Mexico City, were just one of the many delicacies
we tried while traveling around the world.

uring we might need it in places like the deserts of Africa or desolate stretches of Siberia. We had not expected to need it in Mexico, the world's seventh largest oil producer. But we could not find a filling station anywhere. The experience, I decided, was a kind of metaphor for Mexican progress—like the car, Mexico, after a nice stretch of good fortune, seemed to be running out of gas.

After the peso and banking crisis of 1994 and 1995, Mexico's leaders promised to change their inefficient and corrupt ways and build a modern, competitive economy. Initially, they followed through on the promise. They brought inflation down, reined in government spending, and privatized old state-run dinosaurs such as the railroads and airlines, opening the door to competition. The North American Free Trade Agreement opened the economic border between Mexico and the United States and by the time I arrived had brought more than 100,000 new jobs to Mexico. The country subsequently established free-trade agreements with the European Union, Israel, and other Latin American nations.

(In fact, NAFTA has proved beneficial to both nations. Our petroleum imports from south of the Rio Grande make the numbers look bad with Mexico, but many industries in the United States, such as agriculture, have prospered. Corruption, education levels, and a lack of infrastructure—as well as other factors—will make it difficult for Mexico ever to steal away a significant amount of work from the United States.)

A new Mexico caught the eye of the international investment community. Direct foreign investment soared to $13 billion in 2000, up from an annual average of $5.4 billion between 1990 and 1994. Buoyed by strong oil prices and a burgeoning U.S. economy, Mexico was Latin America's tiger economy, with its gross domestic product at the turn of the millennium growing at a rate of 6.9 percent. Politically, things were also looking up. Once hamstrung by a one-party system, the government moved into the hands of an opposition candidate, Fox, in late 1999. Fox is media-savvy and aggressive, more sophisticated than any leader Mexico has seen in generations, smart enough and charismatic enough to curry favor with Mexico's North American neighbors, most important the United States and Canada.

But Fox came in at a difficult time. The downturn in the U.S. economy has curbed the demand for Mexican goods in industries such as electronics, textiles, chemicals, and car parts. With the United States accounting for 90 percent of Mexico's exports, the impact has been significant. Between September 11, 2001, and my arrival in Mexico at the end of October, about 400,000 Mexican workers had been laid off. GDP growth had stalled. The problems were clearly not attributable to Fox, but he was sure to have to take the blame.

The country's state-run oil monopoly, Petróleos Mexicanos, or Pemex, was nationalized in the 1930s. It is Mexico's primary breadwinner, accounting for roughly 40 percent of the federal government's revenues. Roughly 80 percent of the oil it produces goes to the United States. My short take on the company? It is an inefficient operation run by corrupt officials who live on bloated paychecks. Consider that Pemex employs about 137,000 workers to produce three million barrels of oil a day, about twice the workforce of countries such as Venezuela with similar production levels. Trying to find a filling station in Mexico, as I did, exemplifies the company's problems: stations are located where the government and its cronies dictate rather than where the market dictates. And the filling stations do not take credit cards. We ran across only one station in our travels that advertised its acceptance of a card—and it promoted the revolutionary step with a large banner reading WE TAKE VISA.

Clearly the oil-and-gas industry should have been privatized years ago. Fox has tried to sway the unions to no avail and recently tried to appoint four businessmen to the board of directors, a move that was quickly shot down by Mexico's Congress. His problems with Pemex will get worse before they get better. Mexico is running out of oil. Between 1990 and the end of 2000, proven oil reserves fell from 52 billion barrels to about 26 billion. After 2010 production will fall precipitously, reflecting the depleted reserves. Little investment is being made in new exploration. Abu Dhabi can get away with that. The oil-rich nation in the United Arab Emirates also has declining oil reserves, but, given the country's tiny population, those reserves will allow her people to live on what is left for the next hundred years. Mexico, with a population of over 100 million, does not have that luxury, especially with the world's youngest population (the median age is twenty-three, versus thirty-six in the United States).

Little effort has been made to expand the country's refining operations, which are meager at best. In fact, Mexico already imports 25 percent of its gasoline.

In my analysis, declining oil revenues will bring greater instability to an already unstable Mexico, and Fox, through no fault of his own, is going to be in big trouble before his term comes to an end. Foreign direct investment has now declined dramatically. In fact, tens of thousands of jobs have left Mexico for China in the past couple of years.

Even more Mexicans will wind up in the United States, the border being the traditional release valve, where they will help lower our aging demographic. Teach your kids Spanish if they do not want to learn Chinese.

It took us three hours and a visit to three different offices, not all of them located on the border—one of them requiring us to backtrack fifteen miles—to get out of Mexico. We had to buy a tourist license to *leave* the country. It did not surprise us. This was a country, after all, whose criminals—and it was not as though crime and corruption were anything new—would need a full twenty years of day-to-day training at the hands of the Colombians to figure out how to make money in the cocaine business.

We later heard the story of a truck that showed up at the border with 340 donated school desks bound from the United States to Mexico. Mexican Customs officials refused entry in the absence of a high duty payment, and several hundred Mexican schoolchildren went to the border and dragged the desks across one at a time, because as individual units they were allowed in duty-free.

Our experience at the Mexican border was predictably absurd. It was the prospect of the U.S. border that provoked the real sense of anxiety. We had read all the stories about how the border had become a fortress since September 11. We had heard about the interminable backups, the lines of traffic, the hours and hours of waiting to get into the country. We had been across enough borders to know that an agitated, belligerent, or simply unhappy customs or immigration official could make an issue out of anything. We had been out of the country for three years, and we were weird almost by definition—indeed, it was our very weirdness, our out-of-the-ordinariness, that had saved us on many occasions. But how was it going to play at home, a country we had been led to believe was very different from the one we had left?

We faced our arrival in the United States with great excitement; we were thrilled to be home. Our run up to Alaska and everything that followed we envisioned as something of a victory lap. But right now our excitement was tempered. There is a trancelike state you have to impose on yourself when facing the typical border crossing. You cannot be in a hurry, you cannot allow yourself to be unnerved by bureaucratic absurdity, you have to be patient and go with the flow and at the same time stay alert to any opportunities to speed things up.

We crossed at Nogales, Arizona, and my first surprise was the size of the backup. There was not much of a line at all, and it was moving fast. It was a twenty-minute wait at most. By the time we reached the immigration post, a crowd of customs officers, sitting about fifteen yards away, were already on their feet, waving us over. "What's that? Who are you? Bring that car over here. We want to see it." They were all excited. They were no different from any number of local officials in uniform throughout the world—they were all curious to get a look at the car. The immigration officer stamped our passports and waved us over in their direction.

Naturally, we gave the customs people a look at our map. On the inside panel of the trailer hatch, we had installed a map of the world, and for three years I had been tracing the route of our trip on it. From previous expeditions I had discovered this to be a simple, fast, and comprehensive way to explain who we were and what we were doing. When Paige and I were stopped and told to hand over our papers, we would say okay and I would reach into the trailer. Opening the trailer hatch served two immediate purposes: it exposed the contents of the trailer, making it pretty clear that we were not carrying gold bars, guns, or marijuana; and it instantly explained what we were doing. If nothing else, it diverted the attention of whoever was making the demand, and that was always a plus.

So it did take us a while to get into the United States, but only because a couple of the officers at U.S. Customs were car buffs. We had to entertain the crowd. As far as being hassled? It never happened.

We were home.

In Tucson, our first night in country, just as we would in any other corner of the globe, however exotic, we searched out the native cuisine. We passed on the gourmet experience and had dinner at the local Applebee's franchise, where not only the food but also the beer was pictured on the menu. Another first—just like the silkworms and the gallbladder of that snake. As I said, I like to try everything.

It should come as no surprise to you, having followed me this far, that having started my longitudinal crossing of the Western Hemisphere at 55 degrees south latitude, in Ushuaia, Tierra del Fuego, I was not going to quit before I hit that same number driving north of the equator. Indeed, the journey would take us as close to the Arctic Circle as Whitehorse, in the Yukon Territory. We would pass a sign in Watson Lake, welcoming us to the territory and telling us we were "north of 60."

Sixty degrees above the equator and twenty-two degrees below zero. Fahrenheit. And it was only November.

As we drove through the United States and Canada, we ran into—or stopped to see or very often stopped to be seen by—a lot of people who had been "traveling" with us on the Internet. In nearly every city, starting in Tucson, we rendezvoused with people who knew we were there, snapping pictures and shaking hands. And then there was a cop in Utah who was unimpressed by us entirely. Traveling from the Grand Canyon, crossing the Utah border, we were ticketed for speeding by a nice Mormon cop, who was quite forthright in admitting that, yeah, maybe his radar gun was "stuck" on 78. But we were out-of-staters, he said, and did we really want to stick around and go through the trouble of trying to prove he was just collecting fines at random from all the tourists heading north? Utah had to make its money. It was the same conversation I had had with cops in Russia and Mozambique, the same bogus speed trap, the only difference being that this character did not put the money in his pocket. Or so I hoped.

And by the way . . . there is a difference between world-class sights and local-chamber-of-commerce sights. Having been around the world yet again now, I can tell you that the Grand Canyon is world class.

Heading for Canada, we passed through Dillon, Montana, the only city of my experience where the Kentucky Fried Chicken outlet features a casino. We made our way north through Alberta, visiting one of North America's great cities, Calgary, still a bit of a Wild West town but at the same time very sophisticated, like much of western Canada transformed by the oil boom. I probably should not have been surprised, but I was, at how splendid the highways were and how far into northern Alberta they extended. We picked up the Alaska Highway at the Mile Zero post in Dawson Creek, British Columbia, and headed for Whitehorse.

A strategic highway, 1,671 miles long, the Alaska Highway, also known as the Alcan Highway, was built by Canada and the United States over the course of nine months starting in 1942 as a military road. It runs from Dawson Creek to Fairbanks, Alaska, and was not paved in its entirety until 1992, in honor of its fiftieth birthday. I had driven the road twice before, and now, having driven it a third time, I would like to do it a fourth.

"Who wouldn't love this?" said Paige.

The roadhouses we ran across along the way reminded us of similar establishments in the outback of Australia, as did the locals. Bison, moose, elk, caribou, and mountain goats, however, had never crossed our path down under, and those we saw from the Alcan were definitely more laid back than kangaroos. It was almost the dead of winter, and the highway was virtually empty but for the animals and us.

The Yukon is the size of Texas, boasts only thirty thousand people—Texas has twenty million—and twenty-two thousand of them live in Whitehorse, the territorial capital. They found the temperature, twenty-two below (–30 degrees Celsius), to be relatively balmy, telling us to wait a month or two if we wanted to experience the city in really cold weather. In January, they said, it might reach fifty-eight below. We told them we would take their word for it. We drove due south from Whitehorse to Skagway, Alaska, and there we picked up my mother, who had flown up from Alabama to travel with us once again.

Eighty-two years old, and she was ready to go anywhere. Traveling with another of my nieces, Danise this time, she had taken several flights and, despite the arduous trip, arrived in high spirits, perkier than when we had last seen her in Argentina. It had been six months since my dad had died. As frail as she was, she was never too tired unless we told her she was tired, and only then would she go take a rest. From Skagway we took a car ferry down the Inside Passage, traveling as far as Prince Rupert, halfway down the coast of British Columbia, where we spent a day or two before hopping a second boat that would take us to Vancouver Island.

Vancouver, which has fewer than two million people in its metropolitan area (and which is not located on Vancouver Island), is one of the most beautiful cities in the world. Its physical setting is spectacular, with magnificent mountains running down to the sea and an array of public parks beautifully preserved. It offers all that the U.S. Pacific Northwest offers and more. It is a dynamic, prosperous city, in large part because of its status as a modern melting pot, a gateway to and from Asia. Canada actively seeks and encourages immigration as the United States once did. Large numbers of Chinese, Japanese, Koreans, Europeans, Iranians, and others have made the city their home. It reminds me of what New York must have been like at the turn of the twentieth century. In a hundred years, maybe a couple of hundred, unless somebody does something really stupid, Vancouver, one of the great cities of North America, will have become one of the great cities of the world.

In Vancouver we put my mother on a plane for home, and made for the U.S. border.

I expected to find a depression in Seattle, given the cutbacks at Boeing, the departure of the company's headquarters, and the falloff in the dot-com business. Instead, I found a vibrant, flourishing metropolis. It had been several years since my last visit, and since then Seattle had grown up. It was now a real city, with a discernible downtown. There was street life; there was a skyline. A decade earlier, it had been much more provincial, more like Tulsa or Birmingham. Now walking around town was like walking in New York or San Francisco.

I was in a hurry to get home for Christmas, to spend it alone with my mother, so, heading for California, we followed Interstate 5. I had traveled it on a motorcycle ten years before, and since then it had undergone an extraordinary development. Seattle, Tacoma, Portland, as far as Sacramento—it was like driving from New York to Boston, one long urban corridor, but far more up to date, a single, modern, shining, endlessly sprawling city. Moving south, we stopped in San Francisco, Palo Alto, Santa Barbara, and Los Angeles. In traveling the world, whereas I might inquire locally about politics, demographics, and money, Paige will learn a lot about a culture or civilization by studying the local markets and talking with women. So naturally, when we reached Los Angeles, we had to check out Rodeo Drive. Expecting to find a long, never-ending line of shops along this world-famous boulevard that stands as a monument to conspicuous consumption, Paige was crestfallen to discover that it ran for no more than a few blocks.

Christmas was approaching, and everywhere we traveled in the United States, we noticed that the malls, hotels, and restaurants were full, which was not what we had been led to expect. Reading the national press, most of which came out of New York, of course, we had anticipated finding a country deep in the economic tank. While New York was undoubtedly suffering, the rest of the country seemed healthy. We were surprised at how busy and lively the country was in the wake of September 11. We were also surprised to see that patriotism had peaked after the initial surge. Flags were everywhere, but by now they were tattered. No one was replacing them.

In California we met a man who was disbelieving when he heard our story. He and his fiancée, he said, had been stuck with each other for five days, driving from California to Connecticut, and by the time they reached New England, the engagement was off.

I should say a few things about Las Vegas, where we stopped for a couple of days. Not doing so, I think, would be like keeping a journal in biblical times without mentioning Sodom and Gomorrah. I had been to the city several times, usually for speaking engagements, but Paige had never been there and wanted to go. I should start by pointing out that Las Vegas is not my kind of town. In the first place, I do not gamble.

Yes, I know, you are thinking what everyone else thinks, but believe me, nothing could be further from the truth. I do not take risks with my money. Ever. The way of the successful investor is normally to do nothing—not until you see money lying there, somewhere over in the corner, and all that is left for you to do is go over and pick it up. That is how you invest. You wait until you see, or find, or stumble upon, or dig up by way of research something you think is a sure thing. Something without much risk. You do not buy unless it is cheap and unless you see positive change coming. In other words, you do not buy except on rare occasions, and there are not going to be many in life where the money is just lying there.

One of the mistakes that many people make in the stock market is buying something, watching it go up, and thinking they are smart. They find themselves thinking it is easy. They take a big profit and immediately go looking for something else. That's the time they should really do nothing. Self-confidence leading to hubris leading to arrogance—that is when you really should put the money in the bank and go to the beach for a while until you calm down. Because there are not many great opportunities that are ever going to come along. But you do not need many if you do not make many mistakes.

So no, I am not a gambler. Never have been.

Never having particularly liked Las Vegas, I somehow saw it now with new eyes. Perhaps three years and 116 countries made a difference. Paige was fascinated by the neon glitz and over-the-top luxury. I found myself appreciating and understanding the place. In many ways it rivals some of the great cities of history, the great crossroads of vast wealth, astonishing for so enormous an accumulation of talent and money. It is one of the great man-made sites of the world, featuring gigantic complexes arrayed one after the other, each of which cost hundreds of millions. Each in itself is pretty extraordinary. When taken together, they rival by sheer force of will the great temple clusters of ancient civilizations. Many of the world's great architects, however you judge the quality of their work, or lack thereof, are represented there. The great designers of the world, the great restaurants, the famous shops—every brand you have ever heard of is on display there. The Guggenheim Museum had two separate exhibits in Las Vegas when we were there. Even Saint Petersburg's Hermitage Museum is represented. The city is open twenty-four hours a day. You can get anything you want, whenever you want it. You can fly in and out all night long. Its international airport, one of the world's busiest, never closes. The effort, the creativity, the money, the design . . . the flat-out energy . . . All the great entertainers, from classical musicians to pop stars to animal acts, and all the great events, the big prizefights, the tennis matches, the golf tournaments, are attracted to Las Vegas from all over the world, just as they were to ancient Rome. Like it or not, it is one of the great spectacles and sights of the twenty-first century.

And in a hundred years, maybe two, it will be desert again. Whether Miami Beach, Cancún, or Carthage, all this stuff passes. Copán disappeared from the face of the earth for centuries. The Strait of Magellan, once the great passageway on which world commerce and exploration depended, is basically a rickety old ferry now.

We left Las Vegas on December 18. Paige and I wanted to be home for Christmas, she to spend it in North Carolina with her family, I to spend it with my mother in Demopolis. With only a few days to get home, we made a limited number of stops.

Alabama is home to my father's family, extending back several generations, but my mother's family hails from Oklahoma, one set of my great-grandparents having arrived there before it was a state. My mother was born and reared there, my grandparents are buried there, and both my parents and my grandparents had met at the University of Oklahoma at a sorority house next door to a fraternity house. Cousins of mine had been e-mailing us over the course of the trip, and while hurrying east, Paige and I stopped in to see them in Norman.

Oklahoma was on the way home, but New Orleans was not. While the city itself, an absolutely wonderful place, was inducement enough to detour, we had another, equally powerful incentive. There was a woman in New Orleans, Sharon Lambert, who had been "traveling" with us, following our trip on the Web like many people, but she had been doing it for the entire three years, and she had been doing it with her grandchildren. They ranged in age from four to sixteen, she had bought every one of them a globe, and all of them were tracing the journey on their globes as Paige and I circled the earth.

Some of our most faithful followers, Sharon and her grandchildren had been communicating with us throughout the trip, all the kids learning about the world at Granny's insistence. Sharon, in addition to everything else, had gone out of her way for my parents. My mother was not very comfortable with her computer, and Sharon had taken it upon herself to transcribe much of the audio for her. There was no way we were going to miss the opportunity to meet her. She and all the grandchildren joined Paige and me for dinner at Galatoire's.

Paige and I were now faced with the problem of where to end the trip, to bring it to its official close. Numerous places presented themselves as appropriate. It was in Tuscaloosa that my cousins, the Randalls, had thrown a party that commemorated an end of my previous trip. In New Jersey there was Mercedes-Benz of North America, which had supported us morally and physically from the beginning and helped insure we made it. There was also Manhattan Mercedes, which made the final adjustments after the shakedown drive and before our bon voyage. Charlotte, of course, was an obvious choice. It was where Paige and I had met and she had spent her adult life before meeting me. And then of course there was New York.

In the end we celebrated in all those places, as well as Rocky Mount, North Carolina, where Paige's parents threw us a splendid party with champagne and Paige's favorite ham biscuits. Where the trip officially ended, where its completion was formally commemorated, was pretty much up for grabs. And in fact it was of little importance. For in every way that mattered the trip ended for me in Alabama, alone on a cold December day, graveside at the family cemetery, sharing the accomplishment with my father.

The family graveyard is in a town called Letohatchee. There is little there anymore, a railroad crossing, a small post office, the Rogers family cemetery, and a few other graves. It is a classic southern cemetery. If you were making a movie and needed one, this one would be ideal: great stately magnolia trees, Spanish moss, white marble. There are many old graves, and there are picnic grounds within the cemetery. It is here at the picnic tables every year that the Rogers family reunion is held. I remember, when I was a kid, the reunion was held in July, and we would all get together to mow and weed the cemetery lawn. As might be expected of a nine-year-old, I hated it. Weeding was not my idea of summer fun, certainly not in July in the Alabama sun. Somewhere along the way, someone had the sense to suggest moving the event to early May. It was probably the same person who floated the notion of paying somebody to tend the grounds beforehand. After that, the reunion was a lot more fun.

Once my father got cancer, he immediately set out to make a lot of improvements at the house so that my mother would not have to worry about things such as fixing the roof after he was dead. And he did a lot of work at the cemetery, picking out the site, shoring everything up, putting a new fence around the section that was to be ours. He put up a concrete reinforcing wall. He had thought he had only six months to live. Fortunately—or unfortunately—he had plenty of time to do all the work.

*At the family cemetery in Letohatchee, I visit my father's grave
and tell him we finally made it—I dedicate the trip to him
and begin pondering its meaning.*

My mother told me about the funeral. I have four brothers and various nieces and nephews. When the coffin was lowered into the ground, one of my brothers walked over and started shoveling dirt into the grave. My other three brothers and all the grandchildren then took up shovels, and the whole family finished the job together. I had never heard of anyone doing that at a funeral, but when it was described to me, I regretted not having been a part of it. And I regretted not having been there for my mother. When I had announced my intention to make the trip and my father had sat me down with my mother, adamant that I should not interrupt the trip to come home under any circumstances, my mother had made it clear that in her case it was quite the opposite: if anything happened to her, she told me, I was to get home immediately.

When Paige and I had sent flowers, I had implored the Demopolis florist to include a map of the world with the arrangement. It was my way of saying, yes, Daddy, we are doing it, and we are doing it for you, we are continuing the trip, we are traveling the world, as you always wanted to do. The florist was unable to find a map of the world anywhere in town. The only map she could find was a map of Alabama. It was as close as we could come to letting him know that we had honored his wish and were dedicating the trip to him.

It was my first Christmas without my father. I had never been very attentive to Christmas in the past. Once I had gone off to college, especially after I had gotten to England, where the logistics made it difficult, I had fallen into the habit of being away from home at Christmas. I was in the Army, or I was working on Wall Street. Like a lot of other young people, I went through a stage where I did not want to spend time at home; I was too good for it, too busy for it. In the 1990s things started to change, and I began going home a fair amount. When my father was diagnosed with cancer, I began going home that much more, trying to get there as often as possible.

On December 24, two days after I arrived—Paige had continued on to Rocky Mount to celebrate Christmas with her parents—the entire family gathered at home. One of my brothers had been activated for military duty in the Middle East and anticipated being sent overseas. It was the only day he could be there, and so we celebrated the holiday early. On the following day, Christmas Day, my mother and I were the only members of the family at home. There was a calm and a peace that I had never experienced in that house. And though I was not quite sure of the source of it, I experienced a rare sense of inner peace.

Two days later, alone, I visited my father's grave. I am not sure what I expected or wanted, but in any case it was not terribly easy. The place seemed awfully cold, awfully lonesome, and awfully desolate. But in every way I could imagine, it was the most appropriate place to begin gathering perspective on the journey I had undertaken.

# 16

## HOME AGAIN

G IVEN THE SHEER DEDICATION of time, I suppose, it is not particularly profound to point out that I learned more about the
United States in the three years I was away from the country than I
learned in the six weeks that I spent driving it. Perhaps that was to be
expected. No matter how much you think you know, no matter how
far you have traveled across this great land of ours, if you really want
to get to know America, do yourself a favor and get out for a while.

One thing that never ceases to sadden me—and it was reinforced
upon my return from the trip—is how little most Americans know
about the world, or worse, even care to know. And not simply about
the *rest* of the world—ignorance they tend to wear as some twisted
badge of honor—but about the very country in which they live. Indeed, you cannot really understand the latter until you have acquainted yourself with the former.

I returned from the trip exhilarated, surprised to be alive, wondering how I was going to accomplish something so enormous ever
again, only to be disappointed time after time by people who could

not recognize the enormity of the world out there. "We drove around the world," I would tell them. "What airline?" they would ask. Or, "That must have been fun. How long did it take?" "Three years," I would tell them, then have to tell them again, shaking them out of their unconsciousness before it finally sank in: we had covered 152,000 miles, traveling through 116 countries.

For many people, it was incomprehensible. When I speak publicly about the trip, I show the audience a map displaying our itinerary, asking people to pick any six inches of the journey. On a large map of the world it is a mere six inches, but for Paige and me those six inches represent dozens of encounters—ordeals, obstacles, disappointments, and triumphs—a lifetime's worth of exhilaration, depression, and adventure.

On the one hand, I find it disappointing that there are people who have actually never heard of some of the places we visited. On the other, it is somewhat predictable. You will find virtually no reporting on what is happening in the rest of the world by the American news media. We Americans have always been geographically isolated and as a result have always found it easy to be politically isolated as well. Many Americans have never seen any need to understand France or Poland or Chad. And members of the American press are no different.

When the U.S. press does report on the rest of the world, the news is often biased, the media waving the flag in the faces of viewers in foreign countries who are not so naïve or cloistered as the American audience. By the time I returned home, the American press was actually being censored—acceding willingly to National Security Advisor Condoleezza Rice's request that it not report certain events from the Middle East.

To get a broader view of what is going on in the world, I read foreign periodicals and listen to overseas broadcasts, such as Israeli radio, Radio China, and, of course, the BBC. The British have always provided far superior international coverage to that which is provided by U.S. news services. British citizens have always been exposed to news from around the globe; as with all Europeans, they have maintained a worldview, in large part because they have had to. Our media companies have few overseas bureaus now.

If the Central African Republic were to blow up, Americans might never find out, or at best they might find out a couple of weeks after the event, when a U.S. news organization finally got a reporter on the scene. (It is more likely that the U.S. news organization would pick up a BBC feed or pull the story off the Reuters wire.) The average American would never learn what is going on over there, and what is even more painfully clear is that the average American would not care. Even those who say they care usually do not. They do not want to know too much about Malaysia or Zambia or any number of others. We paid a big price for this on September 11, 2001. And this willful ignorance on the part of the nation's citizens finds its logical counterpart in the embarrassing lack of sophistication shown by the people we elect to political office.

Let me own up to my view immediately. My skepticism concerning the people who call themselves public servants in the world is wideranging. The low opinion they enjoy is well deserved. Ask yourself why they are in politics to begin with, and the answer is immediately obvious: these are people who, as schoolchildren, were good out on the playground. When recess came around, they were monumentally successful—out there chatting it up, shooting marbles, skipping rope, playing ball. Studies have shown that the people who in grammar school excelled at recess are the ones who wind up in politics and usually do very well at it.

Very few politicians could build a company, or a country. That is why they go into politics. Harry Truman was a great failure in business, not once but two or three times. Bill Clinton never had a real job. George Bush, the younger: he failed at two or three companies before somebody bought him a baseball team. Not that running a company is necessarily a sign of intelligence or competence, but at least we know that very few people who *are* successful, who *are* good at life, go into politics, and certainly not early. Some of them get rich and then go into politics (indeed, today we see numerous rich people actually buying Senate seats and mayoralties), but few politicians bring anything other than political experience to the job—though many, such as Lyndon Johnson, *leave* office rich, capitalizing on their positions, as has been happening since the beginning, just as Patrick Henry and George Washington did, speculating in frontier land.

In the current administration, the person whose worldview is most sophisticated is the secretary of state, Colin Powell. I suspect it has something to do with his immigrant parents and his background as a military man. The rest of the crowd, for the most part, does not know the world and does not care. Condoleezza Rice, for example, the national security advisor, unlike Powell, is ill served by her background rather than a beneficiary of it. As a student, she studied Russian, and, working her way up through the political establishment, she developed expertise as a Sovietologist. Understanding little about China's place in the world, she supports a Russia-centered foreign policy because she has to—because it confirms the supposed value of her expertise—because in any other scenario she would be out of work.

There are numerous highly paid bureaucrats in the State Department whose careers are founded on anti-China policy. Even if they were able to see the light, they would be unlikely to walk in its direction. The same is true of our Cuba policy. Poor old bankrupt Fidel Castro is not a threat to anybody anymore. The rest of the world recognizes that and is making the best of the opportunities that the future holds in Cuba. To us, Cubans are hopelessly unclean, and we are doing everything we can to destroy our chances there. Why? Because for forty-five years a whole class of bureaucrats has risen to the top based on that policy.

Contemplating the way of the bureaucrat, I am reminded of the various stages of grief: rejection, argument, anger, and acceptance. It is true of terminal disease and the progress of great ideas as well. When somebody first comes up with a new idea, everybody ignores it. Then people ridicule it, coming up with vehement arguments against it, before arriving at acceptance and support. Then, not only do they find themselves explaining why it is a good idea; they go on to say, "Yeah, I thought of it." It has been proved to be true throughout history and is true of politics, economics, and warfare. General Billy Mitchell was drummed out of the service in the 1920s for claiming the aircraft carrier was the wave of the future. Nobody remembers that now, of course, certainly not the people in the armed forces.

In the wake of September 11, 2001, we all understood the need for swift justice. I also felt that maybe somebody in Washington would say, as things unfolded, "We have to reexamine our policies to see if we can do better." What was clear to me as I traveled the world was that the United States had made numerous enemies in the 1990s. It may have been a result of the government's being a bit adrift after the fall of the Berlin Wall. Policy makers had been focusing all their attention in one direction. Suddenly, with the collapse of communism, they were understandably caught off balance. The world changed dramatically without anyone's expecting it; our foreign policy establishment was unprepared for the shift. Perhaps it was surprise or maybe it was incompetence, but either way, we made a lot of enemies in the ten years leading up to the attack on the World Trade Center.

Sadly, that reexamination has yet to take place in Washington. The rhetoric coming out of the halls of power sounds as though it was written in the 1950s. I remember my high school teachers telling me then that the reason the United States had won all its wars—this was before the nation's adventure in Vietnam—was that God was on our side. My teachers all believed it. I believed it. It never occurred to me to question it. It had always been the American view, the rest of the world be damned.

It was only later that I realized that this was a recurring theme in history. The nineteenth-century French historian and statesman François Guizot wrote that Europe was marching in step with divine will—and everyone believed it.

On our way home, I was invited to a think-tank convocation but declined to attend when I was told, "We don't care how the U.S. is perceived in the world, we want you to talk about travel." Not long ago I appeared on a panel with a former U.S. congressman who, in extolling American foreign policy, supported his antic argument that our preeminence was well deserved, that indeed we could accomplish anything, by making the following assertion: that we in America invented the automobile, that we in America invented television. Well, Congressman, it goes like this:

We in America have accomplished some extraordinary things in our history, but our policy must be grounded in reality. We did not invent either the cathode-ray tube, which came out of Germany in 1897, or the television, the first demonstration of which was given in Britain in 1925 using German technology. Nor are we even responsible for the first television service—that was the BBC, in 1936. Not until 1953, more than half a century after the Europeans got going, did we in America, leaping ahead with the first successful transmission of *color* TV, make any significant contribution to television technology.

We did not invent the automobile either. The Europeans (again) were way ahead of us in every aspect of automotive history, starting in 1770—the Germans, the French, the British, the Dutch. A Belgian, in 1860, developed the internal combustion engine. Not until Henry Ford came up with the Model T in 1908—a full twenty-three years after Carl Benz of Germany produced the first petrol-driven motor car—were we in America even in the game.

Reading too deeply into history does not serve the purpose of the nation's politicians, or even, to a certain degree, the State Department. International tension and conflict may be good for votes, good for approval ratings, good for the Pentagon's budget, but have never been good for the citizens, the society, or the economy. And so the responses you get to why the United States has been targeted are completely outside the context of any sense of the world: "They don't like us because we are rich." There are a lot of countries richer than ours on a per capita basis. Japan, Singapore, Switzerland, they are all richer than the United States. Nobody is bombing them. "They hate us because of the freedom we enjoy." People around the world, when they hear George Bush say that, will look at you and ask, "Is he crazy? Nobody hates freedom. If anything, freedom is what we like about America." I have never heard anyone, anywhere, say, "I am going to go out and die for my country so that those who come after me can live under a dictatorship." Many people will tell you that when it comes to the level of freedom enjoyed by its citizens, this country does not even rank first in their view. And nobody is blowing up the Netherlands.

Whatever the answer, you will not find it until you start asking the right questions, and asking them of the right people. Anyone involved in a war, running a company, or simply having an argument has to understand what the enemy, the competition, the other guy is up to or he has no hope of winning the battle, winning market share, or winning the debate. Every military school in the world will tell you that you have to understand how the other guy thinks. The enemy may be crazy, but you have to get into his head if you are ever to have any hope of defeating him.

Paige and I ran into virtually no anti-American sentiment on the ground. Perhaps because there were so few Americans traveling through the countries in question, we were seen as an item of curiosity. Everybody wanted to be hospitable. And virtually everybody we ran into wanted to come to America. People, I think, in general, tend to differentiate between citizens and their government. *Harper's* magazine reported in the summer of 2002 that the United States was the single most favorably viewed country by young Muslims. The same was true after both the First and Second World Wars. Plenty of people are angry at our policies, but they are not necessarily angry at us. People all over the world seem to know the American people are good, but they also seem to know something happens to Americans when they go to Washington.

It is no surprise that they are angry at our policies. Washington, never seeming to think twice about interfering in the affairs of foreign governments, expends effort on the activities of nearly every country in the world and often gets it wrong, even if only by miscalculating. The only beneficiaries seem to be thirty-one-year-old desk managers in D.C. We would be better off in every way if we devoted the same time and money to taking care of things at home.

North Korea is a perfect example of our spending billions on other people's business. North Korea is no conceivable threat to us. If the regime there is as dangerous as we claim it is, it is its neighbors' problem, not ours. Japan, South Korea, Russia, and China are all within a few miles of North Korea; they have vast resources with which to deal with that bankrupt country of only thirty million people. If its unstable leadership and its potential nuclear program are no problem for them—indeed, the current and immediate-past South Korean governments are actively engaging the North to open up—why should we be bothering there, when we have plenty to do at home? We could probably cure cancer with the resources we are wasting on other people's affairs there alone.

Overextension has always been bad for nations, especially nations in debt. England and Spain were great powers at one time, and trying to maintain their presence in too many places brought them down. I do not want to see this happen to the United States. Overextension threatens our currency, our power, and our economy, and ultimately it threatens globalization, which affects all the countries of the world simultaneously. No nation that has gotten itself in this situation has gotten itself out without a crisis, or a semicrisis at best. Overspreading our resources, specifically our financial and military muscle, has the further effect of breeding hostility around the world, creating a vicious circle in which we are required to spend even more money to maintain our safety, security, and prosperity. Butting out as the world's meddling uncle would free up resources we could use elsewhere, including here. We would save hundreds of billions, make fewer enemies, and provide fewer targets if we did not have troops in Europe, Japan, Korea, etc., decades after World War II and fourteen years after the Cold War ended.

Washington is constantly telling us we can do anything we want because we are the world's only superpower. We certainly are the world's strongest military power by far, but we are hardly a superpower. Our navy has only twelve Nimitz-class aircraft carriers now, down from more than one hundred large carriers at the end of the Second World War. The average air force plane is twenty years old, and many of our magnificent fighters will be of little use in wars of the future. Our extraordinary B-1 bombers were flight-ready only 31 percent of the time in 2001. We have only twenty-one AC-130 gunship aircraft. We used up nearly all our cruise missiles in Afghanistan, in what was a relatively small-scale action. This is hardly sufficient to a nation bent on projecting its power all over the world. Spending the money to achieve such a potential would bankrupt the nation and do us more harm than good geopolitically.

Over the period of time we were gone, the U.S. media, the government, and Wall Street were assuring the nation that prices were remaining stable, that inflation was being kept at bay, which on the face of it stretched credulity. It ran contrary to what we thought was happening, what should have been happening, and what we inevitably discovered actually *was* happening. When Paige and I returned home, we were shocked at how much prices had gone up, whether movies or popcorn at the movies, whether dry cleaning, heating, education, lawyers, postage, accountants, dentists, plumbers, electricians, candy, medical care, housing, sporting events, tolls, fees, telephone bills, entertainment, restaurants, suits, insurance, fuel, food, or real estate taxes. All cost significantly more than they had when we had left. The government, not surprisingly, with the help of the media and Wall Street, was involved in a charade, and, like most charades, this one fooled only some of the people and only some of the time.

It was in 1996 that a special presidential commission announced that the government had been reporting the cost of living "improperly" and created a new methodology for measuring inflation. Using "hedonic adjustments," the budget office started reporting price increases as being far lower than previously calculated. The price of a Chevrolet had not really gone up, according to the Bureau of Labor Statistics, because the new Chevrolet was "more comfortable" than the earlier model. The price of gasoline had risen not by 20 percent but by only 15 percent, because the gasoline in question was "better" than before.

A recently published statistic shows 56 percent of the figures that go into the Consumer Price Index are now hedonically adjusted. The term is not one I made up—the BLS uses it to describe the adjustments in question. Because the adjustments keep things like Social Security payments and cost-of-living raises low, making it easier for the government to balance the federal budget, one can assume that the adjustments are here to stay and that 56 percent is not where they will stop. In fact, new "studies" are under way to revise the procedures again.

In November 2002 the BLS reported that heating prices were down by 11.1 percent. Prices, in fact, were up more than 20 percent, according to *The Wall Street Journal* and the markets. Similarly, the BLS reported "cheaper gasoline in May 2000," while the U.S. Department of Energy reported that prices were up by more than 20 percent in May 2000. These are figures that are very easy to verify, yet Wall Street and the press accept the government figures unquestioningly. But then these are the people who said that there was a bull market and a "New Economy" (going so far as to capitalize that phrase in print in the late 1990s) when in fact there was neither.

The Federal Reserve has been printing money at a rapid rate to force interest rates down, to save Wall Street and the stock market. But as always happens, market forces or the forces of nature or the forces of reality eventually come to bear, and interest rates in the end will be higher than they would have been otherwise. So you better refinance your mortgage or buy your lifetime membership to the Princeton club now—do whatever you can to lock yourself in, because prices are going up even faster now.

As I traveled, I found people—those who paid any attention—just incredulous at the U.S. numbers, because prices were going up all over the world. Yes, the price of oil dropped a time or two while I was away, but compared to where it had been in the late 1990s, when we left, it was up a lot. Markets always move up in a zigzag fashion. Nothing goes straight up or down. The real prices of just about everything are up and, thanks to government accounting methods, are working their way unchallenged into the economy. If you learn nothing else in your life, learn not to take your investment advice, or any other advice, from the U.S. government—or any government.

Since my return I have received letters from former employees of the Bureau of Labor Statistics, which reports the inflation numbers, who say that, indeed, they were always instructed to "smooth out" any large increases. The United States has been using similar abracadabra in measuring productivity, economic growth, and the gross national product. Of course, governments all over the world have been announcing numbers for years that we now know to be phony. We know that under the Communists, for example, Russian figures were falsely reported. (But at least the Communists *had* figures; I can tell you from personal experience that nobody over there today is collecting or compiling any real figures at all.)

Europeans frequently point out that if they reported their numbers the way we do, they would have much better-looking books, especially if they employed the techniques devised under Clinton and Alan Greenspan. The rest of the world keeps its accounts differently and gives little credibility to the figures we report. Only a few years ago, all the time Washington was singing hosannas, celebrating the balancing of the budget, the total government debt was rising. If you or I kept our books the way the U.S. government does, we would be thrown in jail.

Which brings us to corporate America.

There is a great hue and cry in the land about faulty accounting by companies. And there is no question that it is serious. During every mania in history people have taken shortcuts, doing things the easy way, and they have always gotten away with it. When things are going up, nobody notices. Nobody cares. In fact, the shenanigans in question are encouraged, because they contribute to the upward trend.

Now, however, not only are stocks down a lot, but many corporate and government pension plans are underfunded, which is not being widely reported. Many employees and current pensioners who are expecting normal pensions may well be surprised in the next few years.

A government agency, the Pension Benefit Guaranty Corporation, guarantees our pensions, but it too is technically bankrupt.

In the 1930s the acting president of the New York Stock Exchange, Richard Whitney, went to jail—Whitney, as in the Whitney family, as in the Whitney Museum. He, too, was involved in shoddy corner cutting. But he got caught with his pants down only after the bubble had burst. During every mania, such behavior is overlooked. It is seen as beneficial—people want it to happen. Only when everything starts collapsing do people ask, "How could you ever have done that?"

What the guys at WorldCom were up to in 1999 and 2000 everyone applauded at the time. Now, of course, those same guys are going to jail. The question is, were they just fools? Very often that is the case, and I would be reluctant to suggest jailing somebody simply because he is a fool. Many others, such as Gary Winnick of Global Crossing, who sold more than $700 million worth of his company's stock and put the money in his pocket, should go to jail. His "company" disappeared a few years after its founding. He created nothing for society or the world. The other employees and investors lost everything on his scam, yet he still has hundreds of millions of dollars. He used to work for Drexel Burnham Lambert, a company that perpetrated an earlier hoax and collapsed when the federal government started shipping people off to prison. The guy has done nothing but lose fortunes for people, yet he is a millionaire several times over. He is just one of many who left ruins but escaped with fat wallets. We can just hope the legal system finally does its work. Or perhaps a more traditional justice will occur. History is full of fast-money guys who die poor because they lose it all, never having really known what they were doing.

While all this was going on, you kept hearing how foreigners wanted to put their money here because the United States had better accounting standards, better regulation than any other country in the world. Which, of course, was total garbage. Now we understand that our accounting standards and practices—both government and corporate— are among the world's worst. In much of the world, accountants and management must certify that financial statements give an accurate reflection of the state of affairs. Here they just have to follow scores of rules. We all know how many ways rules can be interpreted—especially when there are too many of them. But if General Electric, for example, had not used accounting shortcuts, the stock would never have gone to 60. Which everyone loved at the time. Unfortunately, a lot of people— a lot with IRAs—are going to lose a lot more money than they otherwise would have because GE, IBM, Fannie Mae, and many others went up higher than was reasonable. People want the government to do something. And I say the government should do nothing. Reacting to immediate pressures, which is what governments have done throughout history, is invariably the wrong thing to do. Correcting the fundamental problem or letting it correct itself, while temporarily more painful, is the only effective course of action. But try telling that to Alan Greenspan.

Bob Woodward, who wrote the book *Maestro* about Federal Reserve Chairman Alan Greenspan, knows as little about what Greenspan does as the family cocker spaniel. He got sucked into the PR machinery. He probably bought a lot of stocks in 1999, as everybody else did, because he thought Greenspan was a genius. In fact, Greenspan has a long, long history of failure. That is why he has a government job. He has never been very successful.

In 1974, he was head of the Council of Economic Advisors. The country was in the early days of inflation. Greenspan's solution to inflation was to give out little WIN buttons, for Whip Inflation Now. And, of course, during his tenure, inflation went totally out of control. Whatever he tried failed miserably. He went back to work in the private sector, from which he lobbied heavily to get the job as chairman of the Federal Reserve.

Almost immediately after he got the job came the Panic of '87. The stock market went down about 20 percent in one day. Percentagewise, it was the biggest stock market collapse ever. Greenspan and his mutterings were part of the reason for the collapse. The week before, Greenspan had gone on and on about how the U.S. balance of trade was getting much better and things were under control. Two days later, the balance-of-trade figures came out, and they were the worst in the history of the world. Right away, I and a lot of investors— especially internationally—realized, "This guy is either a fool or a liar. He doesn't have any idea what's going on." We now know that Greenspan is no liar. He has simply never understood the stock market. He has never understood the economy.

Cut to 1998 and Long-Term Capital Management, a major fund

that got into terrible trouble, losing billions of dollars. Its collapse was going to have an effect on a lot of Wall Street firms. The investment firms went crying to Greenspan. Instead of letting the company go under and cleaning out the system, as bear markets have done for centuries, Greenspan panicked and put a lot of money into the system, bailing out his friends. That easy money is one of the things that led to the absolute worst of the mania, the bubble that has now burst with such devastating effect.

All of a sudden, there were massive amounts of easy money around, and whenever there is a lot of easy money around, it goes somewhere. And it almost always goes into financial assets first—stocks, bonds, commodities—because that is a simple place for it to go. The worst of the bubble was in those eighteen months after Long-Term Capital Management collapsed. That is when the NASDAQ skyrocketed. Remember, corporate profits in America peaked in 1997. In 1998 the stock market was on its way down. Sixty percent of shares in America were down that year. The same pattern was visible in 1999. Profits had peaked. The economy was slowing down. Yet, if you looked at the averages or you watched TV, you saw everyone going nuts over the "New Economy" and the bull market. That was the period when mutual fund sales started going through the roof. The real trend was masked, because Cisco was going up every day and Microsoft never went down. If you took out about thirty big stocks that were skewing the picture, it was very easy to see that the bear market was well under way. Notwithstanding Greenspan's efforts, the market understood.

But Greenspan, in reaction to a short-term crisis, had panicked. He printed money. He caused the bubble, pure and simple. Rather than calling an end to the party and taking the punch bowl away, rather than pricking the bubble in good times, he let it grow to massive proportions. He kept refilling the punch bowl with stronger stuff. Reading his various testimonies, it is clear that part of the reason is that he actually believed all that claptrap about a New Economy. Had he left things alone and we had had a normal bear market, he would have made some people furious, but that would have been a lot better than the alternative, the outcome that his interference ensured: people losing gigantic amounts of money. In situations like these, the government inevitably reacts to the panic on the other end of the phone, rather than looking back over history and saying, "The best thing that could happen is for you guys to go bankrupt." The government should do its best to do nothing and let the system clean itself out. But politicians have their constituents and their contributors to please.

Greenspan conceivably could have saved Long-Term Capital Management without creating the bubble. He could have loosened up a lot of money and at the same time raised margin requirements, making it more expensive to invest in the stock market. And nobody seems to know why he did not. As recently as 1996, he had spoken about margin requirements as a way to help control speculation. Partly, he came to believe the Wall Street hype, but I can think of no good reason for his not having done so, unless it was in some way connected to helping his friends at Goldman Sachs et al.

In 2001 Greenspan panicked again. That year, the central bank of the United States printed more money on a percentage basis than it had ever printed in the history of the republic. Greenspan has been relentlessly pumping money into the economy; the monetary expansion has never been so great. At the same time, fiscal policy has been loose. The government has been profligate on both sides. President Bush has been spending as fast as Greenspan can print. Both fiscally and monetarily, the world has been hit with a lot of money. "Well," Americans say to themselves, "things are not so bad after all." How long do you suppose that will last? The maestro has now perpetrated a housing and consumption bubble by driving down interest rates. Bubbles always end badly, and even more people will be hurt when this one bursts.

Robert Rubin, secretary of the Treasury, had the good sense to leave the government in 1998. But Rubin is a smart guy, a smart trader. Greenspan did not have enough sense to get out—but then, Greenspan had nowhere to go. He knew he could not get another job, and he is not really smart enough to have realized the damage he was causing.

The idea of central banks and central bankers as gods who can weave magic is a phenomenon of only the last decade in the West. Never before have they enjoyed the exalted status they enjoy now, where everybody knows the name of the head of the central bank in the United States or the name of the Chairman of the Bank of England. This too will pass. If things get bad enough soon enough, we may abolish the Federal Reserve before it collapses. The United States has had three central banks in its history. The first two failed. This one will undoubtedly fail, too.

Where can one find a sound currency? The U.S. dollar is fundamentally flawed; the euro has problems, as does the yen. Alan Greenspan and Federal Reserve Governor Ben Bernanke have officially stated that the Federal Reserve will do everything it can to prevent prices declining in the United States. To prevent deflation, they will print as much money as is necessary and will pump money into the system by buying Treasury bills, bonds, "real estate, gold mines—any asset," whatever is necessary to drive prices higher. That to me is a signal that you must sell U.S. dollars.

Anyone who thinks there will be deflation does not understand twenty-first-century central banking. There may well be a deflationary collapse later, but before that happens the government will print money until the world runs out of trees. The problem is finding a sound alternative currency. Forty years ago the world knew the Swiss franc, the deutsche mark, and a few other currencies were mandated to be sound by their people, but unfortunately politicians have now learned to buy votes by debasing those currencies. I am constantly searching for a sound currency in which to keep my investments but have yet to find one that is satisfactory. I have found only that some are less unsound than others. I own several currencies around the world and have no confidence in any of them.

All knowledgeable economists in history have warned against debasing the currency—which Lenin advised was the most effective way to overturn the existing basis of any society, because it is so subtle and insidious. Observers as wide ranging as John Maynard Keynes and Ernest Hemingway have agreed. Keynes said, "Lenin was certainly right." Hemingway, who saw much of the world close to the ground, observed, "The first panacea for a mismanaged nation is inflation of the currency; the second is war. Both bring temporary prosperity; both bring a permanent ruin. Both are the refuge of political and economic opportunists."

When Nero took power in Rome in A.D. 54, Roman coins were either pure silver or pure gold. By A.D. 268 silver coins consisted of only 0.02 percent silver, and gold coins had disappeared. Smart Romans had moved their wealth out of the depreciating coinage into investments that maintained their value.

Which reminds me: there has been no independent, external audit of the gold in Fort Knox for several decades, which the U.S. government refuses to explain despite repeated inquiries. Perhaps it is because everybody is afraid to go in there. OSHA recently determined that the U.S. Mints in Denver and Philadelphia were "the most dangerous places in the federal government to work" and closed down the Philadelphia operation for weeks.

Everything changes; nothing is permanent, especially one's portfolio. But all bubbles and manias in the financial markets are the same, and have been throughout history. "New Economy, New Economy!" everyone shouts. Well, we have heard that before. The railroad changed the world. Radio changed the world. The Radio Corporation of America became one of the largest corporations in American history and made gigantic profits. But if you had bought shares in RCA in the late 1920s, you would never have made any money, because the shares never again got as high as they got during the mania. Likewise, if you had bought shares in the railroads in the 1840s and '50s.

The railroad industry did not exist before the nineteenth century. Eventually, of course, the whole world was crisscrossed with railroads. The train would become the dominant form of transportation and communication. Yet most of the people who bought railroad shares never made any money. You had to buy them before the mania or after the mania broke. You had to buy them when everybody was saying, "I never want to buy another railroad share as long as I live."

The automobile changed the world. At one time in the United States there were hundreds of automobile companies. And unless you happened to pick the two or three that survived, you never made any money. General Motors became the largest industrial corporation in the world, but unless you happened to be smart enough or lucky enough to pick that one, and pick it at the beginning of the boom, you never struck it rich.

By the time the mania hits, everybody is getting involved: the banana salesman on the corner, the hairdressers, mom and pop; you go to the doctor or the dentist, and the receptionist wants to talk only about stocks, the stocks she has seen people talking about on TV. By the time the bubble has grown that big, the smart money is usually on the run. Bernard Baruch, the legendary financier and adviser to presidents, was having a shoeshine on Wall Street, and the shoeshine boy was giving him hot tips. Baruch went back to his office and sold everything.

The bull market on Wall Street began in the early 1980s. But at the time nobody believed it. The Dow Jones Industrial Average in 1966 was 1000. In 1982 the average was below 800. Sixteen years later it had fallen 20 percent, and that is not adjusting for inflation—and those sixteen years were the worst sixteen-year period of inflation in American history. Well, first of all, so much for long-term investing. Very few people would have sat there over that period waiting for their 401(k)s to mature.

In 1982 you did not see a lot of magazine covers featuring the latest hotshot mutual fund manager; you did not see a lot of investment advisers running around trying to do interviews. People were not borrowing money on credit cards and taking second mortgages on their homes, rushing out to invest in the stock market. In fact, when the Dow Jones went to 1200, rising by 50 percent, many people were saying, "You better sell, because this is crazy. It's going too far too fast."

By 1998 the mania was in full flower. But tell the press, the public, or Wall Street that it was not going to go on forever, and everyone's eyes would glaze over. People would look upon you with pity. Most stocks had already turned down (remember, 60 percent of stocks went down in 1998, and most were down in 1999), yet mutual fund sales went through the roof just in time to guarantee huge losses. "This is different. It's different this time," they would tell you. *The Wall Street Journal, The New York Times,* and *The Washington Post* all ran learned articles explaining that there was no bubble. Whenever you hear somebody tell you that investing is different this time, grab your money and run. It is never different. There never is a "New Economy." There never is a "New Era." The *Financial Times* has reported that the money spent due to exaggerated claims of Information Technology–induced productivity improvements at the end of the last decade has generated a negative return. The press has recently stopped capitalizing "New Economy."

It may have been Meyer Rothschild, the German banker and patriarch of the legendary House of Rothschild who, when asked how he got so rich, attributed his success to two things. He said he always bought when there was blood in the streets—panic, chaos—when despondency gripped the markets. (In old man Rothschild's case, investing amid the turbulence of the Napoleonic wars, the blood was just as likely to be literal as it was to be figurative.) And he always sold "too soon." He did not wait for enthusiasm to peak. He always knew when to get out, and he got out in time with all his money.

I doubt Meyer would be buying U.S. stocks these days, since he always waited for serious despair. After all, many on Wall Street are still raking in big money, employment there is down only slightly, stocks are not cheap by historical measures, and mutual funds are still thriving. He would probably point out that Japanese equity mutual funds lost 80 percent of their assets in the bear market after 1990; that is more like real blood in the streets.

I suspect that old Meyer, if he were around today, would have moved his investments to commodities, after having gotten out of stocks earlier. There have been long periods when stocks did well while raw materials did horribly—the 1980s and 1990s, say. The late 1960s and the 1970s saw the reverse. From 1906 to the early 1920s stocks did nothing while commodities boomed. It may sound radical, but it has occurred repeatedly. These cycles always have occurred as supply and demand patterns have shifted. Everyone invested in stocks in the 1980s and 1990s, but little money went into productive capacity for natural resources. There was a glut after the great boom of the 1970s, so no one was calling us to invest in sugar plantations or lead mines or offshore drilling rigs. Demand has continued growing worldwide, eventually to exceed supply, which has been flat for years. Asia alone has become a huge buyer; China is now already one of the world's largest importers. Excess inventories built up in the Cold War have been liquidated. We now have a classic change. Raw materials supply and demand are out of whack again, and inventories are down. Commodities will do well for years, while stocks, recovering from the bubble, will do little.

The new commodity bull market has started, but few realize it yet, just as few recognized that a new bull market in stocks had started in the 1980s. Commodities rose more than 150 percent between the end of 1998, when Paige and I left, and mid-2004, while shares were down substantially. The government, Wall Street, and the media keep telling us that prices are not rising, but one can go over to the com-

modity pages to check reality. War and the printing of money just ensure that the commodity boom will last even longer.

But it will not last forever. Someday, in several years, we will have
to sell our commodities and go back to stocks. Merrill Lynch no
longer has commodity brokers because it is such a bad business.
When Merrill Lynch goes back into the commodity business and
CNBC starts broadcasting from the soybean pits in Chicago, sell out
and buy stocks.

While the rules governing markets remain unchanged since the founding of the Rothschild dynasty, the same cannot be said of very much
else. When Paige and I set out to circle the globe, we envisioned our
journey as an investigation of change. We wanted literally to seize the
moment. The next opportunity to measure the world's heart rate as it
jumped a millennial divide was, by definition, a thousand years out.

Of course, a thousand years back, on January 1 in the year 1000,
there were only a few people in the world who would have identified
the day as signaling the arrival of a new millennium; back then, most
people in the world did not use the Julian calendar. (Christian calendars in centuries past have had New Year's Day in various months.)
There were many more Muslims than there were Christians in the
world, and the Muslims had their own calendar. Asians, who outnumbered both, were familiar with the calendars of neither. In the
Western Hemisphere the Maya, who were brilliant astronomers, observed what is known as the Long Count calendar, which measures
mankind's history in cycles of fifty-two hundred years. The year 1000
to us was the year 3188 to them. By their calculation, the fall of civilization, making way for renewal, is scheduled for the winter solstice
in our year 2012. (Start making plans.)

And now, not even we use the Julian calendar anymore. We have
not used it in the English-speaking world since 1752, 170 years after
the Gregorian calendar, the one we *do* use, was introduced to the rest
of the Christian world. If history is any guide, the world, as likely as
not, will never experience a January 1, 3000. Who knows what calendar will be in use a thousand years from now?

Who knows which culture will be on top? Who of the world's
270 million people in the year 1000 would have supposed that in
the year 2000 there was going to be this country in North America

that . . . *North what?* Had you been familiar with all the civilizations on earth, you might have moved to one of the great empires of modern-day Latin America, to one of the great empires of the Arab world, or maybe Asia. You might have moved to Africa, to Timbuktu.

The largest and most prosperous city at the end of the last millennium was Córdoba, Spain. One of the wealthiest was Seville. Both were more culturally significant at the time than Constantinople, the center of the Byzantine Empire. At the close of the tenth century, the Toltecs, supplanting the great civilization of the Maya, were commencing their two-hundred-year domination of Mesoamerica. What will the world look like a thousand years from now? I have spent five of the past thirteen years driving around the world, and by simply gauging the changes it underwent between the fall of the Berlin Wall and the fall of the World Trade Center, I can assure you that in a thousand years it will be all but unrecognizable. Trying to get an accurate read on things requires a metaphysical stopwatch.

In a magnificent showcase on Piazza San Marco one can see the names of all the leaders of the former Republic of Venice, a world power that for a thousand years flourished under a democracy that no nation would approximate until the nineteenth century. The listing of names ends with the demise of the Venetian constitution, eliminated by Napoleon when he marched into the defeated city-state with his army in 1797. At the turn of the last millennium, Venice was rising to absolute naval supremacy; it achieved a monopoly on Mediterranean trade and controlled European trade with the East. This was the city that gave rise to Marco Polo and helped impel the High Renaissance.

And I suspect that without the help of that showcase, none of us can name a single one of its leaders. I doubt that many Italians can. And I promise you that the time will come, however unfortunate, if not four hundred years from now, then certainly by the turn of the next millennium, that few will be able to name a single American president, not even George Washington.

*Sic transit gloria mundi.*

The glory of the world may pass away, but mankind will prevail.

I think of those cities carved into the mountains of Cappadocia or the homes in Coober Pedy in the Australian desert, a physical testament to mankind's ingenuity and ability to survive. The Cornish lan-

guage may disappear, Gaelic may disappear, Venice may be swal-
lowed by the sea, but despite all the doomsayers, mankind will not
perish from the earth. Even if we blow ourselves up—if we overheat,
if we overcool—we will figure out a way to survive. We will dig deep
enough below the mountain to reveal an underground stream, dig
deep enough to source a well. The winds of change are irresistible, but
equally as powerful a natural force is mankind's ability to withstand
them.

The inner peace I felt upon arriving in Demopolis did not last. A
vague sense of unease, a feeling I can only describe as postpartum depression, maybe post-periplus despondency, set in almost immediately after I arrived in New York—as it had, I might add, after my
previous trip.

A year earlier I had been driving from the Taj Mahal to Calcutta.
Two years earlier I had been about to drive through thirty-two countries in Africa. Now here I was in my house in New York after having
been away for three years, trying to remember the name of the fur-
nace company. What was the plumber's phone number? Worse, I had
nothing to look forward to—waking up in the morning, I had
nowhere to go, no place I had to get to. Every day for the previous
three years, Paige and I had awakened with an adventure ahead of us.
There had been a reason to get up, a challenge, a threat; there was
something to do, some excitement. Now I did not get to go anywhere.

I knew instantly when I walked through my door that I wanted to
simplify my life. I wanted to clean out the stables of clutter and junk.
I wanted never to buy anything again. I became protective of my calendar, which before we left had always been full: a dinner or lunch or
a trip or a speech, a project, a party, an interview. I did not want that
to happen again. I had gotten along just fine without a calendar for
three years. For three years I had made absolutely no entries. But as
predictably as the rains in Africa, it threatened to fill up as soon as I
was home. If you go back to your old ways, I told myself, if you come
home and on day one you end up back where you started, then you
probably should not have left in the first place.

As much time as I spent trying to acclimate to being home, I spent
more asking myself what was next. It is said that once a parent dies,
you instantly become a generation older. I wondered if it was time to

settle down. Or was there a road out there that needed traveling before the sense of mortality I was feeling really took hold?

The wars in Angola and East Timor have ended. I know great successes come to people in such places. Shanghai, soon to be the most exciting city in the world . . . should I go? Or go to Ethiopia or Tanzania or Myanmar, all opening after being closed for decades? Or the exciting new frontier in Bolivia and western South America? The Atlantic coast of southern Spain? Several months driving through Brazil or India or China?

Looking back out there, reading the papers, I wanted to be in all those places.

And I knew that wherever we went, Paige and I would go not as a couple but as a threesome. We were now setting out on a new adventure: eight months after we got home, after waiting for all the vaccines to clear our systems, we started a family.

Before meeting Paige, I had never set out purposely to have children. I had always understood that raising a child requires a lot of time, energy, attention, money, and devotion—even if you do it wrong. I had gone through years actively *not* wanting a child. I remember, when I was about twelve, my father's turning down a promotion because it required relocating. He never said so directly, but the implication was that he had done so because it would have meant uprooting the children, that he would have taken the promotion if he had not had us.

Whereas my father had sacrificed adventure because he had children, I had sacrificed having children because I wanted to experience as much adventure as possible. The dream of traveling around the world is one most people act on *after* raising a family. Having skipped this natural stage of maturity, I wonder now if it would have enriched the traveling I did. I wonder what my father would have said. It occurred to me as soon as Paige got pregnant that I had never gotten to talk to him about fatherhood.

Of all the adventures I have had in my life, this will be the ultimate adventure. The child will show me a world I have never seen.

If fatherhood enriches one's travels, I am certain the reverse is also true. I think of all the things I have gained from my travels that I will now be able to give to our new daughter. I cannot wait to show her how to drive, how to read a map—all the things my father taught me.

I have already bought her an atlas and a globe. After English, what language will we teach her first? Will it be some dialect of Chinese? Will it be Spanish?

I think of all the places I have not been—the interior of Brazil, southern India, Eritrea, Iran, Israel. These and other places I will be able to show her on our next trip around the world. Paige has been pushing to move to Shanghai or southwestern Spain, to spend time in Punta del Este or Cochabamba. Perhaps the child will grow up in one of those places. Or who knows, maybe I will build a house on property I own on the Warrior River in Alabama, sit in a rocker, and sing "Old Man River," rearing a family where my father reared his. I suspect my father would have liked that—and in his wisdom, would have expected it all along.

She is here!

Hilton Augusta Parker Rogers arrived May 30, 2003. I had always felt sorry for people who had children before, but boy, was I dead wrong! She is pure ecstasy for me every hour of every day. What if I had never experienced this?

And I now understand my parents and all parents whereas I never did before.

# APPENDIX

*Jim Rogers and Paige Parker*
*Millennium Adventure 1999–2001*

| | |
|---|---|
| ICELAND | DECEMBER 29, 1998–JANUARY 12, 1999 |
| UNITED KINGDOM | JANUARY 12–20, 1999 |
| IRELAND | JANUARY 20–24, 1999 |
| UNITED KINGDOM | JANUARY 24–30, 1999 |
| FRANCE | JANUARY 30, 1999 |
| BELGIUM | JANUARY 31, 1999 |
| GERMANY | JANUARY 31–FEBRUARY 9, 1999 |
| AUSTRIA | FEBRUARY 9–11, 1999 |
| HUNGARY | FEBRUARY 11–15, 1999 |
| YUGOSLAVIA | FEBRUARY 15–16, 1999 |
| BULGARIA | FEBRUARY 16, 1999 |
| TURKEY | FEBRUARY 16–23, 1999 |
| GEORGIA | FEBRUARY 23–26, 1999 |
| AZERBAIJAN | FEBRUARY 26–MARCH 4, 1999 |
| (CASPIAN SEA | MARCH 4–5, 1999) |
| TURKMENISTAN | MARCH 5–11, 1999 |
| UZBEKISTAN | MARCH 11–20, 1999 |
| KYRGYZSTAN | MARCH 20–21, 1999 |
| KAZAKHSTAN | MARCH 21–APRIL 1, 1999 |
| CHINA | APRIL 1–MAY 17, 1999 |
| (YELLOW SEA | MAY 17–18, 1999) |
| SOUTH KOREA | MAY 18–31, 1999 |
| (KOREA STRAIT | MAY 31–JUNE 1, 1999) |
| JAPAN | JUNE 1–JULY 2, 1999 |
| (SEA OF JAPAN | JULY 2–4, 1999) |
| RUSSIA | JULY 4–28, 1999 |

| | |
|---|---|
| Mongolia | July 28–August 3, 1999 |
| Russia | August 3–20, 1999 |
| Kazakhstan | August 20, 1999 |
| Russia | August 20–September 4, 1999 |
| Belorussia | September 4–6, 1999 |
| Lithuania | September 6–7, 1999 |
| Russia | September 7–8, 1999 |
| Lithuania | September 8, 1999 |
| Latvia | September 8–10, 1999 |
| Estonia | September 10–11, 1999 |
| Russia | September 11–15, 1999 |
| Finland | September 15–19, 1999 |
| Sweden | September 19–29, 1999 |
| Norway | September 29–October 4, 1999 |
| Sweden | October 4–5, 1999 |
| Denmark | October 5–11, 1999 |
| Germany | October 11–28, 1999 |
| Switzerland | October 28, 1999 |
| Italy | October 29–November 4, 1999 |
| Vatican City | November 4, 1999 |
| Italy | November 4–8, 1999 |
| San Marino | November 8, 1999 |
| Italy | November 8–11, 1999 |
| Slovenia | November 11, 1999 |
| Austria | November 11–13, 1999 |
| Slovakia | November 13, 1999 |
| Czech Republic | November 13–20, 1999 |
| Germany | November 20–21, 1999 |
| Liechtenstein | November 21–22, 1999 |
| Switzerland | November 22–24, 1999 |
| Italy | November 24–25, 1999 |
| France | November 25, 1999 |
| Monaco | November 25–27, 1999 |
| France | November 27–29, 1999 |
| Spain | November 29–December 1, 1999 |
| Andorra | December 1–2, 1999 |
| France | December 2–12, 1999 |
| Luxembourg | December 12–14, 1999 |
| Belgium | December 14, 1999 |
| Netherlands | December 14–17, 1999 |
| Belgium | December 17–18, 1999 |
| United Kingdom | December 18–21, 1999 |
| Ireland | December 21–24, 1999 |
| United Kingdom | December 24–January 25, 2000 |

| | |
|---|---|
| BELGIUM | JANUARY 25–FEBRUARY 2, 2000 |
| FRANCE | FEBRUARY 2–5, 2000 |
| SPAIN | FEBRUARY 5–10, 2000 |
| PORTUGAL | FEBRUARY 10–13, 2000 |
| SPAIN | FEBRUARY 13–18, 2000 |
| GIBRALTAR | FEBRUARY 18–20, 2000 |
| SPAIN | FEBRUARY 20, 2000 |
| MOROCCO | FEBRUARY 20–MARCH 5, 2000 |
| WESTERN SAHARA | MARCH 5–11, 2000 |
| MAURITANIA | MARCH 11–21, 2000 |
| SENEGAL | MARCH 21–25, 2000 |
| GAMBIA | MARCH 25–28, 2000 |
| SENEGAL | MARCH 28–29, 2000 |
| MALI | MARCH 29–APRIL 7, 2000 |
| BURKINA FASO | APRIL 7–9, 2000 |
| IVORY COAST | APRIL 9–16, 2000 |
| GHANA | APRIL 16–24, 2000 |
| TOGO | APRIL 24–25, 2000 |
| BENIN | APRIL 25–27, 2000 |
| NIGERIA | APRIL 27–MAY 3, 2000 |
| CAMEROON | MAY 3–10, 2000 |
| EQUATORIAL GUINEA | MAY 10, 2000 |
| GABON | MAY 10–24, 2000 |
| (ATLANTIC OCEAN | MAY 24–25, 2000) |
| REPUBLIC OF CONGO | MAY 25–28, 2000 |
| ANGOLA | MAY 28–JUNE 8, 2000 |
| NAMIBIA | JUNE 8–14, 2000 |
| BOTSWANA | JUNE 14, 2000 |
| ZIMBABWE | JUNE 14–15, 2000 |
| ZAMBIA | JUNE 15, 2000 |
| ZIMBABWE | JUNE 15–16, 2000 |
| BOTSWANA | JUNE 16–18, 2000 |
| NAMIBIA | JUNE 18–22, 2000 |
| SOUTH AFRICA | JUNE 22–JULY 2, 2000 |
| LESOTHO | JULY 2–3, 2000 |
| SOUTH AFRICA | JULY 3–8, 2000 |
| MADAGASCAR | JULY 8–11, 2000 |
| SOUTH AFRICA | JULY 11–18, 2000 |
| SWAZILAND | JULY 18–21, 2000 |
| MOZAMBIQUE | JULY 21–30, 2000 |
| MALAWI | JULY 30–AUGUST 5, 2000 |
| TANZANIA | AUGUST 5–30, 2000 |
| KENYA | AUGUST 30–SEPTEMBER 10, 2000 |
| ETHIOPIA | SEPTEMBER 10–27, 2000 |

| | |
|---|---|
| Sudan | September 27–October 20, 2000 |
| (Nile River | October 20–23, 2000) |
| Egypt | October 23–November 10, 2000 |
| (Red Sea | November 10–11, 2000) |
| Saudi Arabia | November 11–25, 2000 |
| Qatar | November 25–28, 2000 |
| Saudi Arabia | November 28, 2000 |
| United Arab Emirates | November 28–December 5, 2000 |
| Iran | December 5–6, 2000 |
| Bahrain | December 6–7, 2000 |
| United Arab Emirates | December 7–8, 2000 |
| Oman | December 8–23, 2000 |
| (Gulf of Oman | December 23–27, 2000) |
| Pakistan | December 27, 2000–January 9, 2001 |
| India | January 9–February 22, 2001 |
| Bangladesh | February 22–28, 2001 |
| India | February 28–March 7, 2001 |
| Myanmar | March 7–24, 2001 |
| Thailand | March 24–26, 2001 |
| Malaysia | March 26–30, 2001 |
| Singapore | March 30–April 10, 2001 |
| (Strait of Malacca | April 10–12, 2001) |
| Indonesia | April 12–28, 2001 |
| East Timor | April 28–29, 2001 |
| Australia | April 29–June 4, 2001 |
| Vanuatu | June 4–6, 2001 |
| New Zealand | June 6–21, 2001 |
| French Polynesia | June 21–29, 2001 |
| Chile | June 29–July 13, 2001 |
| Argentina | July 13–20, 2001 |
| Chile | July 20, 2001 |
| Argentina | July 20–22, 2001 |
| Chile | July 22–23, 2001 |
| Argentina | July 23–August 10, 2001 |
| Uruguay | August 10–13, 2001 |
| Brazil | August 13–17, 2001 |
| Argentina | August 17, 2001 |
| Paraguay | August 17–21, 2001 |
| Argentina | August 21–23, 2001 |
| Bolivia | August 23–September 6, 2001 |
| Peru | September 6–23, 2001 |
| Ecuador | September 23–October 3, 2001 |
| Colombia | October 3–4, 2001 |
| Venezuela | October 4–7, 2001 |

| | |
|---|---|
| PANAMA | OCTOBER 7–10, 2001 |
| COSTA RICA | OCTOBER 10–14, 2001 |
| NICARAGUA | OCTOBER 14–17, 2001 |
| HONDURAS | OCTOBER 17–20, 2001 |
| EL SALVADOR | OCTOBER 20–23, 2001 |
| GUATEMALA | OCTOBER 23–27, 2001 |
| BELIZE | OCTOBER 27–29, 2001 |
| MEXICO | OCTOBER 29–NOVEMBER 13, 2001 |
| UNITED STATES OF AMERICA | NOVEMBER 13–20, 2001 |
| CANADA | NOVEMBER 20–28, 2001 |
| UNITED STATES OF AMERICA | NOVEMBER 28–DECEMBER 2, 2001 |
| CANADA | DECEMBER 2–8, 2001 |
| UNITED STATES OF AMERICA | DECEMBER 8–JANUARY 5, 2002 |

# INDEX

# And look for
## *Hot Commodities*

If you want to know what is happening in the booming commodities market and how to invest in it successfully, read *HOT COMMODITIES*, Jim Rogers' first book of practical, straight-forward business advice.

www.atrandom.com | RANDOM HOUSE